STRAIGHT FROM THE HEART

Jean Chrétien

KEY PORTER BOOKS

Canadian Cataloguing in Publication Data

Chrétien, Jean, 1934–
  Straight from the heart

Rev. ed.
Includes index.
ISBN 1-55013-576-7

1. Chrétien, Jean, 1934–   . 2. Canada — Politics
and government — 1963–1984.* 3. Canada —
Politics and government — 1984–   .* 4. Prime
ministers — Canada — Biography. 5. Cabinet
ministers — Canada — Biography.* 6. Politicians —
Canada — Biography. 7. Liberal Party of Canada
— Biography. I. Title.

FC626.C47A3 1994   971.064'092   C94-930200-7
F1059.C47A3 1994

Key Porter Books Limited
70 The Esplanade
Toronto, Ontario
Canada M5E 1R2

Design: Don Fernley
Typesetting: Compeer Typographic Services Limited
Printed and bound in Canada

94 95 96 97 98 99 6 5 4 3 2 1

CONTENTS

TO ALINE

PREFACE

N O ONE WAS more surprised to discover that Jean Chrétien had
written a book than Jean Chrétien. I'm a politician, after all, not
a man of letters.

The idea wasn't entirely mine. After the defeat of the Liberal government in 1984, I gave a long interview to Ron Graham, a journalist
who was working on a book on Canadian politics from 1980 to 1985.
With more time on my hands than I had been used to in more than
seventeen years as a minister, I was relaxed, philosophical, anecdotal
and loquacious.

Graham recorded the interview and agreed to give me the transcripts. Since I had never kept any regular record during my career, I
found the process useful as a way of preserving some recollections and
re-examining the great issues Canada has confronted in the past twenty
years. Over lunch one day in Toronto, Graham mentioned the exis-
tence of these transcripts to Anna Porter, the president of Key Porter
Books. She approached me to write a book of experiences and obser-
vations drawing on the material in the transcripts. I used to make
audiences laugh by telling a story about what happened next.

"Madame," I replied, "I will never write a book, because you need
a big ego to write a book and mine is big enough."

She said, "You have to write a book."

I said, "Madame, I will never write a book, because a politician only writes a book to justify himself, and I don't want to justify myself to anyone."

She said, "You have to write a book."

I said, "Madame, I will never write a book."

She wrote a cheque. I wrote a book.

Obviously I wanted it to appear simultaneously in French and English. While I worked on the French version with the help of my old friend Pierre Garceau, Graham agreed to work with Key Porter as an editor of the English version. As well, both texts benefited from the advice and comments of many friends. I was particularly indebted to John Rae and Eddie Goldenberg, who spent many hours reviewing the material with me; Mitchell and Jeannette Sharp, who made many valuable contributions; the late Pierre Genest; the secretaries at Lang Michener, who prepared the original manuscript for publication; and Phyllis Bruce of Key Porter, who had the responsibility for seeing that it all made sense. The encouragement of these people, and many others, enabled me to complete my task. The errors and omissions, of course, remained mine.

The marvellous reaction to the hardcover edition of *Straight from the Heart* came as a pleasant shock to me. Despite my initial doubts, I had imagined that it would do reasonably well in a country where books that sell over 10,000 are usually considered best-sellers. I had even dreamed of matching the sales of some previous political blockbusters, which experts in the publishing industry told me had sold around 75,000 copies. But I never expected to sell 120,000 hardcover books in French and English, and another 130,000 in paperback.

Because I had discussed the writing of the book with many friends, I had discovered much interest about it. "I hear you're threatening us with a book," a good friend said to me, as though he had heard that a hockey player was planning to become a figure skater. But the first real hint of success occurred when *Straight from the Heart* was launched at a great party in Montreal in October, 1985. Hundreds of people showed up, including Pierre Trudeau, John Turner, many former Liberal cabinet ministers, many friends from Shawinigan, and all my family. The book was national news on television and radio that night and a front-page story in many newspapers the next morning.

Then the reviews came out, and almost all of them were favourable. I was pleased that most people found the book both informative and readable, and I was expecially pleased by those who said that reading it was like hearing Chrétien talking frankly in their own home. The only negative comment was from those who thought that I hadn't been nasty enough, that there wasn't enough blood in the book, and therefore that I hadn't written "straight from the heart." In fact, though I suppose I could have elaborated in interesting or even damaging ways in places, I left out nothing that was fundamental. Occasionally I chose to omit someone's name or the full details of a private conversation, because I didn't want to humiliate anyone unnecessarily or be vengeful, but the omissions would have been marginal.

Even with all the positive media attention, I admit I was very nervous when I went to my first public book signing. It was at an Ottawa bookstore during lunch hour, and all the way there I kept thinking to myself, "If no one shows up, I'll look like a damn fool." Then I ran into a friend, a former Deputy Minister of Public Works, who had just come from the store. "Jean," he said, "I wanted to have you sign your book, but the line's too long for me to wait." At another lunch-hour signing in Ottawa, the line stretched more than two blocks, right under the windows of Prime Minister Mulroney's office, even though the day was so cold that a restaurant handed out cups of hot soup to my customers.

Long lines turned out to be the case across Canada. I found a couple of hundred people waiting in the old Tory town of Kingston, Ontario. Bookstores in Halifax sold all their copies of *Straight from the Heart* in one weekend, and in Charlottetown two Conservative provincial ministers showed up in the queue for an autograph. I was certain that a signing session in Calgary was going to be a flop, but at seven-thirty my breakfast was interrupted by news that scores of people had already gathered in the hotel lobby. Whether in Kitchener or Victoria, people were extremely nice to me. Many of them came to see a celebrity or collect an autograph, but many more spent their time and money simply to say thank you. In a world where politicians seldom receive much thanks, I was deeply touched by everyone's kindness.

At the end of the first week my book was seventh on the national best-seller lists. At the end of the second week it was third. "It's tough to be number one," I joked to the press. "It means beating Lee Iacocca and the sex life of Elvis Presley." In the third week, however, *Straight from the Heart* went into first place and stayed there for months.

Naturally the political crowd bought it. I heard of one highly political man who went into hospital for an operation and received *four* copies of my book from different members of his family. But I was always fascinated to see the variety of people who came up to me in the lines: young and old, intellectuals and labourers, students and housewives. It was explained to me by a man I met in London, Ontario. He was wearing a bright red tie, so in my usual exuberant fashion I congratulated him for bring a Grit. "I'm not a Grit, Mr. Chrétien," he said, "but I came to ask you to keep writing. I'm a professor of political science at the University of Western Ontario, and in reading your book a lot of things became clearer to me. You have a talent for putting complicated issues into understandable terms."

In the past that "talent" had earned me the wrath of many intellectuals, but now I am delighted when people say they understood constitutional reform or the Charter of Rights or the relationship between ministers and bureaucrats for the first time when they read this book. Everyone seemed to have a favourite section. Some found the chapters on my family background and early years in politics particularly entertaining. Some found what I had to say about Quebec or the business community especially interesting. Many people were intrigued by the drama of the 1984 Liberal leadership race.

My objective was not to write a political autobiography. I wasn't trying to fight any old battles or create new ones. Instead, I wanted to give some perspective on the political process in Canada as seen by an active participant. A person cannot ask for much more than the chance to make a difference in his or her chosen field of work. And because politics is my vocation, I will be forever grateful for the opportunities I have had to contribute to this great country of ours. I know I am a better person for it.

Between the first edition of *Straight from the Heart* in October, 1984, and the paperback edition a year later, I left my seat in the House of Commons to work in the private sector. I returned to public life in 1990 as leader of the Liberal Party and leader of the Opposition. On November 4, 1993, I became Prime Minister of Canada. My publisher wished, therefore, to bring out a new edition of my memoirs to take into account some of the events that have occurred since the paperback appeared. I agreed, on condition that all my royalties from this new edition be given to the Institut de recherches cliniques de Montréal. I took a part of the Christmas holidays to work with Ron Graham on making some changes to the introduction and conclusion.

Politics has been a constant source of excitement and challenge for me. I hope that you, the reader, while reading this updated version, will gain some appreciation of the satisfactions and frustrations I have encountered while serving this great country.

My political career has been the result of the help of many people from all walks of life. Some of them are mentioned in this book, others aren't. But every one of them played an important part, and I am the first to recognize their contribution. What we have achieved was achieved together.

Of all the people who have stood by me, none has been more faithful than my wife Aline. Certainly her judgment helped shape this book. It is to her that I dedicate it, in appreciation of her great support and love throughout the years.

CHAPTER ONE

A PASSION FOR POLITICS

I HAVE ALWAYS been interested in politics. My father, Wellie Chrétien, was a machinist in a Shawinigan paper mill, but politics was his favourite hobby. He was a Liberal organizer, and I used to help him distribute pamphlets when I was quite young. During the 1949 federal election, when I was fifteen, I argued for the Liberals in the poolroom near our home. At eighteen I was taking on Union Nationale supporters in the cafeteria of the mill where I worked during the summer. Some of the boys would get me to give hell to the older guys who were deeply committed to Maurice Duplessis, the Union Nationale Premier of Quebec in those days. I'd do it just for fun. I'd say things like, "You guys pray in front of the picture of Duplessis every morning," and the old guys would get really angry. The boys thought it was a good show.

My family has always been *rouge*, Liberal in the free-thinking, anti-clerical, anti-establishment tradition of the nineteenth century. My grandfather, François Chrétien, had also been a Liberal organizer and mayor of the village of St-Etienne-des-Grès for thirty years. There is a great story about him. During the election of 1896 he and a Doctor Millette handed out alcohol among the voters. It was a common practice; my grandfather's father-in-law, Laforme, had done the same thing for the Tories. It was also a sin. The priest, however, gave absolution to my Tory great-grandfather but not to my Liberal grandfather or Doctor Millette. He told them that only the Bishop of Trois-Rivières could

11

absolve someone of such a terrible sin. The bishop was Monsignor Louis-François Laflèche, an ardent Conservative who used to emphasize in his sermons that Heaven is blue and Hell is red, *rouge*. At that time people were excommunicated for their liberalism, which advocated the separation of church and state among other radical measures. My grandfather replied that he wasn't important enough to confess to Bishop Laflèche. So Sunday after Sunday, all through Lent, the entire village saw the mayor and Doctor Millette singing near the altar but never going to communion. It was a big scandal.

My poor grandmother was going crazy, and every night she recited the rosary at home for the sake of her stubborn husband. Easter came and he still hadn't given in. If he didn't receive Holy Communion by the next Sunday, he was going to Hell for sure. My grandmother began reciting three rosaries a day. Then the bishop gave in. He sent a Franciscan priest to confess my grandfather and Doctor Millette. My father was very proud of that, and I was pleased years later when the bishop's name was dropped from the name of my riding, St-Maurice-Laflèche.

The first time I met Duplessis I was a student at the Collège des Trois-Rivières, his alma mater. Everyone was introduced to him, and when he heard my name, he asked, "From Shawinigan?"

"Yes," I said.

"Your father is Wellie Chrétien?"

"Yes."

"Your grandfather was François Chrétien, mayor of St-Etienne-des-Grès?"

"Yes."

"Then you're a damn *rouge*!" Duplessis said.

Later, when I studied law at Laval University in Quebec City, I became president of the Liberal Club. The late 1950s were not great years to be a Liberal; in fact, they looked a bit like 1985. Diefenbaker was in power in Ottawa and Duplessis was entrenched in Quebec. Things were so bad that many students were afraid of losing their government bursaries if they were seen to be Liberals. That didn't worry me too much, because I had a private scholarship and a summer job in the paper mill. Besides, I didn't believe the government would take

12

away my small bursary. It didn't, but my family used to worry about me, and I had difficulty attracting members to the Liberal Club.

In those days politics penetrated every aspect of Quebec life. Partisan considerations decided if your village got an asphalt road, if your organization got a grant to hold a sports event, if your restaurant got a liquor licence, and if your university got funding. Duplessis seemed omnipotent. His enemies, such as Pierre Trudeau, were denied teaching jobs; his friends' illegalities were overlooked by the police; and corruption was so much part of the system that most people just came to accept it and hope for a piece of the action.

"I'm helping my friends," Duplessis used to say to the crowds. "What would you do in my place?"

And the crowds would reply, "We'd help our friends, Maurice."

His authority was backed by the Roman Catholic Church, which used its position as an arbiter of what was right or wrong for the people to become an instrument of Duplessis. They shared an interest in keeping Quebeckers poor, rural, uneducated, and bound to the church teaching that life on earth is just a grim passage to Heaven. Society was based on privileges, not rights; obedience and gratitude were essential parts of the people's mentality. Even as late as 1960 I had a fight with my parish priest, who suggested in his weekly newsletter that we owed our allegiance to the Union Nationale because it had given us a tennis court. It was as scandalous then as in my grandfather's day for a feisty young lawyer to tell a priest to mind his own damn business during an election. Maybe it was more scandalous, as I used to yell at him through a loudspeaker aimed at the church.

Nationalism was the other cover for Duplessis's patronage and corruption. As a friend of mine used to say, "Duplessis made a skirt out of the Quebec flag in order to hide his dirty parts." My father, on the other hand, taught me that the survival of the French fact in North America was due to Quebec's association with Canada. He had learned from experience. My father spent his early years in New Hampshire, because his family was part of the wave of Quebeckers who moved to the United States in search of work. They returned to the Mauricie when the economic situation improved; but my father never lost his interest in the fate of francophones outside Canada. He was a director of the *Association Canado-Américaine*, an organization dedicated to the survival of the French in New England, for forty-five years; he subscribed to French-language newsweeklies from Massachusetts and even from Michigan, and knew about the history of the French in Louisiana and the American West.

The assimilation and loss of influence of the French in the United States contrasted dramatically with what had happened in Canada, so my father always looked on Canada as a good protector. He was aware, of course, of the difficulties French Canadians had outside Quebec, and he used to worry about how francophone minorities would survive and flourish from coast to coast, but he never blamed the English for that. His attitude was always positive, concerned with the future rather than obsessed with the past.

My father had become a strong Canadian under Laurier, a *rouge* Liberal whom he greatly admired. When the Liberals introduced the new flag, Dad said, "Laurier said we would have a Canadian flag, and now we have it." He proudly bought one for each of his children. Sometimes he represented me at flag-raising ceremonies in the villages of my riding and gave short, patriotic speeches.

That same patriotism made him one of the few people in the Mauricie to support conscription during the Second World War. Many French Canadians felt that it was Europe's war and they shouldn't intervene. In retrospect that seems a wrong judgment; but at the time the pacifist arguments were strong, particularly since the United States was reluctant to get involved and France itself had given up. But my Dad thought that Canada should be at war and the allies should keep up the fight. Not only did he vote "Yes" in the referendum on whether to impose conscription, but he felt it was his duty to convince his sons to volunteer for the army. Two weren't accepted, one because he was a doctor and the other because of his poor eyesight, but a third enlisted and became a captain in the artillery. My Dad was very pleased to be able to put a star in the window of our living-room to indicate that a member of the family had volunteered. As a boy I used to pack boxes of food and clothes to send to my brother. But ours wasn't the common

14

experience, and my family's willingness to go against the trend may have shaped the attitude that has carried me through my political life.

Although my political involvement began in fun, as an intellectual exercise, I came to understand it as an influential instrument for social change. Once, for example, I organized a student rally for democracy in Quebec. Between fifty and seventy-five students were to go into the visitors' gallery of the Legislative Assembly and drop pamphlets onto the members. But someone leaked the plan, so when the group arrived in the gallery, there were about two policemen per student. I think a couple of guys might have shouted a slogan or two, but the others were too scared to do anything and the protest was a big flop.

Another time I protested to Duplessis himself. In the first year of law school every student needed a copy of the Revised Statutes of Quebec. If you were a supporter of the Union Nationale, you could go to the Renaissance Club, an elegant, old stone building on the Grande-Allée for party members, and pick up one for free. The rest of us had to pay $10. That seemed like a great injustice. So a friend and I decided to complain to Duplessis. My friend was also a Liberal, but he was from one of the old Trois-Rivières families that had produced lawyers for generations. His parents knew Duplessis's family well, and Duplessis's secretary knew my friend's mother. She also knew some of my family, because my grandfather had been a Liberal organizer in Duplessis's riding.

"We want to see Mr. Duplessis," we said to her.

"Why?" she asked.

"Because we have a protest. Will he talk to us?"

Duplessis greeted us in the premier's corner suite in the Parliament Buildings. It was filled with flowers and Krieghoff paintings, and showed the taste for good things that was part of Duplessis's character. Another part was a taste for good times, boxing, and baseball. Though he came from the establishment of Trois-Rivières, Duplessis was seen as an anti-establishment politician; and though he was very conservative and religious, he was extremely fun-loving.

Certainly he had a lot of fun with us. His eyes sparkled and he had a forceful presence in spite of his small size. He defended the notion that

15

no one has rights in society, only privileges. "If you are at university," he said, "it is because you are privileged." We took the opposite approach and maintained that it was unfair for Union Nationale students to get free books.

"It's because you aren't true believers," Duplessis said. "These other students have the faith, and the faith rewards people. But I'm glad you came and I'll make you a deal. Rather than pay $10 each, pay $10 and I'll give you two sets."

As president of the Liberal Club I got heavily involved in the 1956 Quebec election. It was a rough one. The provincial member from St-Maurice was René Hamel. He was a great orator who had been one of the two candidates elected federally in 1945 by the Bloc Populaire, the leftist, Quebec nationalist party that had arisen in protest to the imposition of conscription in 1942. In 1952 Hamel became a Liberal MPP. He was so effective in opposition that Duplessis detested him; they were like fire and water. Duplessis used to come into our riding and say, "If you vote for Hamel, you won't get the bridge you want." So I'd reply in my speeches, "I will cross the river swimming, but I will never cross the river on my knees!"

We had terrific political rallies in those days. Every night I teamed up with Hamel and a good friend named Fernand D. Lavergne to speak in the riding. Lavergne was an important influence on me. He had started the unions in Shawinigan and had been their local president for years. He had had no formal education, but Pierre Trudeau said that Lavergne was one of the most intelligent union leaders he had ever met. He also had a wonderful outlook. At one point he was so fed up with Duplessis that he quit a good job and moved to Saskatchewan; but even though he spoke English, his huge family didn't. Since they weren't able to adjust, they came back. In the 1957 federal election he deserted the Liberals and ran as a CCF candidate in St-Maurice-Laflèche. He did well. I might even have voted for him. Certainly I remember being tempted.

Hamel won in 1956, and I helped him in his race against Jean Lesage for the leadership of the Quebec Liberal Party in 1958. We had no money for the campaign, and though Hamel had been a good member and occasionally acted as leader during the illness of the departing leader, Georges Lapalme, he had been in the Bloc Populaire and was seen as something of a troublemaker. Hamel suffered a very humiliating defeat; but Lesage went on to win the provincial election of 1960. I was a practising lawyer by then and a principal election organizer in Shawinigan.

Our federal Member of Parliament was J.A. Richard. He had won the biggest Liberal majority in Canada during the Diefenbaker sweep of 1958. St-Maurice can't be called a safe Liberal seat — it had gone Bloc Populaire in 1945, after all, and later it would go Union Nationale and Parti Québécois provincially — but in 1958 it gave Richard a sympathy vote. He wasn't a flashy communicator and he didn't make many speeches in the House of Commons, but he was well loved, a hard worker, and a nice gentleman. By 1962, however, his age had become a problem. Many Liberal organizers thought we'd lose with him, and some of them wanted me to run. They knew I had become a lawyer in order to become a politician, and they were ready to nominate me to run against Richard.

I knew Richard very well, because one of his sons was a close friend of mine, and with the candour that has been both a weakness and an asset in my political career, I told him what was happening. "Some people think you may be a bit too old," I said, "and they would like me to run against you. If you don't run, I will run. But if you run, I will not run against you."

"Jean," he said, "you're younger than my youngest son. I will do another term and then I will give you the chance."

So Mr. Richard was nominated as the Liberal candidate for the 1962 federal election. We had rented a big hall for the nomination meeting, but the crowd was very small. A few weeks later the Créditistes got a huge crowd in the same hall to their rally. Social Credit arose as a phenomenon in rural Quebec during an unusual period. Diefenbaker's Tories had been a disaster since 1958, yet there was a strong feeling among ordinary French Canadians that the Liberal Party didn't belong to them. It looked a bit too élitist, a bit too Montreal. Into that vacuum stepped the Créditistes under their provincial leader, Réal

Caouette, who had been born in my riding. Caouette was not a sophisticated person, but he could read the mood of the people extremely well and articulate their frustrations in a very colourful way. He stood up for the small people of the province, the wage-earners, the unemployed, and those who struggled all their lives to pay their mortgages. And he did it in the language of the people. "You're born on credit and you'll die on credit," he used to say, as he attacked the financial and intellectual establishments for their arrogance and hypocrisy.

His attacks were particularly effective because they spoke to the uncertainties created by the Quiet Revolution that shook the province after the death of Duplessis and the victory of Lesage. Those two events unleashed the forces of modernization that had been present but suppressed in Quebec for almost two decades. The whole society took a great leap forward in a remarkably short period of time. The priests and nuns began to be replaced by secular teachers, and the school system was reorganized into bigger and more centralized units. Books that had been banned became available; television opened the province to what was going on in the whole world; and the state became a positive force in the economy and in every corner of the society, bringing with it higher taxes and greater public debt. While this explosion produced welcomed progress in education, the arts and business, it also acted like a bulldozer on the old institutions with which the people had become comfortable; and it smashed a lot of traditions with such speed that it caused a reaction. Caouette personified that conservative, populist reaction and expressed it better than anyone else.

He didn't have a solution, however, other than the "funny money" ideas of Social Credit. "Something is wrong in a system in which the stores are full of goods but no one buys," he said. "People don't buy because they don't have money. If the government printed more money, people would have more money and would buy more. Buying more would create more jobs, and jobs would create more goods and more money, and everyone would buy even more. There's not enough money in circulation because some stubborn banker in Ottawa won't start the printing machine."

As simplistic as this argument was, it was hard to refute to ordinary people and it appealed to their sense that the bankers and the bureau-crats were against them.

Though the Créditistes were usually dismissed by the media, they attracted and convinced a lot of people, especially when Caouette spoke. He served a useful function by demystifying many sacred cows, including the language itself and the idea of Quebec independence, and the crowds loved him for it. In that 1962 election the Créditistes defeated J.A. Richard by 10,000 votes. I was in his kitchen when the results came over the radio and I gave him the bad news. "Mr. Richard, we've been clobbered this time," I said. There was even a rumour that the local returning officer put extra votes into the box so that Richard wouldn't lose his deposit.

The federal Tories under John Diefenbaker won only a minority government, however, and they were forced to call another election in 1963. Richard stepped aside and the local Liberals had a nominating convention. I got about 500 votes and my opponent got about ten. Unfortunately, it was harder to win the election. I was up against the Social Credit incumbent who had trounced Richard nine months before. "Nine months," I used to say, "just time for Mr. Lamy to give birth to a defeat."

Gérard Lamy was a rather successful small businessman, but he was not very sophisticated politically and had really won the 1962 election by a fluke. His big pitch was that he had experience and fifteen children and Chrétien was only twenty-nine years old. Fernand D. Lavergne used to make speeches on my behalf, and he was extremely funny. He had a stutter that he exploited to win over the audience and to time his punch lines.

"Mr. Lamy wa-wa-wa-wants us to vo-vo-vo-vote for him because he had fif-fif-fifteen kids," he said. "Mr. Pellerin, the Tory candidate, wa-wa-wants us to vo-vo-vote for him because he had fourteen k-k-kids. I did not run this time because I could not compete: I only have nine k-k-kids. Mr. Lamy has a lot of merit in having fif-fif-fifteen kids. But if he is like the rest of us, he must have had some fun, too. It's true that Jean is only twenty-nine. In our religion we're only allowed one wo-wo-wo-woman. So if he had fif-fif-fifteen k-k-kids, we would have a few questions to ask him. Ladies and gentlemen, what we're looking for is a representative, not a re-re-reproducer.''

I used the same argument against Lamy in the all-candidates debate in Grand'Mère. "If it was a question of kids, my Dad should be prime minister, because he and my Mom had nineteen kids.''

Lamy got really mad, raging and swearing. Some of his own supporters turned against him, and people were yelling at him to go to hell and insulting him. There was a big brouhaha. So I went to the microphone and said, "Ladies and gentlemen, Mr. Lamy is your Member of Parliament. Will you listen to him, please? In two weeks no one will have to listen to him anymore.'' Lamy became twice as angry, of course, and that's when he lost the campaign. Everyone was embarrassed. In the end I beat him by 2,000 votes.

I have always had to pay a political price among the intellectuals of Quebec for using slang, emotion, and jokes in my speeches, but the St-Maurice valley was a region of populist politicians famous for their colourful style. Duplessis and J.A. Mongrain were in Trois-Rivières, Hamel and Lavergne were in Shawinigan, Maurice Bellemare was in Champlain, and Réal Caouette and Camille Samson of the Créditistes were also from the Mauricie. Since I had to fight populists, I learned from them and even tried to outdo them. That has often shocked and annoyed the intellectuals, who exaggerate my humble beginnings or conclude I am not educated.

In fact, though my family was far from rich, we were seen as successful, almost aristocratic, in the working-class village of La Baie Shawinigan where I grew up. My father worked in the mill, he was the secretary of the municipality, and he took on other jobs in order to send his kids to college. My mother Marie was equally energetic in her ambitions for us. She had married at seventeen and had nineteen children, nine of whom survived infancy — I was the eighteenth. In those days God decided how many kids people had. Most of the deliveries were done at home, and Dad's first remark was always, "I hope it's not twins.'' Then he asked about the health of the mother and baby and said, "Well, a bit more water in the soup will do.''

We lived in a brick house with a large garden in which my mother

20

grew vegetables, strawberries, rhubarb, and so on. She worked very hard, canning goods for the winter and making jam, and looking after the five or six children still at home. So we were hardly poverty-stricken, though the three youngest children shared an allowance of a nickel a day and got the hand-me-downs of the older kids. All my parents' savings went toward education, which was a real sacrifice because there were no classical colleges in Shawinigan, so we had to go away to boarding schools. For my parents the grass was greener on the other side of the fence, and education was the way their children could get into that greener field. It was a rare obsession for that time and place, and it made my parents stand out in a community where most families just raised their kids to go into the mill. In a village of a couple of thousand people only three or four families sent their children to college. In fact, my mother didn't mix easily with the neighbours because she was pre-occupied with her children's education and the proper use of language. My parents' effort produced wonderful results. My eldest brother Maurice, who is twenty-three years older than I, became a noted gynaecologist and arts patron; my youngest brother, Michel, became a well-known medical researcher in Montreal. One brother is a druggist; two others have done well in business; two sisters are nurses, and another is a social worker.

If anything, I was seen as the black sheep of the family. The three youngest boys, Guy, myself and Michel, were always getting into so much mischief that the director of our school in Joliette wrote my unfortunate parents, "I don't want them back again, not one of them. I've had enough." My Dad used to say that the three of us didn't get enough marks for good conduct to make enough good conduct for one, but that was just youthful exuberance.

My particular problem, however, was that for a period I gave up trying to do well in the classroom. A large part of the problem was that I had missed a year of school because of sickness, and so I was in the same class as my smart younger brother. In the first, second, and third months Michel came first and I came second. In the fourth month he came first and I came fifth. In the seventh month he came first and I came thirtieth. As well, I was shy about the birth defect that had left me deaf in my right ear and distorted my mouth, although I had become quite good at defending myself with my fists after years of hanging out in the neighbourhood poolroom, which could become pretty lively on payday or during a political campaign.

My mother spent a lot of effort to make sure I didn't turn out bad. She knew that I was having difficulties and that I hated boarding school more than my brothers did, so she paid extra attention to me. For example, when I was at school in Trois-Rivières I was already dating my future wife. My mother used to bring Aline with her on visits and leave us alone for the afternoon while she went off to visit cousins. Unfortunately my mother died suddenly of a heart attack at the age of sixty-two and never saw how I turned out.

My Dad, however, lived to be ninety-three, and he was very pleased to have a politician in the family: it had been his dream. He always urged me to become a lawyer in order to get into politics, which is exactly what I decided to do at the age of twenty. He would also have been pleased when my daughter, France, became a lawyer and married André Desmarais, a son of Paul Desmarais, the chairman of Power Corporation. It owns Consolidated-Bathurst, the paper company for which my father had worked all his life. He used to say, "I never thought I'd see the day when a French Canadian would own that mill."

He was full of vigour to the end. After decades of hard work, he began to travel the world when he was seventy. Until he was eighty-five he went on organized tours of about thirty-five countries, including the USSR, Israel, Turkey, Syria, Greece, Italy and Mexico; and at the age of ninety he climbed all the steps at Mont St-Michel in France and visited the beautiful little Loire village of Loches where the Chrétiens originally came from.

So the language I often use in my speeches has nothing to do with a lack of education or a poor upbringing. It stems from my wish to remain close to the working-class people of my riding. I was quite left wing when I began in politics. I wasn't obsessed with making money, or else I wouldn't have given up a $30,000-a-year law practice for the $10,000 that a member of Parliament received in those days. I was a working-class lawyer and I deliberately built my first house in a working-class area, Shawinigan North, while most of the professionals were going to Shawinigan South. My oldest friends are working-class people, though many of them have moved into administration or started businesses, and the president of my riding association has always been a blue-collar worker. When the lawyers ask what they can do to help me, I say, "Stay home."

My pitch was always to the working class because the Liberal Party in my riding is supported by the unions and the workers. We were the party that fought Duplessis, and I was an authentic descendant of those gutsy *rouges* who had fought against the bishops for liberal principles. Many of those old, reformist Liberals showed up at the all-candidates debate in Grand'Mère because they saw me as the bearer of their strong fighting tradition.

However, my organization consisted mostly of people my own age. They pushed out the old gang on the riding executive, which was more or less René Hamel's provincial team, and took over the key party functions such as finance, publicity and canvassing. Below them I had a chief in every parish, which usually had about ten polls, and each chief had a team of poll captains. They met from time to time to go over the voting lists, check off the known Liberals, and pinpoint the undecided voters who should be lobbied or invited to meet the candidate. That still happens, though it's more difficult now that party affiliations are not so rigid. Basically the organization was, and remains, a group of people who believed in me, liked politics, and developed a lot of friendships.

Politics is a game of friends. They want to do well for each other and they take a great deal of pride in what they do. In a small town or village a poll captain and a parish chief are local big shots because they have a responsibility to deliver several hundred votes to their candidate and everyone knows it. They even consider it a service to society. My father looked after four or five polls all his life, and he liked to boast that he had always delivered them to the Liberals. He worked at that, talked to people, and occasionally offered them a helping hand in the hope it would bring some to vote Liberal. We were proud of him. Between elections there are meetings with speakers and fund-raising get-togethers.

I meet the party workers three or four times a year, for example, and every Christmas I have a reception for more than 500 Liberals in the riding.

People come and people go. Sometimes you have to hunt for new blood when workers get tired; sometimes you have to push out old-timers who want to stay but don't want to work. That's particularly difficult when you've had a series of easy victories, and the machine gets too rusty to fight a real fight, because there's little excuse to oust those who aren't doing much to make room for new enthusiasts. After all, everyone is a volunteer. One of the most regrettable mistakes I ever made in politics was to try to build a compact, powerful machine in my riding at the start of my career. It became a small clique that had its finger in every activity of the district. People used to approach us to get permission to be on the school boards, to be aldermen, to be mayor, and we used to decide if they were suitable, now or ever.

But I learned my lesson early and I learned it well. Shortly after I became a Member of Parliament, I was asked by René Lévesque, then a minister in Lesage's government, if I had some suggestions for a good candidate for the provincial Liberal nomination in Shawinigan. I mentioned Clive Liddle, a popular doctor who spoke French with an English accent and wanted to be in the Quebec Assembly, but Lévesque thought it was bad politics to nominate an anglophone in a period of nationalist fervour, and I was crazy enough to buy his silly argument. When Liddle tried for the nomination anyway, I instructed my machine to vote against him, and he lost to a less capable person. In revenge Liddle ran against me as the federal NDP candidate in the 1965 election. He took a lot of votes away from me, but he took even more away from the Créditistes so I was returned with a bigger majority than the previous election.

He taught me something, however: it was dangerous to interfere where I had no business because that made enemies out of friends. For every person I backed, there were a score of good Liberals who were offended or annoyed. So I closed down the operation, even though its myth still exists twenty years later. Some people still believe they win or lose only because of the blessing of the Chrétien machine, which isn't

24

true at all. As for Liddle, after the 1965 election I went to him and said, "You deserve respect for trying to do to me what I did to you." Eventually he returned to the Liberal fold and we remained good friends until his death.

Once my team was in place for an election campaign, I simply went out and met people, in the street, at their doors, at the gates of their factories, everywhere. Shaking hands and being seen are still very important, despite the increase in television coverage. It's a great psychological moment in politics when a voter first meets a candidate; and it's both an art that must be learned and a natural talent that some people are born with. If you make the voter feel happy or comfortable, you'll get his vote. If you're pushy or tense or clumsy or self-satisfied, you'll lose that vote forever. That's the general rule but, of course, there are many successful MPs who don't fit the mold. Hard work, intelligence, party affiliation, and luck are also factors, and ridings send personalities to Ottawa that range from older, sombre representatives to exuberant, unorthodox characters. My own riding has been rather eccentric in its choice of parties and personalities at both the federal and provincial levels.

In April 1963, at the age of twenty-nine, I was elected to the House of Commons as part of a minority Liberal government under Lester "Mike" Pearson. Members of Parliament may have lost prestige in recent times, but for them and their families getting elected is always a very emotional moment. Despite the cruelties of political life, we all take some joy and pride in that moment. I had been to Ottawa a couple of times before, once for the Liberal convention at which Lester Pearson was elected leader, but I remember first walking under the Peace Tower as an MP. I was moved, thinking of my mother, who had died when I was twenty; but I was pleased that my father's dream of having a politician in the family had come true at last.

Ottawa was a very English town in 1963. Very little French was spoken, except by security guards, waitresses, and maintenance men. French Canadians felt strange there, as if it wasn't our national capital at all. Slowly we began to change that. The arrival of a number of very rural, unilingual Créditistes made a difference. Though rather uneducated, they were quite articulate and not shy in complaining about the lack of French services. Liberals and even some Tories made similar noises, and Pearson was sympathetic. Once he said to me, "The biggest mistake we ever made in Canada was when Queen Victoria chose Ottawa over Montreal as the capital. It was a bad move because it made the capital an English city." He was determined to correct that mistake, and we made gradual progress. All sorts of services became available in both languages, and more people insisted on speaking French at work and around town. The city's character has changed completely now.

When I arrived I hardly spoke any English. I could read it a bit but communicating and understanding were very difficult. I was determined to learn, however. Since there were no language teachers on Parliament Hill, I had to develop by myself. One way was to read *Time* and *Newsweek* thoroughly every week, which also helped me learn about American issues. I kept a dictionary at hand and I got assistance on pronunciation from my wife, who was bilingual. I often joke that I resolved to learn English so that I wouldn't feel inferior to Aline, but as soon as I became functionally bilingual she learned Spanish. She has a great facility for languages, she speaks four now, and she found me a poor student.

The more practical and enjoyable way was to become friends with many of the anglophone parliamentarians, guys such as Rick Cashin from Newfoundland, Ron Basford from British Columbia, and Donald Macdonald and "Mo" Moreau from Toronto. They all went on to highly successful careers: Cashin as head of the fishermen's union in Newfoundland, Basford as Minister of Justice, Macdonald as Minister of Finance, and Moreau as president of a mining company. Moreau was particularly helpful. He had been French-speaking in his youth but had become anglicized later on, so I helped him learn back his French and he helped me with my English. We were part of a group of ambitious young mavericks who used to meet regularly, usually in Rick Cashin's office. Cashin was a lively Newfoundlander whom we called "Prime Minister" because he supplied the booze. I didn't drink—that was one of the promises I had made to my wife when I went into politics—but I spent hours listening to the talk in order to improve my English. For a long while I never knew whether they were laughing at me when they were making jokes, but I picked up new words and I was never shy about trying out my English. That led to many funny incidents.

Once there was a big argument between Cashin and Gerry Regan, a Liberal MP from Halifax who became Premier of Nova Scotia and later a Trudeau cabinet minister, about whether Newfoundland or Nova Scotia produced the best lobsters. So I was called upon to be a judge at a party at the Cashins'. There was a lot of white wine that night so nobody cared about who won. The talk was all about politics, and since most of the guests were from the Maritimes, the talk was all in English. Someone asked me how I had won my riding in spite of the huge Créditiste majority of the previous election. I answered falteringly.

"Work hard, vary hard," I said. "I went to all the fact-or-ies and I shaked hands with every-body. Sometimes when the work was finish at five o'clock, the man and the woman were passing by so fast that I did not have the time to shake their hand, so I just touched them on the *bras*." Of course I meant "arms." Everyone roared with laughter. "So that's how you won your election, you damn Frenchman!" they said.

Another time I was asked about Claude Ryan, then the editor of *Le Devoir*. "Vary important," I said. "Every politician read him. He love to be consulted and he give good advice. But he can be a little bit pompous. When you are in the presence of Mr. Ryan, you feel you are in front of a bishop. You almost have to put your knee on the floor and kiss his *bague*." The word "bague" had come into my head instead of "ring." People were laughing so hard that I couldn't continue speaking, but I didn't know what I had said that was so funny.

I still have problems in English. There are mistakes that I made at the beginning and I haven't been able to shake them. But many Canadians are very sympathetic. They have followed my progress on television and in speeches over the years and that has given them a rapport with me. "You were pretty bad last year, but you're getting better," they used to say to me on the street and in airports, or "I understood everything you said tonight."

I went to a language teacher for a while. She corrected me on my grammar and my pronunciation mostly. "You should learn to say

'Japan' and not 'Chapan' " and so on. One day I asked her to help me with my accent, but she refused. "Never," she said. "When I turn on the radio and you're speaking, I know it's you and the rest of Canada knows it's you. You have to keep it." That's often led me to say that Maurice Chevalier and I had to practise to keep our French accent in English. It has become a kind of trademark.

My first chat on Parliament Hill was with Doug Fisher, then an NDP member, now an Ottawa journalist. It was a difficult conversation because he knew little more French than I knew English, but it was a pleasant encounter. I had an introduction to Fisher from Fernand D. Lavergne, who admired him as the guy who had defeated C.D. Howe in Port Arthur, and Fisher took me to the House of Commons. "You'll be sitting there," he said pointing to the back row.

"Yes," I replied, "but someday I'll be *there*." I pointed to the front bench.

Then Fisher gave me some good advice. "The guys who go to the front bench are the ones who work."

"Don't worry," I said. "I will work."

The early 1960s were a turbulent period in Canadian politics. Quebec nationalism had become literally explosive, with bombs going off in the province. Pearson understood the seriousness of the tensions and he dedicated himself to resolving them. He laid the foundation for the "French fact" in Ottawa that many people later attributed entirely to Pierre Trudeau. Trudeau built on Pearson's groundwork. But Pearson met much resistance and he had many frustrations. He had good ministers, such as Guy Favreau, Maurice Lamontagne, and René Tremblay, who were treated unjustly by the opposition and the press. That was a shame, and I still get angry thinking about it.

Favreau was a brilliant man, who had been an excellent Assistant Deputy Minister of Justice before leaving the public service for politics. Pearson made him Minister of Justice, House Leader, and his Quebec lieutenant and relied on his advice a great deal, perhaps too much for a newcomer. Favreau accepted every responsibility, worried about all the details, and eventually was killed by the work. He was harassed because of a minor influence-peddling charge against junior officials in the bureaucracy. According to the subsequent inquiry, Favreau had made the right decision in the matter but had failed to consult his department. For that he was hounded without mercy.

As for Lamontagne and Tremblay, they were very bright professors from Quebec who had the misfortune to buy furniture from a dealer just before he went bankrupt. Because their names appeared on the list of debtors, their reputations were smeared with innuendo and they chose to resign rather than fight. Lamontagne was a man of great moral and intellectual integrity, and Tremblay was a decent gentleman who never had an enemy in his life. They did nothing wrong, yet their careers were ruined and their families were hurt by the unfair accusations of scandal that Diefenbaker exploited for his own political reasons. He was cruel, and we all felt it was not coincidental that the targets of his attacks were French Canadians.

Diefenbaker didn't hate French Canadians, but he was bitter that Quebec had abandoned him after his great majority of 1958. He was a strange man in many ways. He had a great opinion of himself — as he showed when he prepared his own magnificent funeral and memorials—and he used to make wonderfully crazy speeches. I enjoyed listening to him in the House of Commons because he put on such a great show without notes, and despite our political differences we liked each other for being House of Commons men. Whenever I got off a good line against any of his enemies in his own party, he would send me a note of congratulations! But he could be very unjust. When you compare us to other countries, you see that Canada has very honest politicians and a highly dedicated public service. That's not to say there are never people who have made mistakes, but that's probably as true in the private sector as in government. Diefenbaker's real purpose in attacking Favreau, Lamontagne, and Tremblay was not to throw out the bad apples but to get revenge on the Liberals.

There may have been some bigotry among the Tories, too. Certainly their opposition to a new Canadian flag to replace the Red Ensign seemed foolish and emotional. I call it "The Empire Strikes Back." The debate in the House of Commons, with Tories singing "God Save the Queen" and making obscene gestures, was out of proportion to the simple thing we were trying to achieve and of which all Canadians are now so proud. Perhaps it was the trauma of becoming mature as a nation.

One night during the flag debate I was on an elevator in the Parliament Building with a crowd of other members. The elevator stopped at the second floor where more members were waiting to go up, but the operator — a francophone — decided there wasn't enough room for them and closed the doors. At the third floor there was only a page-boy waiting so the operator let him squeeze on. Bob Coates, one of the Tories with us, called the operator a typical incompetent French Canadian for letting the kid on but not the members. George McIlraith, who was then the Minister of Public Works, said, "Don't give the guy hell, he's only doing his job and I'm his boss." You could feel the tension.

When we all got off, Coates grabbed McIlraith by the tie and began to push him around. So I grabbed Coates by the lapels of his jacket and pushed him back against a wall. We stared each other down and walked away. That was in 1965. Times have changed. Now Coates and I are quite good friends and he was a very strong supporter of Brian Mulroney for leader of the Progressive Conservatives, because Mulroney would bring Quebeckers into the Tory party.

As I had promised Fisher, I worked hard, and before very long I developed a good relationship with Mike Pearson. He appointed me his parliamentary secretary. That was more or less an honorary position since the prime minister has no department per se with budget estimates to defend, documents to table, written questions to answer, speeches to make, ceremonies to attend, and all the other duties that preoccupy the parliamentary secretaries assigned to ordinary ministers.

Parliamentary secretaries don't have any formal or legal role, they're just to help their ministers in whatever way the ministers find useful and to whatever degree their ministers permit, but in Pearson's day the post was usually a sign that you were considered to be ministerial calibre and were on your way to the cabinet. Later Trudeau changed the system to give experience to more members: you would have your turn working with a minister and then you would return to the back benches. Both approaches have their advantages, and it's hard to know which is better.

I've always joked that Pearson noticed me because of his love of baseball. I have never been a star at sports but I have always been able to play most positions reasonably well. If a short stop was needed, I was just good enough to be a short stop. If a catcher was needed, I was just good enough to be a catcher. Like my career in the cabinet, I was good at plugging holes. I wasn't a sports star because I lacked practice more than agility, but it was more fun to be a goalie one day, a centre the next day, and a defenceman the day after that. Anyway, Pearson asked me to pitch a softball game between the politicians and the press. He was our coach and Charles Lynch of Southam News was theirs. Lynch had bushy hair and made lots of noise. He surprised me because I had the notion that anglophones were rather dull and subdued. We won the game, and I think Pearson was so pleased that he made me his parliamentary secretary.

There was a more serious incident that made us close. In 1964 René Hamel, Shawinigan's MPP who had become Attorney General in the Lesage cabinet, was named a judge. His seat was surrounded by Union Nationale ridings, so it was a weak spot for the provincial Liberals. René Lévesque was at the start of his political career as Minister of Natural Resources in the Quebec government, and he was put in charge of the by-election. He either asked for the job or was given it, but my guess is that he asked for it because it would teach him about organization and get him into rural Quebec. In retrospect it is evident that he had great ambition. When he visited Shawinigan, he talked to a friend of mine, Jean-Paul Gignac, a businessman from an old Liberal family who later became close to Lévesque and president of Sidbec, the Quebec-owned steel company. Gignac said, "The best man to replace Hamel in this riding and to have influence in this region is the young federal member, Jean Chrétien." So Lévesque called me and I went to see him in Quebec City.

Those were the days of the Quiet Revolution, and Quebec City was an exciting place to be. Lévesque had been responsible for the nationalization of the hydro-electric companies, and I had supported the idea even though Shawinigan was threatened. The town had been built on the special price for electricity that Shawinigan Water and Power gave to Shawinigan Chemicals and the other local industries. Lévesque had more or less guaranteed us that the deal would continue, and it did last for a few years. But gradually the notion grew that everyone in Quebec should pay the same, and Hydro-Quebec eventually stopped giving the Shawinigan factories special rates. That contributed to the decline of Shawinigan.

Lévesque and I had lunch at the Georges V. He drove me there and made a parking space for himself in a narrow gap. He had needed a little more room and simply created it by bumping back and forth into two parked cars. He didn't do any damage, but I thought it was a gutsy thing to do and enjoyed it. Over a delicious lunch he tried to persuade me to leave federal politics. I was tempted, but I wondered why I should give up what I had already achieved in federal politics. "I have a bright future in Ottawa," I told him. "I'm thirty years old, I'm chairman of the Justice Committee of the House of Commons, and I'm beginning to be known." I suppose I was fishing for an offer of a cabinet post, though I never asked directly.

"Jean, you have no future in Ottawa," Lévesque said, "because in five years Ottawa will not exist for us."

I was shocked, because this was the Liberal Minister of Natural Resources speaking. "But, Lévesque, are you a separatist?"

"No, no, I'm a federalist," he said. "Just forget about it, Jean." He had said too much.

From that day I knew that Lévesque was a separatist and concluded a great deal about his intellectual honesty. Now, in 1985, he claims that he is no longer a separatist, but that is typical: he is like trying to pin Jello to the wall.

Anyway, he was in no position to promise me a job in the Quebec cabinet, but he took me to see Jean Lesage. I had met Lesage when he was a minister in the St. Laurent government before he left Ottawa to become leader of the Quebec Liberal Party, and he knew me well from the provincial election of 1960. I found him formal and rather self-satisfied, but he was seductive. He said I would do very well in

Quebec, that I was a man of the future, and that he needed someone young and experienced. In other words, if I was interested, he was interested. I remember it was the first week of Advent because he recited a passage from the Gospel that he had heard the previous Sunday: "Behold the fig tree, and all the trees. When they now put forth their buds, you know that summer is near." It was his way of telling me that I would be in the cabinet, I suppose.

I must have looked convinced because word soon got back to Ottawa that Lesage had persuaded me to quit the federal caucus and run in the Shawinigan by-election. There was a lot of rivalry between the federal and Quebec Liberals then, and the rumours were carried quickly to Pearson. He called me into his office and asked me if the reports were true. "Yes, I'm thinking of going," I replied.

Those were difficult days for Pearson. He was trying to do so much to help French Canadians and combat the incipient separatism, yet every time he moved forward, something made him roll back. It was like dragging a car from the mud. He asked me, "Jean, do you believe in Canada?"

"Of course I believe in Canada," I said, somewhat taken aback. "If you wish, I will not go, Prime Minister."

"No, don't make that decision right away," he said. "Go home and take a week to think about it."

"But we're in a minority situation."

"Don't worry, we'll survive," he said. "Just take your time."

So I went back to Shawinigan and consulted nineteen friends and my wife about what I should do. Seventeen of them told me to go to Quebec City. In those days there wasn't much happening federally beyond the post office, some quays, and unemployment insurance claims. All the activities that mattered locally, whether jobs or schools or patronage, were provincial because that's where the money was. But two friends—Fernand D. Lavergne and Marcel Crête, a very intelligent lawyer who is now Chief Justice of Quebec—urged me to stay in Ottawa. They felt I was doing well there and perhaps they detected the troubles that Lesage was to have by 1966. My own inclination was to go to Quebec, but I usually respected the advice of Lavergne and Crête. They were like weights that balanced my judgments, because Lavergne was a union leader and quite left wing while Crête sat on the boards of companies and was more conservative. Both had an extremely good understanding of politics.

Crête had been present at one occasion that was partly responsible for my going to Ottawa in the first place. We were lawyers together in the courts of Trois-Rivières and often we lunched with friends at the Château de Bois, a grand old hotel that unfortunately has burned down. One day there were four of us at lunch and we were debating the case of Marcel Chaput, a federal civil servant who had been fired for advocating separatism in the early days of the Quiet Revolution. I have never been a separatist but I was rather left wing and I believed in defending my own kind, so I sided with Chaput and launched into an attack on the English.

One of the other lawyers, Guy Lebrun, lit into me. "You're talking through your hat, Chrétien," he said. "You don't know any of the English, you've hardly even met them. You've never talked to them, you don't know their language. You've only been to Ottawa once or twice in your life, so I'm surprised at you. I thought you were an intelligent guy. The English may have their narrow-minded 'square heads,' but it looks like we have ours, too."

It was tough to take, particularly from a good friend. Lebrun had hit me hard and I was hurt. Later I drove back to Shawinigan alone, about twenty miles. For the first five miles I was screaming at that son of a gun. For the second five miles I was plotting how to get even. For the third five miles I began to think about what he had said. There was a lot of truth in it. By the time I reached home, I said to myself, "Yes, I should be more careful. I shouldn't get emotional and shoot off my mouth without any knowledge." Before that incident all my thinking and background would have led me into provincial politics. After it I became more interested in the broader field, all of Canada.

My wife was also telling me to stay in Ottawa, so I followed the opinion of my three closest advisers and telephoned Pearson at the end of the week to say I would not be going to Quebec. I expected him to be joyful, but his voice sounded dead. All he said was, "Thank you very much, Jean." Later I learned that he had just heard that another of his French-Canadian ministers was allegedly implicated in another scandal, this one involving influence-peddling, of which he was eventually acquitted. The next day, however, Pearson was his usual bouncy self. He came over to me in the Commons and shook my hand. Though he didn't promise me anything, he seemed grateful that I had chosen Canada.

CHAPTER TWO

LEARNING THE ROPES

MANY CANADIANS don't understand the House of Commons. They turn on their televisions, see us yelling at one another, and dismiss us as a bunch of fools. Sometimes even my wife will say, "Jean, you're shouting too much in the House." But often I have to shout. There is a reason for that, beyond the wish to be heard. The House of Commons is primarily a debating society. People tune in and wonder why we aren't looking after their welfare cheques or putting commas in the legislation, but our concern is the broad direction of policy.

The model is, of course, the British House of Commons, in which members have seats rather than desks to encourage them to speak without notes — the British Speaker can rule members out of order if they rely too heavily on a written text. Views are not delivered in speeches from a podium, as in France, or written by unknown assistants. In the disagreements over policies or actions there can be interruptions, questions, and clashes of personality: Why have you done this? What about that? It is a human experience, and the purpose is to discover the truth, affect changes, and seek the mind of the government. We are not talking to the nation: we are individuals confronting individuals.

That can create a bad impression on television. We forget that the cameras are there and that millions of people are listening in on what is essentially a personal discussion among elected members. Television is an intruder in a sense, and though I'm not against its presence, it has changed the institution. More and more texts are read at length and no one knows if they reflect the opinions of the speaker or some back-room speechwriter. Great debates and great debaters have become rarer, as homeviewing takes away from the exciting atmosphere created when the public galleries are overflowing, the press gallery is packed, and everyone is eager to witness history in the flesh. The cut and thrust seem more artificial as members speak to the cameras instead of to each other, and the House itself seems to have lost its aura of almost sacred mystery by being taken out of its context and placed in every living room.

The old spirit still exists during question period. With its tough questions, catcalls, and laughter, it puts the ministers on the spot. They cannot hide from the public or behind their officials. "Be honest! Be honest!" That is the call of the House of Commons. If we go too far in our attacks, we have to withdraw or earn the anger of the Speaker and the people. On the other hand, if a minister makes a big mistake, the whole government can tremble for weeks. No matter how many back-benchers a governing party has for a vote, everyone on the front bench is under pressure not to look incompetent or ridiculous; and, human nature being what it is, sometimes the back-benchers will pass notes to the opposition in order to keep the heat on a certain minister in the hope that he'll be fired and they'll have a chance to get into the cabinet.

That gives the House of Commons real power. For example, in December 1984, the question period forced Prime Minister Mulroney to define his position on the universality of social programs. He had many options and he had been waffling, but under pressure from opposition attacks he pulled the rug from under his Minister of Finance and said that money would be taken from the rich and given to the poor. Came the spring and Mulroney changed his mind, accepting in the budget the de-indexing of pensions. Because of renewed pressure in the House of Commons, he pulled the rug again from under his poor minister. The House once more had done a fantastic piece of work by changing something for the better.

Many Canadians believe that the House of Commons can do nothing but rubber stamp what the government wants. Obviously, not everyone can be preoccupied with details in the Excise Act and how money will be collected at the border. But many television viewers aren't aware of the work of the committees to which the bills are referred. There the fine points of legislation are examined by members who have become specialists in that field. A member with an interest in external affairs may be appointed to that committee and then become an authority on NATO, for instance, and his or her authority may have an impact on the government. The committees may call witnesses when studying a bill or departmental budgets, and they may form into sub-committees that travel and listen to the people and make recommendations. Often committees produce non-partisan proposals that the government can accept easily, unless the cost is prohibitive.

Members from Quebec probably aren't too knowledgeable about transportation in the West and members from Alberta probably aren't too concerned about the fisheries in the Atlantic. In such cases the general tendency is to vote with your party in good faith. That doesn't mean that members are nothing but sheep. I know because I was accused of being a sheep the first day I arrived in the House of Commons.

The issue was whether Canada should agree to placing Bomarc missiles on its soil. The policy of the Liberal Party was to accept them, because Canada had a commitment to do so, but during the election I had said that I was against the policy. Pearson got a message to me to keep quiet until after the campaign, but there were already headlines that a Liberal candidate in Quebec was opposed to the Bomarcs. So the damage had been done, if speaking frankly was indeed damage.

Certainly I had a hell of a problem because there was a vote of confidence on the issue as soon as Parliament met and the Liberals were a minority government. Lucien Cardin, the Associate Minister of Defence, came to see me. I asked, "Lucien, are we really committed or not? You know, I'm a Quebec lawyer, so I want to see the text. Is there a commitment on paper?" Cardin did something very unusual. He arranged for me to see some confidential documents. I was taken to a little room in the Privy Council Office, the documents were brought, and I was left alone. Unfortunately everything was in English. There were many words I didn't know, there was nobody I could ask for a translation, and I wouldn't have wanted to admit that my English was so poor anyway. In the end, of course, I was no more convinced than before.

Then I ran into Douglas Harkness washing his hands in the men's room outside the House. He was a great gentleman who had been Minister of Defence in the Conservative government until he resigned because Diefenbaker had refused the Bomarcs. In my very painful English I told him my problem, and he replied, "Young man, if you knew me, you'd know what a Tory I am. To have resigned from the cabinet was not a light matter for me. I did it because Canada did have a commitment." That convinced me; I went into the House and voted with my party. The next day, however, I made a naive mistake: I stood to explain my vote. It was awful. I got catcalls and *Le Devoir* said I was a sheep. My father was quite humiliated and very angry that his son was called a sheep.

Nevertheless, my parliamentary career was launched with a bang and I moved quickly. The Speaker, Alan Macnaughton, liked me, and when it was time to let a Liberal back-bencher ask a question of his own cabinet ministers, he often looked over to where I sat with Cashin, Basford, and the other "rebels." We asked a lot of questions and took turns talking out opposition bills so that they wouldn't pass in the allotted time. Before too long I had learned the ropes sufficiently to accomplish a significant reform.

In 1964 I wanted to change the name of Trans-Canada Airlines to Air Canada. This was the period of rampant, sometimes violent nationalism in Quebec, and the old name had become a hateful symbol because it didn't translate easily into French. I had tried in my first session in the House to pass a private member's bill, but it had failed. This wasn't surprising, because it is almost impossible for a back-bencher to get a bill passed. There's only an hour a day, between five and six o'clock, for the discussion of private members' bills, so not many come up in a session. Those that do must be passed in the hour or they're sent back to the bottom of the list, and seldom surface again. Each party can speak on the bill, and the government can always kill it by getting a member to talk till six o'clock. I wondered how I could avoid another setback. By the time I got my bill back to the top of the order paper in the next session, I had figured out a sort of trick.

I went to see Rémi Paul, a Tory member from Quebec, who was very conservative but quite pleasant. I said to him, "I have my bill on Air Canada coming up and you guys will kill it. That's not very good for Quebec. Help me. At least say nice things about it." Paul agreed. Then I went and asked the same of Bob Prittie, an NDPer from Vancouver who spoke French, and Réal Caouette of the Social Credit. So I had lined up all the speakers in my favour. Then I went back to each of them and said, "If you don't speak too long, the bill will pass." The toughest to convince was Rémi Paul, because the Tories were strongly opposed to the change, but eventually he agreed.

So when my bill came up, I rose and made a very short, deliberately unprovocative speech. I may have mentioned the bilingual advantage of the new name, but I stuck to plain arguments: Air Canada was shorter, the airline was no longer just flying across Canada, and there were two other TCAs: Trans-Caribbean and Trans-Continental. Then Paul got up and said, "I agree," and Prittie got up and said, "I agree," and Caouette got up and said, "I agree." By 5:15 there were no more speakers, so my bill passed second reading. Under the rules it would have to stay on the order paper until fully passed. In effect that would have delayed all the other private members' bills for the rest of the session. The government wasn't happy about the change, primarily because of the cost, but by six o'clock it was accomplished. Later I received a very generous letter from Pearson, thanking me for solving a problem in a painless way.

It was an interesting example of what effect a lone MP can have and it is unfortunate when the press ignores the ordinary member of Parliament. MPs are very important in their ridings, and the community service they provide for their constituents is both valuable and demanding, even when it's not visible or newsworthy. They are like local ombudsmen, linking the people with the government, or ambassadors from the ridings to Parliament. They have thousands of concerns, from people having problems getting their old-age pensions or unemployment insurance to families wanting assistance with immigration, and from businessmen seeking grants to municipalities requesting industries. They receive delegations, arrange meetings with cabinet ministers or bureaucrats, serve as patrons to community activities, and even rush to get passports for last-minute travellers. Since the MPs have no boss except the voters at election time, they can do nothing or they can make a full-time job out of serving people well. Most of them work extremely hard in order to get re-elected.

Moreover, they have an influence on ministers that the public rarely appreciates. At a party function shortly after the 1963 election I reminded the ministers that they were in the front benches because we were in the back. It was the cockiness of a twenty-nine-year-old, but I never forgot that even when I became a minister. It is essential to maintain a good rapport with the party MPs and keep them on side. During the constitution debates I always listened to the arguments of the Liberal back-benchers who opposed the constitution package. One of the dissidents even supported my candidacy for the leadership of the party shortly afterwards.

The most effective contributions of many MPs go unreported because they often take place in the party caucuses, which are secret. There are regional caucuses and special caucuses on various subjects, such as agriculture or regional development, but the key one is the general caucus that meets every week when Parliament is sitting. It's a chance for questions and complaints, reports and policy development, topical problems and general discussions. The caucus of the governing party includes the prime minister and his cabinet, of course, so it's a place for significant back-bench input. Sometimes MPs don't get much press attention because they don't make much use of the House of Commons, but they'll get up now and then in the caucus and speak so much sense that their views are noted; and ministers are often more devastated by a frank, well-reasoned attack from one of their own MPs than from a slew of opposition critics and reporters.

Occasionally an MP who is unknown to the press and the public will be appointed to the cabinet as if from nowhere and for no particular reason. Often the appointment results from a series of intelligent interventions in caucus that brought the MP to the attention of the leadership. The more common story, unfortunately, is that many good MPs never get the recognition or the reward their influence deserves. Those who have achieved a stunning coup in caucus are the least likely to boast about it in public, because they know they would be the prime suspects in any breach of confidentiality. Many times they don't even realize that they have changed a decision by convincing a minister with a pertinent intervention. Seldom does the minister go back to them and say, "It's because of your little speech that I decided to do things this way." I regret I didn't do that more often when in cabinet, but in the crazy world of politics such a gesture might have looked like insincere back-slapping. As a result there are frustrations built into the process, because input and consultation aren't the same as decision-making, and every back-bencher knows that the decisions are made in the cabinet — where the glory also happens to be.

The problem is one of ego. Because some MPs are selected to be in the cabinet in the parliamentary system, two classes of politician are created. That's discouraging. Some people are content to stay on the back benches, look after their constituents, make contributions in caucus or committees, and leave no deep mark on history. I had a good friend like that, a very good member of Parliament, an extremely intelligent guy, who was never off the beam when he spoke, but he had no ambition. He was pressured into politics by his friends because he was a popular lawyer who had a chance to defeat the local Tory. When he arrived in Ottawa he served his constituents but never worked to become a minister because he didn't give a damn about being a minister. Later he became a Superior Court judge and wouldn't accept an elevation to the Appeal Court. He was comfortable with himself and knew what he wanted in life.

No doubt many more MPs want to go into the cabinet, and they often fail for reasons that have nothing to do with their capabilities or intellects. On the one hand, I like to argue that anyone who wants to be a minister badly enough, works hard, and has the talent usually becomes a minister. On the other hand, I have to recognize that because of regional representation or representation by age, sex, and ethnic background, the cabinet frequently contains people who aren't first-rate and excludes talent that should be there. Nor is long service automatically rewarded as it was in the United States, where seniority made senators and congressmen chairmen of important, high-profile committees. The personal disappointment of MPs is compounded when public attention is focused on the leadership and the work of the ordinary member is ignored.

Not only is that focus unfair to individuals, it undermines the whole system. Parliament has lost some of its relevance because the media have made elections more presidential than parliamentary. The classic notion of a parliamentary election is that 282 individuals are elected to represent their ridings. In theory, the people of Shawinigan vote for Jean Chrétien, who just happens to be a Liberal. Tomorrow I could become a Tory or an independent or a Communist and I would not have to resign my seat. Again in theory, elected individuals gather in an assembly, select a speaker as referee, and form alliances according to policies. Gradually a cabinet and a prime minister emerge. That is the traditional British system, which began when the nobles used to come together to resolve the problems of the nation.

More and more, however, perhaps because of the nature of the media and Canada's proximity to the American presidential system, elections are fought among party leaders. In a sweep such as the Tory victory in 1984, good members are swept out with the same broom as bad ones, while bad ones are carried in on the coattails of the victorious party. So the work, personality, and intelligence of MPs count for less and less in the riding campaigns. In my judgment maybe no more than fifty MPs make a personal difference in the outcome of their elections. The rest tend to rely on the appeal of their leader and the luck of belonging to the winning party. The risk is that MPs will become more marginal, more expendable, and at the mercy of the leadership. Certainly fewer back-benchers will be prepared to give their leaders frank advice or tell them to go to hell if they know they can be replaced.

This is a danger for our system because we don't have the same checks and balances that are built into the American presidency. I prefer Canada's parliamentary system, but I see a problem in its evolution if

43

too many people become dependent on the will and popularity of the leaders. That is happening largely because the personalities of a few people have usurped the normal political debate in the media. I had a vivid experience of that when I ran for the leadership of the Liberal Party in 1984. For a couple of months everything I said and did was big news, but during the federal election a few weeks later nobody bothered with me even though I campaigned in ninety-five ridings for the party.

In my opinion the media have more impact by deciding what is news than in their editorials. Politicians and bureaucrats may read editorials and be influenced by them in the course of governing, but I don't think many voters are swayed by what an editor thinks during an election. In 1980, if I recall correctly, Trudeau received the endorsement of only four newspaper editors out of more than a hundred, yet he won a majority. In 1965 I was very pleased when Claude Ryan mentioned me in an editorial in *Le Devoir* as one of five Quebec Liberals who ought to be elected in their ridings. He preferred to support individuals rather than parties. (I still smile at the thought that he recommended me but not Trudeau — I don't think Trudeau ever forgave Ryan.) I felt so good about that editorial that I almost went back to bed the morning I read it. I boasted about it in my speeches for days. But do you know how many of my constituents commented on what Ryan had written? One hundred? Two hundred? The answer is two — a brother of mine and a well-educated accountant.

On the whole I am not critical of the press in Canada. Personally, I have been treated reasonably well and generally I have a good relationship with journalists, though there are some with whom I'm less than comfortable. I would rather deal with a tough, professional press than operate in the old ways of Maurice Duplessis, who rewarded good stories with envelopes of money and blackballed newspapers that printed unfavourable stories. I have found that if you treat journalists professionally, they will treat you the same way. Nowadays pride in their work is likely more important than money for most reporters. But when you talk to reporters you have to be careful of the circumstances. If you're off the record and you reveal something that they know may hurt you, they will usually play straight with you if you have played straight with

44

them in the past, too. If you've tried to use them, however, they aren't fools and they'll sock it to you.

One of my worst run-ins came in 1975 when *The Globe and Mail* reported a statement of Mr. Justice Kenneth Mackay of Quebec that I had tried to influence another judge. A company in my riding had been closed down for six months and its 400 employees laid off because the company's assets had been frozen pending a court decision about a bankruptcy. Since I felt it was my duty and since there was no other route open at the time, I called the judge who was to decide the case and said, "When are you going to make up your mind? I've got 400 guys out of work. I don't care what you decide, just decide something so these guys can go back to work."

When the story broke, I phoned the judge again and he was happy to dictate a letter denying that I had tried to influence him. I sent a copy of the letter to Mr. Justice Mackay, who promptly retracted his accusation and admitted in a letter to my lawyer that he had made a mistake. However, that letter was misplaced for several days, during which my name continued to be muddied in the *Globe*. Finally it published Mackay's letter and an apology. I was still angry, however, so I called the national editor and said, "Yesterday I gave a full explanation in the House and you didn't print it."

"We didn't have a translator," he said.

"Come on," I replied. "If I had said I was guilty, I bet you would have found a translator pretty quickly. If you don't do better than that, I'll sue."

"Is that a threat?" he asked.

I wasn't intending to sue, but I was trapped. "No," I said. "It's a promise." I called my lawyer and very good friend, Pierre Genest.

The matter dragged on for years. The problem was that I was claiming damages while my career continued to soar. Eventually, however, I got $3,000. My lawyer gave it to my wife, saying, "Buy whatever you want because your husband doesn't deserve a dime." So she bought a piano. Now whenever anyone comes to visit I introduce my wife, my kids, and my "*Globe and Mail* piano."

The best approach is to see journalists as professionals with a job to do. No one wants to be seen in a bad light, but it is better to be candid about your weaknesses and shortcomings than to try to manipulate the press. I have always worked to be accessible and to deal with all reporters equally. The press has my home phone number and it is not unusual for a reporter to call me on a Sunday night, often after failing to reach anybody else. Naturally I see some reporters more than others, because of their specialization or personality, but I have not gone out of my way to be buddy-buddy with any of them.

Some politicians look on the press as being primarily left wing. Certainly most reporters aren't among the financial élite. They're usually well-educated but they live the lives of average citizens. So their viewpoints tend to reflect society from that position. Furthermore, many journalists are by nature independent people who like to fight establishments — or else they would be doing something more lucrative or settled — and there is a tradition in their profession to oppose governments rather than support governments. An ironic example of that occurred when Patrick O'Callaghan, the publisher of the *Edmonton Journal* who fought me tooth and nail when I worked to get a charter of rights as Minister of Justice, became one of the first people to win a case on the basis of the charter, after some documents were seized from his offices during a police search. It was with some relish that I phoned him to tease him about it.

What is disturbing, however, is that fewer and fewer reporters seem to want to be reporters these days. They sound like frustrated columnists or editorialists. In the old days reporters strived to present the facts, and their pride rested in their accuracy. They used wonderful descriptions and created the atmosphere of events, but their basis was fact. Now it seems that the pride of reporters rests in being commentators. Every page is filled with disguised opinions. That can be annoying when it goes too far, as it often did in Quebec on the matter of separation; but I learned to live with that, even to laugh at it. That's the freedom of the press, after all. Many times the editors themselves didn't know what was going on, and they were under a lot of peer pressure.

By 1965 I was often mentioned favourably in the Quebec press as an active, "new guard" Liberal. I was the Prime Minister's parliamentary secretary, I had seconded the Speech from the Throne in my second session, I had brought in the name Air Canada, and I was working hard in the committees. Soon my name began to show up in the newspapers in the short lists of potential cabinet ministers. At one point there was speculation that if George McIlraith became Minister of Justice, I would be appointed Solicitor General; but Lucien Cardin was promoted to the Justice portfolio, so he was complemented by an English Canadian, Larry Pennell. Still, my hopes were high that something might happen after the 1965 election.

Pearson had consulted me about calling that election as a gamble to secure a majority government, and I had advised him against it. "We have a minority and we should tough it out," I said. But he was pressured into it by the cabinet, particularly Walter Gordon, his close adviser and Minister of Finance. Pearson invited me to make a speech at his nomination meeting in Algoma, Ontario, and later in the campaign he sent me back there with Mary Macdonald, his influential Executive Assistant, on his behalf. I gave little speeches in my terrible English, and as a laugh I once got Mary to get up and translate one into French, which she did. She used to give me notes about all the people I was to meet — what they did or some character trait — and I used to annoy her by repeating her information to the people themselves: "I'm supposed to know this about you or I'm supposed to say that to you." We had great fun.

I was campaigning in Algoma East with Mike Pearson when he told me of a new development. The Liberals had recruited three exceptional candidates in Quebec: Jean Marchand, Gérard Pelletier, and Pierre Elliott Trudeau. I had heard of them, of course. Marchand was a well-known union leader who had been one of the first to stand up to Duplessis in a tough, energetic way; Pelletier was a distinguished journalist who had worked closely with Marchand; and Trudeau had a reputation as a radical intellectual. I had never met Trudeau, but he was a friend of Fernand D. Lavergne and occasionally visited Shawinigan on union business.

"What do you think of them coming with us?" Pearson asked me.

47

I thought it would be a good thing. The coming of the "three wise men" to Ottawa would buck the trend of bright Quebeckers staying in Quebec, and it would be Pearson's greatest achievement in rebuilding the federal Liberal Party. "But I have a problem with this guy Trudeau," I said. "We'll never get him elected anywhere." In fact, it proved difficult to find a riding for him. I was told he wanted a French-speaking seat, but he ended up in an English-speaking suburb of Montreal.

Then Pearson said, "You know, Jean, this might mean that you won't come into the cabinet as quickly as hoped."

I didn't feel bad because I understood the situation. "Prime Minister," I said, "if you have better people than me, you should promote them before me."

After the election, which produced another minority, Marchand went into the cabinet, but Pelletier and Trudeau hung back in order to learn their way around Parliament. So it looked like there was an opening for me. I was a parliamentary secretary; I was from rural Quebec, which balanced the preponderance of ministers from Montreal and Quebec City; I had refused to go into provincial politics at Pearson's request. Marchand said publicly that I was ready to be a minister, and Pearson indicated to me that I would be appointed. It seemed a sure thing, and the press was phoning me regularly with questions and speculations. But when the new cabinet was announced, Jean-Pierre Côté, a Montreal-area MP and later Quebec's Lieutenant-Governor, was named instead. Nobody had expected that, and I suspected a little intrigue. That isn't an accusation. I have no evidence, and Côté turned out to be a good minister as well as a friend. He was older than I, a very likeable fellow, and his riding organizer was the brother-in-law of Guy Favreau, then Pearson's Quebec leader. My case may not have been helped by having the support of Marchand, who represented a shift of power that threatened Favreau, and I was not part of any gang that might have advanced my interest. I have always been independent, something of a loner, and I was even more of a maverick in those days. So I can't blame Favreau for wanting someone closer and more reliable in the cabinet with him. The story I heard was that Jack Pickersgill, the veteran Liberal strategist who was then Minister of Transport, went to

Pearson on Favreau's behalf and asked that Côté be put in the cabinet as a favour to the Quebec leader.

I was standing near the Prime Minister's Office when Pearson spotted me and called me in. "Jean," he said, "you're mad at me because I named Côté a minister instead of you."

"I cannot be mad at you, Mr. Pearson," I said, though I was very disappointed, "because I'm not in a position to question your judgment." Besides, Pearson could disarm anyone with a pat on the back and his warm charm.

Then he said, "Someday you will understand, Jean. I am going to appoint you parliamentary secretary to Mitchell Sharp in Finance. You will learn things there, and I hope you will become the first French-Canadian Minister of Finance. If I had taken you into the cabinet today, in the traditional French-Canadian portfolio of Postmaster General that I have given to Côté, it might not lead you to greater things."

That was very kind of him, and though I cannot be sure if it was more kindness than sincerity, it turned out to be prophetic.

There was a reason he thought in terms of Finance. When I was first elected, Pearson circulated a form on which he asked all the Liberal MPs what committees they wished to be on. I mentioned the form to my friend Jean-Paul Gignac one day when we were driving between Shawinigan and Montreal. I said I was tempted to apply for Finance. Having had to fight the Créditistes, I had become interested in monetary policy in order to challenge their "funny money" theory.

"That's a good idea," Gignac said, "You're young, you could learn something important, and there aren't too many French Canadians who know much about finance."

So I put Finance as my first and only choice. Later Pearson told me that that had struck him because I was the only member, English or French, who had done so. He put me on the House Finance and Banking Committee and that gave him the idea of sending me to Sharp. It served two purposes that had consequences down the line: it gave me the ambition to become the first French-Canadian Minister of Finance; and it allowed Pearson to make Pierre Trudeau his parliamentary secretary.

My association with Mitchell Sharp, who had been a senior public servant before becoming a cabinet minister, was a fantastic experience. He became my mentor in politics. He taught me everything about the operations of government, and he gave me a post-graduate course in economics. I had been impressed by him from a distance, but I had been closer to Walter Gordon. I was seen to be on the left wing of the party, and Sharp was seen on the right. It was a period of great battles, with the party arguing about the introduction of medicare and debating protectionism versus free trade, and very often Gordon and the progressives were lined up against Sharp. My ideas didn't shift too much, but I felt obliged to defend my minister in these fights. In time he influenced me a great deal.

Because of the Liberals' minority we had to remain on hand in case there was a sudden vote, so there were countless evenings when I talked for hours with Mitchell in his office, his ill wife often by his side. Since my own family was usually in Shawinigan, I used to drop in on Mitchell and eventually I became part of the furniture. He let me stay no matter who showed up, and I listened. After decisions were made, I would ask him why he had done this or why he hadn't done that, and he would explain. We discussed the mechanisms of governments, the motivation of bureaucrats, the international monetary system — everything.

I got to know such great public servants as Bob Bryce, Louis Rasminsky, Simon Reisman and Edgar Gallant. They were men of long experience, with brilliant minds and great integrity, who shunned intrigues and the cocktail circuit in order to dedicate themselves to the public good. They always made me feel welcome among them, they were extremely patient and helpful, and I felt that their company was better than a university.

The first day after my appointment Mitchell invited me into a meeting where there were nothing but big shots: the Governor of the Bank of Canada, the Deputy Governor, the Deputy Minister of Finance, and so on. For an hour and a half they discussed bond issues and tariff rates and balance of payments, and I listened with wonder and awe. Finance was still a very mysterious thing for me. After the meeting Mitchell came up to me and said, "Jean, what you have heard today is very secret. You must not say a word to anybody about it."

"Don't be worried, Mitchell," I said. "I didn't understand a bloody thing."

His education gave me the background to prepare two major speeches on the economic effects of Quebec separation. I knew I would be attacked as the mouthpiece of the anglo establishment, so I deliberately chose four francophones from the Department of Finance—Edgar Gallant, Gérard Veilleux, Michel Vennat, and Jacques Malouin — to work with me. I wanted to be able to say that my arguments represented the work of five French Canadians and no one else.

Sure enough, René Lévesque accused me of being the mouthpiece of the "mandarins." He was still a Liberal in 1966, but he was developing the idea of sovereignty-association. He discussed it with Liberal Robert Bourassa, and apparently the future Liberal Premier of Quebec said, "This is serious stuff that Chrétien is producing." Certainly those speeches earned me a lot of attention by arguing against separation on the basis of economics.

Pearson obviously got good reports of my work with Sharp, and my public reputation had continued to grow, so my name was bandied about once again for the cabinet. One morning in April 1967, I was summoned to Pearson's office. There were rumours of a cabinet shuffle. Though I knew that other members were lobbying, I had expected to be promoted since the New Year; and in my ambitious little mind I felt that I deserved to be a cabinet minister. Pierre Trudeau waited with me that morning, and when he was the first to be called in by Pearson, I figured he was to get the bigger job. He became Minister of Justice, and I became Minister without Portfolio attached to Finance. I felt great. Trudeau and I were sworn in on April 4 along with John Turner, who was elevated from Minister without Portfolio to Registrar General.

There was some complaint among the "old guard" in the Quebec caucus about two "new guard" members going into the cabinet, but I found that ironic when I remembered my first political encounter with Trudeau. It must have been just after the 1965 election. The artificial division of the Quebec Liberal MPs into the "old" and "new" guard— essentially pre-1963 and post-1963 — was unfair and arbitrary; but the press had established the distinction and everyone was aware of it. So when there was an election for the chairman of the Quebec caucus, the two groups tended to line up behind their own candidates. A friend of mine, Gérald Laniel, ran for the "new guard" and I supported him; indeed I proposed him. As it happened, he lost by one vote. Trudeau hadn't voted. Had it been a tie, the chairman had been expected to vote for our guy. In other words, Trudeau lost us the election. I went over and gave him hell.

"But, Jean," he said, "I don't know these guys. They didn't make any speeches, so how could I have decided to vote for one or the other?"

"But you should have had some indication when you saw me propose Laniel," I said. "That was a sign that he's the 'new guard' guy."

"Pardon me," Trudeau replied. "There is no 'new guard' or 'old guard' for me. I didn't know those guys, so I didn't vote for either of them."

"But weren't you impressed by the fact that I proposed Laniel?"

"I wasn't impressed at all," he said.

"Gee, Pierre," I said, "you'd better learn something about politics or you won't go very far." I was disappointed, and all the "new guard" guys were angry at this beatnik. The worst part was that, in his logic and his objectivity, he was right.

Six or eight months after that, as I recall, he and I were part of the federal delegation at a closed-door meeting of the federal and provincial ministers of Finance. We both marvelled at how Sharp dominated the proceedings. He was knowledgeable, he was calm, and he was able to see through the problems. At one point Trudeau remarked, "This guy would make a good prime minister if only he could speak French." Afterwards, Sharp held a press conference, and Trudeau said to me, "It might be a good idea if we stood behind Mitchell and got our pictures in the newspapers." Not only would it help us in our ridings, he implied, it would show that Quebec MPs were participating in the meeting.

"You learn fast, Trudeau," I said.

In those days the cabinet met in what is now part of the East Block muscum. There weren't enough seats for everyone around the table, so there was a second row of chairs. You certainly felt very junior sitting in the second row. If someone didn't show up, you could move to the table, and that was always a thrill. The first day after I was sworn in, I was walking with Bob Bryce, the brilliant Deputy Minister of Finance. Usually I let him pass first into a room because he was older and wiser than I, but this day he motioned for me to go first. "Now you're a minister," he said.

"No, no, Bob," I said. "I know that you bureaucrats are the ones with the real power. I have no illusions. You go first." But he insisted, so I went ahead.

By the time I joined the cabinet, I had a pretty good understanding of how it operated from all of my talks with Mitchell Sharp. Backbenchers are frustrated because they think that all the decisions are made by the cabinet, but ministers feel a similar frustration because they see that the power is really with the prime minister. There are no votes in cabinet, except on marginal issues such as whether ministers should be allowed to smoke during the meeting. There is a discussion, and then there is a decision. In theory the prime minister makes all the decisions. If he always goes against the consensus of his cabinet, of course, ministers will resign and he will not survive long. Contrary to the public perception, Pearson was much less consensual than Trudeau. He had his own views, and most of the time he just did what he wanted to do. There would be great storms in cabinet, with ministers pounding the table and raging at each other. Then Pearson would say in the middle of the mess, "It's time to go to lunch, so I'll take care of the matter." Few people would realize that he was accomplishing exactly what he wanted.

Pearson's administration looked chaotic, but it wasn't a case of weak management or lack of direction. He was very, very tough in managing his ministers, and he knew what had to be tackled. It was a tormented era, however, and the problems that overtook him were controversial, often emotional ones, such as the flag and bilingualism. There were also the normal difficulties of minority governments, compounded by a Leader of the Opposition who was highly irresponsible. Diefenbaker said anything about everything if it suited his political purpose. That was my impression, at least. It looked as if he thought that God had chosen him prime minister, and Pearson had got in the way of his destiny. He always seemed in an angry mood — perhaps because his own party was trying to stab him in the back — so he exploited the bad luck of some of Pearson's ministers by exaggerating the so-called scandals.

That gave the wrong impression of Pearson's cabinet. Obviously not all the ministers were strong, but history has confirmed the strength of people such as Mitchell Sharp, Walter Gordon, Allan MacEachen, Paul Martin, Lionel Chévrier, and Guy Favreau. Many of Pearson's ministers had powerful backgrounds and firm ideas. That sometimes made for a fractious and leaky cabinet, in which there were plenty of ideological and political fights that showed up in the press day after day. Public feuding among departments and cabinet members is more common in the United States than in Canada, because the Americans aren't bound by cabinet solidarity. Maybe Pearson learned to be rather tolerant during his time in Washington with External Affairs. Normally his ministers rallied around Pearson when he had troubles. Despite his toughness, he seldom seemed heavy-handed, and his diplomatic experience allowed him to perform well when trapped in a crisis. His cheery awkwardness made everyone want to come to his rescue, and there was a lot of warmth for him that didn't exist for Trudeau later. People respected Trudeau's intellect, whereas with Pearson they respected his personality. We all thought he was a great man.

I got into trouble with the first speech I made as a minister. It was to the German Association of Canada in Toronto on the subject of whether Quebec should have a special status as a province. That was an important debate at the time. Because I was to speak in English, I enlisted the help of my assistant, John Rae, an extremely bright, perfectly bilingual kid and older brother of Bob Rae, now leader of the Ontario NDP. I had spotted him in 1965 in Switzerland, where his father was Canadian ambassador, and I had said to my wife, "If ever I become a minister, I will have a guy like that as my assistant."

When I offered him the job, he had just earned the right to vote because he had just turned twenty-one years old. He had been the editor of the Queen's University newspaper, and at one point his ambition had been to be a journalist, so he used to get a big thrill when the speeches he wrote to express my ideas were reported and commented upon in newspapers across the country. "Do you know how long it would have taken me to get on the editorial page as a reporter?" he used to laugh. Eventually he became a vice-president of Power Corporation in Montreal, and he was the manager of my leadership campaign in 1984.

Anyway, in this first speech I said, "Those who are in favour of special status are often separatists who don't want to admit that they are separatists." Because the subject fell under the prerogatives of the minister of justice, I showed my draft to Trudeau, who said, "You are absolutely right. It's going to hurt, and you'll have some problems, but you're right."

Being full of bravado I thought, "If that's what I believe, that's what I'll say." So I went off to Toronto with my speech under my arm and John Rae at my side. When we arrived at the hotel, Rae went up to the desk and said, "I'd like the keys for the rooms of the Honourable Jean Chrétien and his assistant."

"Who are you?" the clerk asked. You have to remember that Rae was twenty-one and looked fifteen.

"I'm the assistant."

"Go away, kid," the clerk said.

Rae came back, very embarrassed, but I said, "Don't worry about it, John, I'll fix it up." So I went up to the desk and said, "I'd like the keys for the rooms of the Honourable Jean Chrétien and his assistant."

"Who are you?" the clerk said. You have to remember that I became a minister when I was thirty-three.

"I'm the minister."

But the clerk wouldn't give me the keys either. It wasn't an auspicious start.

The speech was well-received, but there was a problem in the translation. Rae's draft had been translated into French, but I hadn't checked the French version thoroughly enough before it was released to the press. The translator had dropped the word "often" so my statement read, "Those who are in favour of special status are separatists who don't want to admit that they are separatists." That little error caused me a political storm in Quebec. I felt I was finished forever in politics. The Quebec press howled, every intellectual in the province jumped on me, and even my family and friends thought I had blundered. It was really bad.

In retrospect, what was significant about the incident was what Trudeau had said to me when I showed him the text. "Jean," he said, "we have always known what we wanted." I assumed that he meant "I" when he said "we," because I was fifteen years younger than he and had been a student when he was articulating his ideas in *Cité Libre* in the 1950s. "We have always been federalists," he went on. "Look at these intellectuals who want special status for Quebec. They are the same ones who wanted the federal government to take over education because Duplessis wasn't doing enough in that field. We opposed that idea then. We said that we have to respect the constitution, that education is a provincial responsibility, and that if we feel Duplessis isn't doing a good job, we should kick him out. We still believe in the constitution. If it's inadequate, we can work to change it, but in the meantime we have to respect it. We have been consistent, and in the long run we will be proven to have been the right ones because we knew where we were going." I could not have guessed that a year later this man would be the Prime Minister of Canada.

By the fall of 1967 there were indications that Pearson was ready to step down. I think he was simply tired after all the battles of a decade. In November I heard from an inside source that Pearson would be announcing his resignation within weeks. I remember telling that to Donald Macdonald, a very good friend who was to become Minister of Finance under Trudeau. He was discontented because he was still a parliamentary secretary after five or six years in the House of Commons, and he was thinking seriously about returning to his law practice in Toronto after the next election. "Don't say anything," I advised him. "Something big will happen in the next few weeks that might change your mind." Sure enough, it did happen and Macdonald decided to stay in politics.

Before Pearson went, however, he named me Minister of National Revenue in January 1968. It wasn't a controversial portfolio and I had two good deputy ministers, one for customs and excise and one for taxation, so I can't say I made a great impact in that department, though I suppose my photograph is hanging somewhere in its corridors. Everyone was distracted by the leadership campaign. In the fall of 1967 there had been a party convention in Alberta. So many ministers — Paul Martin, Robert Winters, Paul Hellyer, John Turner, Allan MacEachen, Joe Greene and Mitchell Sharp — had agreed to speak at it as a prelude to their campaigning that Pearson got angry. He told them all to stay in Ottawa. "Chrétien will go to represent the federal party," he said. It was one of the toughest assignments in my life. The Albertans were disappointed that all the big ministers had cancelled, they were furious at Pearson, and along came this little guy from Shawinigan who could barely speak English. I didn't feel very welcome, but somehow I survived. Actually, I was beginning to be known in the West. During the summer of Canada's Centennial, I had travelled across the country in a government railway car with my wife and daughter, France. It was one of the greatest trips of my life. For ten days we went from town to town, while I made speeches in Manitoba and Saskatchewan, saw the Calgary Stampede, visited Vancouver and Edmonton, and everywhere met Liberals who remained close friends and supporters.

As soon as the leadership convention was called, I committed myself to Mitchell Sharp. He had asked me if he should run and I had encouraged him to declare himself. Sharp was my mentor and I had felt a duty as his parliamentary secretary and junior minister to support his cause. Often I had to defend my support against my left-wing colleagues, who considered Sharp to be on the right of the party.

My position may have looked more difficult from the outside than from the inside. I have never been doctrinaire on issues. That is one of the great things about being a Liberal; you can base your decisions on the circumstances without having to worry about your established public image. If you are a socialist, all your decisions have to conform to the socialist slant, even if that slant doesn't offer a good solution to a particular problem, or else you have to justify your actions to your party and the press. Similarly, if you are a conservative, your solutions must conform to the conservative slant. Either way, the slant becomes more important than the decision.

To a lesser extent that happens within the Liberal Party; certain ministers become preoccupied about whether they are on the left or right wing of the party. If they see themselves on the left, they feel pressured to be seen on the left side of every argument; if they belong on the right, they feel obliged to stick to the right. I never belonged to any clan in cabinet, and that freed me to move among the clans as a minister. I could look at the problems directly, hear the debates, and make up my own mind about what to do. Some may have seen that as shifting and opportunism, but I saw it as independence and good sense. I backed Sharp because I thought he was the best man as well as a good friend. It didn't bother me when Quebec MPs said we should support one of our own or when the left wing accused me of desertion.

There was much speculation that Jean Marchand would run, but I knew he was worried about his weak grasp of English and his health. Then, around Christmas, the idea began to grow that Trudeau would be a good candidate. He was an unusual person and attracted a lot of favourable attention as Minister of Justice at a constitutional conference in February 1968, when he won an exchange with Daniel Johnson, the Premier of Quebec. Traditionally Quebec premiers liked to belittle federal ministers from their province. Johnson tried to dismiss Trudeau by calling him "the member from Mount Royal," a cheap shot to remind Quebeckers that Trudeau had been elected by the anglophones. Trudeau won the confrontation and became a media star at the same time.

In the same period there was a Liberal convention in Montreal at which I was working for Sharp. Marchand arranged to give the platform to Trudeau, who was not yet a candidate, and Trudeau gave a terrific speech about special status for Quebec in Confederation. Many Quebec Liberals were looking at special status as a compromise solution to the rise of the independence movement, but Trudeau hit them with the same arguments he had raised with me. "We are not better," he said. "We're equal." He was strong, and he created a hell of an impression. He demonstrated a remarkable talent as a speaker. He was one of the first politicians I had seen who tried to talk to people rather than shout at them.

Meanwhile Marchand, who could be a tough operator, was trying to get everyone to support Trudeau. "You have to vote for our man," he said to me. "We cannot divide the family."

"No, I'm sorry," I replied. "I'm with Sharp and that's that." Marchand didn't like it, but he never held it against me.

It wasn't long before Trudeaumania swept the country. At a party meeting in Toronto in February 1968, he walked into a room full of delegates, and everyone jumped to see the new phenomenon. An excitement pervaded the hotel, and even those who were supporting Sharp rushed out to see Trudeau. Our goose was probably cooked even without the parliamentary incident that crippled Sharp's candidacy and almost brought down the Liberal government in the middle of the leadership race.

This is what happened: one night in February in the House of Commons Sharp called for a vote on the third reading of a surtax bill. The party whip had told him that there were enough Liberals present to pass the bill, as indeed there were. But a few Tory MPs who had gone off to a movie decided to drop into the Commons to see what was going on. So, by accident, the Liberals lost the vote. Allan MacEachen rose and, in a marvellous demonstration of parliamentary skill, regained control of the House of Commons by seizing the initiative from the Tories and proposing an adjournment. The majority agreed, partly because the new Conservative leader, Robert Stanfield, who had replaced Diefenbaker in 1967, didn't have his predecessor's intuitive sense of the Commons. He must still dream about that adjournment, because it gained enough time for Pearson to fly back from his holiday in Jamaica and find a diplomatic solution that let his government survive by the skin of its teeth. The next day Réal Caouette said, "I defeated the measure, but I did not defeat the government." This was an unprecedented statement because normally in a parliamentary system a government that has been defeated on a money matter is expected to resign.

Since the bill had been his, Sharp felt responsible for what occurred. He gathered his key supporters in his office one night and told them that he intended to withdraw from the race. I arrived late from the Commons and found everyone with long faces. "Don't withdraw, Mitchell," I said. "If you withdraw now, you're finished. You may be Minister of Finance until the end of this regime, but your career will be over. Stay in as a candidate. Then make a statement that because of the extreme pressure on the dollar and so on, your first duty is to the country. Meanwhile your friends will campaign on your behalf."

He did that, and I went off to help him. At one point I flew to the West on a private jet belonging to an oil tycoon. He had a drinking problem, he hated paying taxes, and he didn't care for French Canadians very much. I was a non-drinking, French-Canadian minister who collected taxes. I had to take a lot of abuse from him. But the trip was free, and he lent me the plane for the weekend.

In Edmonton someone asked me what I thought of Robert Winters, the handsome, smiling Bay Street candidate who had been Minister of Public Works under St. Laurent, gone into the private sector in Toronto in 1958, and been brought back by Pearson in 1965 to bolster the Liberal Party's reputation in the business community. He was one of those guys who look perfect for the private sector when they're in the public sector and perfect for the public sector when they're in the private sector, but he seemed badly out of touch when he returned to government despite the fanfare that preceded him.

I was bitter about Winters. He had told Sharp that he didn't intend to enter the race and that he would support Sharp, but he changed his mind under pressure, and this weakened Sharp's power base and game plan. So I said something tough. I called Winters "a Cadillac with a Volkswagen engine." That wasn't deserved, for he was better than that, but I wanted to be funny. Apparently the remark was reported back to him, and I assumed that if Winters had become prime minister—which he almost did — Jean Chrétien could have packed up for Shawinigan.

My main work for Sharp was in Quebec, of course. I lined up about seventy delegates for him. I would go into a riding where I knew the head of the party association and I would say, "Everybody is for Trudeau, so that won't help you much. Why not help me by voting for Sharp?" In that way I convinced old friends and people from my own riding, and they held, even though they weren't too happy about all the explaining they had to do. Sharp was a very meticulous person, and a week before the convention he hired a firm to double-check his real support. Often delegates commit themselves to two or three candidates or simply lie. I didn't see the results of his survey, but he told me that his biggest surprise was that my Quebec list proved to be the most solid. On the whole, however, his numbers weren't good enough, and he decided to pull out and go to Trudeau, along with most of his supporters, including C.M. "Bud" Drury, Jean-Luc Pepin, and myself. Personally I was somewhat relieved despite my sympathy for Sharp, because I didn't want to see him hurt at the convention.

Sharp asked me to call Trudeau to tell him what was about to happen and arrange a meeting. I found Trudeau at his mother's home in Montreal, where he had gone to rest up for convention week. When he got to Ottawa and met with Sharp, I was assigned to integrate their two organizations. In the end, Sharp's move was an important factor in Trudeau's victory, because the race against Winters was close, and Trudeau was helped by being seen to have momentum.

Trudeau won the convention on April 6, 1968, and went on to win a majority government in the June election. He dazzled the nation and excited the press with his novel style and his brilliant mind. The mood was captured for me shortly after the convention by André Laurendeau, the respected Quebec thinker who was co-chairman of the Royal Commission on Bilingualism and Biculturalism until his sudden death.

"It's unbelievable, Jean," Laurendeau said. "I never thought that a guy like Trudeau — an intellectual, a writer, a man so far away from the political scene — might end up prime minister of Canada. After the convention I woke up in the middle of the night and I didn't know if I had dreamed it."

CHAPTER THREE

THE BUSINESS OF POLITICS

DURING THE 1968 ELECTION I was campaigning in British Columbia when someone asked, "Mr. Chrétien, what will the policies of the Trudeau government be for the Indians of Canada?"

As I was Minister of National Revenue at the time, I was somewhat taken aback. "Do you want a frank answer? I don't know a damn thing about it!" Everyone laughed. Three weeks later Trudeau invited me to become Minister of Indian Affairs and Northern Development.

I didn't think I could accept after what I had said in Vancouver, but Trudeau looked at it another way. "Nobody will be able to say that you have any preconceived views of the problems," he argued. "In fact, you represent a similar background. You're from a minority group, you don't speak much English, you've known poverty. You might become a minister who understands the Indians." I was also being pressured to accept by my young assistants, John Rae and Jean Fournier, both of whom had worked in the North as students and were in love with it.

So I agreed. Before me the Indians had had seven ministers in seven years. I stayed six years, one month, three days, and two hours, and I loved every minute of it. My fondest memories are of travelling in the North in those years, the kind people, the remote villages, the scenes of unusual beauty and isolation. After fifteen years, for example, I vividly recall many wonderful moments such as a visit to Coppermine, NWT with my wife, two of my children, and a sister in early 1970, the

North's centennial year. The day was extremely cold but sunny, and there was a ceremony for us in the assembly hall of the Anglican church. The men were laughing and the women were feeding their babies, and there was a nice exchange of gifts and good wishes. The town had never seen a cabinet minister before.

At the end of the formalities the Inuit wanted to do something special, so they sang "God Save the Queen" in their own language, with all the verses that are sung in church, finishing with a recognizable "Amen." French Canadians have often felt uncomfortable with the monarchy, because it has represented the Conquest for many of them, but that day I understood a dimension that had eluded me; these people were singing a hymn to the head of their Church. And they sang with such beauty and respect that my sister had tears in her eyes.

The department was a fascinating one, and because of its range and authority, I used to refer to myself jokingly as the last emperor in North America. This time was probably the most productive of my career in terms of the number of decisions made and initiatives taken. An excitement seemed to seize the entire department, perhaps because everyone knew that Trudeau had a great personal interest in the native peoples and the North. He had said to me, "Jean, you do something there," and he was involved in the problems and debates that arose from my policy paper on Indian affairs in 1969.

Trudeau and I had been bothered by the charges that the Indians were the victims of discrimination because they lived on reserves and came under the authority of the Indian Act. They described themselves as second-class citizens, and the reserves looked like ghettos to outsiders. But when we offered in all sincerity to abolish the department, to give the Indians their land to do with as they pleased, and to make them fully equal with other Canadians, they were shocked by the challenge. "If you do that," leaders such as Harold Cardinal said, "you'll assimilate us and we'll disappear as a people." They talked about the threat of cultural "genocide" and admitted they needed affirmative action in their favour. After that, no one could use the old rhetorical exaggerations about the reserves or the special laws because the Indians themselves had chosen to keep them.

These were very controversial issues at the time, and anything to do with the Indians usually made the front pages of the major newspapers, perhaps because there was a pervasive feeling of guilt in Canadian society. Some people accused me of creating my own problems by deliberately consulting with the Indians, helping organize Indian associations across the country as instruments for negotiation and discussion, and in effect financing my own opposition. That may be true, but I felt it was essential that the native peoples be given opportunities to express their views even if they put me in an awkward position.

I used to go to meetings with the Indians and they would give me hell. "White man, you speak with forked tongue, you cheated us, you gave us bad land, you broke the treaties." They would say this time after time, and time after time the press would report that Chrétien got another beating. I was always looking bad; it became an image problem. To correct it, I asked to speak first at these meetings and then I invited the Indians to give me hell. "Sock it to me, you guys," I would say. "Tell me that the white man speaks with a forked tongue or a crooked mouth or whatever, that we stole your land from you, that we didn't respect the treaties. Speak your mind." In that way I tried to defuse the public-relations problem while encouraging the Indians to vent their anger and frustration. They felt better for it and we were able to move on to practical matters afterwards.

Once an old chief in northern Saskatchewan told me, "Mr. Chrétien, in the old days I paddled a hundred miles by canoe to see the Minister of Indian Affairs, and he just passed by on a train and waved. Now I am sitting with you, speaking to you, and you are listening to me for hours into the night." That was a necessary start to an evolution that may take a couple of generations to complete, but one of my greatest satisfactions was to enshrine aboriginal rights in the constitution more than a decade later.

Besides funding our own opposition, my department gave money to the Inuit and Cree of northern Quebec to help them fight the provincial hydro-electricity development in the James Bay region until the natives obtained a fair compensation settlement for their land. That was a political risk for me because it meant opposing Liberal Premier Robert

Bourassa, who was selling the project as a key to Quebec's economic growth, and the strong unions, who didn't like the idea of losing tens of thousands of jobs over the rights of a few thousand natives; but I believed in the rights of the native peoples.

The fight was in the courts. The natives' lawyer, James O'Reilly, succeeded in getting an injunction to stop the project. To me that was a great tool with which to pry a deal out of Bourassa. I said to the native leaders, "Suspend the injunction and let the construction proceed while you negotiate. The threat that you can stop the work any time you choose will be like a sword over Bourassa's head." My feeling as a lawyer and the advice of federal government lawyers was that the injunction might not be upheld if the case were appealed. I thought O'Reilly should quit while he was ahead.

O'Reilly is a good lawyer who has done much good work for the native peoples; but in my opinion he got carried away on this issue and thought he could preserve the favourable judgment all the way to the Supreme Court. We argued about that, and once I asked him bluntly, "Jim, are you for the Crees, the trees or the fees?" The leaders supported him. Unfortunately they lost their case, and their bargaining tool, in the Appeal Court. In the meantime, however, Bourassa had begun to negotiate and, on my advice, he appointed John Ciaccia as his negotiator. Ciaccia was a member of the Quebec Assembly, who had been my Assistant Deputy Minister of Indian Affairs. When he came to see me on behalf of the Quebec government, I handed him a memo he had written while in the department on what would constitute a fair settlement. It became the basis for the agreement worked out among the Cree, the Inuit, and Quebec. It wasn't a perfect deal, of course, but it was the first big native settlement with a provincial government, with trust funds, land, and hunting and fishing privileges, and it was the first settlement since the treaties.

I also tried to use development to bring about a good settlement for the native peoples of the Mackenzie River Valley. There the issue was a scheme to bring American natural gas from Prudhoe Bay in Alaska to the American markets. A pipeline would be built down the valley, where the natives had certain unsettled rights. My role in the James Bay project had been clear, but now I was in conflict with myself: as Minister of Indian Affairs I was on the side of the Indians; as Minister of Northern Development I was in favour of development.

I believed that the pipeline would be good for Canada, because the Americans would pay for a project that could eventually transport Canadian gas from the North to Canadian markets, but I felt I needed public pressure from native groups and environmentalists to get the best deal for the Indians. So the federal government decided to set up an inquiry to examine the matter in 1972. On my recommendation it appointed as commissioner Mr. Justice Thomas Berger, a former leader of the British Columbia NDP who had been involved in native land-claim cases as a lawyer.

Berger travelled around the country, held hearings, and got marvellous press. That was good, because it allowed the Indians to speak and participate, but he interpreted their opposition to the pipeline as an opposition to all development. I knew that most Indians didn't want to return to a life of trapping and fishing, and I was hoping that Berger would show how the project could benefit them, in terms of both a general settlement and meaningful jobs. He could have told the American companies to train and employ hundreds of Indians for important work; he could have suggested that the companies invest in local native enterprises, buy from them even if at a loss, lend money to build hunting and fishing camps managed by Indians that the companies' directors or employees or clients could hire. Berger's mandate was to tell us how to build the pipeline. Instead he told us not to build it. He recommended that the construction be postponed for ten years.

I was disappointed, but the recommendation was a popular one and the government was forced to agree. Most people missed the point. They thought the postponement was to block the Americans or to block Ottawa. In fact, it took a bargaining tool away from the Indians. The minute the pipeline was stopped, there was no more pressure to settle the native claims.

Public opinion is always influential in politics, but decision-making is more than a matter of polls. Sometimes Trudeau was accused of governing by polls, but he wasn't the type of person to change his mind on important issues if he thought he was right, no matter what the numbers said. If he had a marginal commitment to a question, however, he might look at the numbers because they were convenient. They are also extremely volatile. A successful politician must not only be able to read the mood of the public, he must have the skill to get the public on his side. The public is moved by mood more than logic, by instinct more than reason, and that is something that every politician must make use of or guard against.

When faced with a difficulty, particularly in negotiations, I often tried to make the issue a public one, because the participation of the public can have a very important effect. For example, someone who steps forward from a riding association can have great influence. Government policy can't always be the same as the policy of the party, because the government must take the broad interests of the whole community into account, but leaders can't be out of step with the party members too often without risking dissatisfaction at the grass roots. So there are many exchanges between the ministers and the membership that have real, though not always visible, influence.

Participation is not the same as decision-making, however. Often when a decision is at odds with their position, people will say that they weren't consulted. That is always a difficulty, because there are always many opinions on every issue, but ultimately someone has to call the shots. That doesn't mean the participation had no effect; but the decision-maker has to make a political judgment about what is right, what is the real issue, who speaks for whom and on what. For example, labour leaders may present a certain point of view, but do they really speak for the Canadian workers all the time? If their organizations are truly representative, why don't the workers support the NDP? So the politician has to weigh all this and decide. If he calls the shots right, he will be in power for a long time. If he calls the shots wrong, he'll be kicked out.

Trying to mobilize public opinion can be tricky, as I discovered with the Berger inquiry, but it can also be highly effective. While I was Minister of Indian Affairs and Northern Development we created ten new national parks in four years. Only four had been created in the previous forty years. How was that possible? By harnessing the power of public opinion, by using the public in public administration.

The period around 1970 was the beginning of the conservation and ecology movement, and that became useful to us. In British Columbia we wanted to create the Pacific Rim National Park, to preserve the beaches and rare forests on the western coast of Vancouver Island. We rallied the support of the people of Victoria and of the ecologists at the universities; then I went to see the Premier, W.A.C. Bennett, in his office. I always liked Bennett, even though he wasn't a Liberal and ran a rather single-handed government. He was the kind of jolly, rural, populist politician I was familiar with in Quebec. (When I became Minister of Finance, he was dying. I used to phone him for advice and he would talk happily for an hour. I think he enjoyed listening to me too, because my troubles with English amused him.)

"Mr. Bennett," I said, "I have two speeches prepared for tonight. If you say no to helping us build the Pacific Rim National Park, I will say you're a son of a gun. If you say yes, I will say you're a hell of a good guy. Which speech do you want me to use?"

He laughed and said, "Okay, let's have a national park."

It was easier to create parks in the North because I only had to get the consent of the Minister of Indian Affairs and the Minister of Northern Development, and I was both. But I still had to fight the resource interests that wanted access to the minerals or oil or hydro-electricity of the entire area. I've never been a fanatical conservationist, but I've always been a lover of nature. Canada has such beautiful land that I felt it was my duty to preserve the best of it for future generations. When I saw the Nahanni River in the Northwest Territories and the Kluane Range in the Yukon, I wanted to protect them forever and eventually did.

Once I was flying from Pangnirtung on Baffin Island to Broughton Island, and we passed low over the huge, spectacular fjords there — walls of rock topped with magnificent ice caps and plunging thousands of feet into the ocean. I was so excited that I said to my wife, "Aline, I will make these a national park for you." When I got back to the office, I asked for a map, and with a pen I circled off 5,100 square kilometres. I felt very big that day, believe me, and I remember thinking, three hundred years from now no one will know who did this; but maybe some guys will say, "They were smart, whoever they were."

On another occasion I was touring the Cape Breton National Park with Allan MacEachen, and he asked, "Why don't you make a park in your riding?" There were no national parks in Quebec, and I knew that all previous efforts to create one there hadn't succeeded; but I decided to try again. When I first mentioned the idea of a park in the St Maurice valley, one of my bureaucrats said, "You need a beautiful area for a park. You don't build national parks in swamps."

"You come with me," I said. He didn't come, but he sent an assistant. We climbed to a natural lookout on the top of a hill near Shawinigan, and I pointed to the beautiful lakes, the untouched forests, and the ancient rocks of the Laurentians. "Look at my swamps," I said.

It was more difficult to convince the Quebec government that a park in the Mauricie was a good idea. There was a split in the Union Nationale cabinet between Gabriel Loubier, the Minister of Tourism who wanted a park, and Marcel Masse, now the federal Tory Minister of Communications, then the provincial Minister of Intergovernmental Affairs who opposed the idea for nationalist reasons. Loubier liked to tease him in front of me. "Look at him, Jean," he said. "Marcel has a great future. He's young, good-looking, intelligent, articulate, ambitious, hard working. I'm telling you, Jean, with a little more experience he could become . . . my successor as Minister of Tourism!" You could see Masse's chest expand and deflate.

The negotiations dragged on, and at one point they looked dead. The Quebec government announced there would be no national parks in the province. Loubier was furious when we met just before a benefit hockey game between the federal MPs and the provincial MNAs in the Montreal Forum. "I lost because of Masse," he said, "so don't miss him on the ice."

It was a fun game, played before 12,000 people, and I knew Masse wasn't a great player because I had been at college with him in Joliette. So when he got the puck, I grabbed my golden opportunity and slammed into him.

Still, I didn't give up on the park. I organized a local movement in

favour of it to put pressure on the provincial politicians. Everyone —
from the chamber of commerce to the trade unions — got involved.
There were citizens' committees, slogans, petitions, and every politician was put on the spot in public: "Are you for the national park? Yes
or no?" The issue became a local factor in the 1970 provincial election:
the Liberals supported the park and the nationalists opposed it as federal interference. The Liberals won, and Bourassa allowed us to go ahead
shortly after he came to power.

Enlisting the help of the conservationists and building these parks
had benefits for some of my other work as minister. One of my responsibilities was northern development, and my belief in balanced development did not contradict my dedication to parks. Certainly I took some
chances in allowing oil exploration in the Beaufort Sea. I felt it was essential for Canada's energy policies to find out if we had oil reserves there
or not, and the only way to find out was to permit drilling. After I left
the department, one of my successors, Judd Buchanan, was trying to
get permission to extend the drilling season in the Beaufort Sea and
allow drilling from ships. He was meeting resistance from Trudeau, who
must have been getting advice from the environmentalists, so Buchanan
asked me to intervene. I argued his case in cabinet, saying that drilling
from ships was safer than drilling from man-made islands and ice plat-
forms, which the exploration companies already had permission to do.

"But who gave them permission in the first place?" Trudeau asked,
rather surprised.

"I did," I said.

"But what would have happened if there had been a blowout?"

"I knew, Prime Minister, that I would have been blown out," I
said. Both of us understood that I had taken the risk and the decision: if
I had made a mistake, it would have been on my shoulders. The point
was that, because I had done so much for the North and created the
parks, the conservationists knew I was well-meaning and they had a
problem attacking my credibility on development.

Besides the political manoeuvrings on the outside, the other essential
ingredient for getting things done in Ottawa is to mobilize the bureau-

cracy in your favour on the inside. My first lessons about bureaucracy had come from Mitchell Sharp, who had been a bureaucrat before he had become a politician, and no one could have been a more knowledgeable tutor. I saw how he led his officials to respect his wishes once he had made up his mind without ever getting into conflicts with them. Very quickly I realized how important it was to create a closeness between the minister and his bureaucrats. There is, after all, a community of interest between the two.

A minister must convince his bureaucrats that he is their friend and that they are his strongest allies. Then everyone can work as a team. If a minister doesn't trust his officials, he won't get anywhere. Personally I have never resented or feared a bureaucrat with strong views, a will, and persistence, as these are qualities I admire. I never pretended to know everything, and many Ottawa bureaucrats are extremely well-educated, well-read, and nobody's fool. Knowledge is power, and in many cases these people got to power because of their knowledge. Of course, a minister must place the facts and opinions in a political perspective and not be overwhelmed by them, but on the whole the stronger and more intelligent the officials, the better the minister.

When I suggest that the ministers and the officials must have a close relationship, I don't mean that the bureaucracy should be politically partisan. I'm always surprised when people accuse the federal civil service of being full of Liberals. For one thing, Ottawa ridings elect at least as many Tories as Liberals. For another thing, I can't recall ever asking a bureaucrat about his political leanings.

When I was Minister of Finance in 1979, I had a deputy minister named Bill Hood, who I thought was a Tory by his background and his occasional remarks, but I never asked and I didn't care. In fact, I had asked Trudeau to appoint him Deputy Minister, because he was an extremely good official. The irony is that the Tories replaced him during Joe Clark's government; and in so doing they probably contributed to their own downfall, because such an experienced bureaucrat would have seen the political dangers in the budget of December 1979.

The Canadian bureaucracy has a tradition of great loyalty to the system and the institutions, not to the party in power. Naturally when they serve a department, they serve a minister at the same time. They fight his battles, celebrate his successes, and suffer his failures, but their goal is not the victory of a particular party. Their goal is the good of the nation. At times the distinction between the political and administrative levels has seemed a thin one because the Liberal Party was the government for so long, but the distinction did exist. This was demonstrated when the Tories came to power and were served well by most of the same people who had served the Liberals. In my experience, if you tell the bureaucrats what you want with no ambiguity or confusion, there's no problem.

My time in Indian Affairs and Northern Development coincided with a period of expansion, and that helped my reputation and my popularity among the bureaucrats and in the country. In a period of expansion ministers are judged by how much money they can spend and how well they can extract money from the system for their projects. Spending was easy, because there was no end to the useful and imaginative initiatives bubbling up in the department. Those were its glory days. Getting money was trickier. There wasn't much problem selling ideas to the cabinet, particularly as Trudeau was usually sympathetic; but then I had to get them passed by the Treasury Board, a committee that decided how to finance cabinet decisions, in what order of priority, and so on. It didn't take me long to figure out that the Treasury Board was where the real decisions were made, and I got appointed to the committee early in my career. Let the philosophers philosophize elsewhere, I thought; I want to be where the cash is.

At one point I heard a rumour that Trudeau was going to replace me on the Treasury Board with a more powerful minister. It is part of my pride that I never complained to Trudeau or asked for anything, but this time I went to him and asked to stay on the committee. Fortunately he agreed. Many people found the Treasury Board boring because there were a lot of documents to read, a lot of submissions to assess, and a lot of endless meetings, but I really liked it. What I liked was that it was always making decisions. I've always been more comfortable making decisions than engaging in long and intellectually satisfying discourses, perhaps because I'm an impatient person. So I was happy to attend regularly, sit through the scores of submissions, and stay until the bitter end. In fact, staying to the end was part of my strategy.

In those days the President of the Treasury Board and chairman of the meetings was Bud Drury, a distinguished gentleman who was the MP from Westmount, Quebec. His background and his manner earned him the confidence of the business community, but he was much less right-wing than most people imagined. I discovered that he was very concerned with social problems. I also discovered that his meetings were extremely long. After three hours or so, most of the ministers would excuse themselves, and soon only Drury and Chrétien were left. So I learned to put my items at the bottom of the weekly agenda, knowing that by eight o'clock Drury would be ready to go home.

"Gee, Bud," I would say shortly before eight, "we have a chance to make another national park that will last forever. It's not a question of money, because in fifty years the land will be developed and never available again."

"Fine, Jean," Drury would answer. "Go and do it."

The myth is that no one did anything without Trudeau's permission. Yet in my experience he was happy to have a minister who ran a good shop and didn't create any problems. I had my own northern empire, I was on the Treasury Board, and I was satisfied with the job I had to do; so I didn't pester him just to bask in the Prime Minister's sun like some ministers did. In fact, once he took me aside and said, "Jean, are you mad at me? You haven't spoken to me for a long time."

"No, everything is fine, so why should I bother you? I'm not mad or anything. My job is not to be a bother."

One of the great disappointments in politics is that you have a lot of colleagues but very few friends. Political life is more demanding than most people realize. Every day of every week you meet the same people in cabinet or committee or the House of Commons, but everyone is busy and in a rush. In the evenings there are social occasions such as a reception at an embassy or a fund-raising dinner or a valuable opportunity to be with your family; so you haven't got the time to develop friendships. Usually you end up closest to those who work with you, who are there at the end of a long day when you have a half-hour to put your feet up and talk about something besides work. These may be members of Parliament or parliamentary assistants or aides who drop in when your door is open, but seldom are they cabinet colleagues, who are usually working overtime in their own offices.

Some people made a career out of being seen close to Trudeau, but I chose to keep my distance because I wanted to keep my independence. I wasn't as powerful as those who dropped Trudeau's name all the time, and nobody said that Trudeau called me every morning to know what to eat for breakfast; but I had to remain my own man to be effective in politics, and what I lost in influence I gained in not making enemies. Though I never tried to be his pal, I found him generous in his comments. Some ministers, even important ones, used to complain that he never complimented them, but compliments were not his nature. He felt that a professional relationship didn't require him to be constantly patting his ministers on the back as if they were kids.

Years later, after Trudeau and I fought the Quebec referendum and the constitution issue, we became closer. I wouldn't say I became a confidant, because Trudeau didn't seem to need confidants, but I would hope that if he drew up a list of his good friends my name would be on it. He's an extremely private person, apparently self-sufficient, like a monk in some ways. Certainly I never dared stop at his house, knock on the door, and invite him out for a beer. When we were sitting beside each other in the House of Commons, I used to pass him interesting newspaper articles or mention some book he might have missed (he rarely talked about what he read, as if it would be an invasion of his private life); those were very pleasant conversations, but on the whole our friendship was strictly professional.

All that said, I remember a wonderful occasion with Trudeau. In January 1984, my wife organized a surprise party for my fiftieth birthday. She invited Trudeau and got him to sing an old-fashioned, rural song that had been very popular in Quebec during the Depression. He sang and recited poetry and was very relaxed. It was a fantastic evening. The party began at five o'clock in the afternoon and didn't finish until five o'clock the next morning. Even I sang in my terrible voice.

In cabinet Trudeau listened more and compromised more than most Canadians imagine. Of course he had his own ideas, his vision of the country, and his goals, and they weren't always shared by the cabinet or the party; but the leader has a right to lead and it's never easy to be prime minister. He has to hurt the feelings of a lot of people on a regular basis; he has to operate in the public eye with MPs who fret and bureaucrats who gossip and colleagues who disagree.

When his ideas were challenged or when he wanted to get to the heart of a matter in cabinet, Trudeau could be ruthless in debate, asking probing questions that demolished the logic underlying the counterarguments, and applying the full force of his intellect and knowledge. Occasionally I saw him get his way simply by interjecting a phrase that indicated his position. Since most ministers assumed that Trudeau had thought through everything, and since even more ministers wanted to please the boss, he was able to rally a majority to his side without much difficulty. That was human nature, of course, but it could be annoying when ministers constantly played to Trudeau, sensed his direction, and automatically followed. At times Trudeau tested for sycophancy by suddenly supporting the opposite argument and seeing who really believed what they had held.

But I never subscribed to the notion that Trudeau was a dictator. Often, knowing what he thought, I saw him accepting the views of his ministers despite his own wishes. He was extraordinarily patient, he let everyone have a say, and he listened attentively. Sometimes he was too patient, too generous. When a bunch of people meet for four or five hours every week in cabinet and again in committees, it's not long before you begin to hear the same arguments, the same anecdotes, the same rhetorical tricks repeated over and over. More often than not, you wished that Trudeau would bring down the gavel.

Most times I found that ministers who talked too much defeated their own purpose. Their ideas became repetitive, boring, and predictable, and therefore lost clout. Often I advised new ministers to keep quiet, and there were long periods in which I didn't say anything myself; because a relevant, timely intervention usually had more effect and drew more notice from Trudeau than a series of interventions that merely aimed to attract attention or bolster the Prime Minister's case. The talkers did less well than the listeners, so I stifled my own love of talking.

I also discovered that letting Trudeau win the arguments seemed to satisfy his appetite, so that he was a great deal softer in practice than people imagined, perhaps because he realized that those who lost to his intellectual ferocity needed some soothing. His nature was to challenge, to provoke, to buck the trend, and he didn't mind making enemies in the process, but that didn't mean he acted in an authoritarian manner when the debate turned to decision.

As a close observer of politics, I have noticed some qualities necessary to leadership. The first is knowledge. A leader has to know how the system functions — not just the system of government but the whole social and economic system, including business, the unions, and the universities. Trudeau was a student of the system all his life. He even knew more about business than he let on. Whether he was right or wrong about economics may be debatable, but no one can say he wasn't interested in or knowledgeable about the economy. He had studied economics at university and, despite his socialist image, he had managed his family's fortune before entering politics.

The second quality of leadership is a strong personality. You have to be a saleable commodity, someone who attracts people by your ability to do the tough jobs. You also have to be interesting, different — intriguing somehow. You need strong nerves, a thick skin, and a control on your temper. Without control you'll make mistakes, because the game is frustrating, annoying, tough and mean. It may be tough and mean in the private sector, too, but if you fail, your failure is known only to a few colleagues and your family. It is not the subject of public scrutiny that can humiliate you in front of all your relatives and total strangers. That's why ambitious politicians often take failure very badly and very personally. So a leader must be able to keep the support of people who see their egos attacked in public every day.

Trudeau has been criticized for losing some important cabinet ministers over the years, including John Turner, Donald Macdonald, Mitchell Sharp, and Bud Drury, but Canada's political system may have been the cause more than any weakness in management. In the United States, for example, the president can only stay in office for eight years, and the members of his cabinet seem to come and go even more frequently. More than eight years would be an eternity for people such as Henry Kissinger or George Schultz. They came into government from a university or a business, served for a while, and went back to their old jobs with added prestige and a title.

In Canada the prime minister can stay for decades, and his ministers are expected to stay with him even if their own ambitions are frustrated; and it's not easy to come back once you've left. Obviously if a prime minister is successful for as long as Trudeau was, some people will move on to do other things, some people will step aside to let younger MPs have a chance in cabinet, and some people will stay with reduced expectations. If Trudeau had had to retire after eight years, you can be certain that John Turner and Donald Macdonald would not have left the cabinet. Meanwhile, it became harder to recruit good people from other sectors because few of them wanted to give up their comforts, get into government for the long haul, and suffer the abuse that public life requires, particularly if they knew that when they did leave public service, they might be impeded from getting many good jobs because their political affiliation branded them as either too close to the government or too unsympathetic to it. Many of us stayed on because we felt that politics was the handiest instrument for influence. Traditionally francophones have never been a comfortable part of the banking and business élites — though there have been notable exceptions — so we tended to remain politicians for life while many of our English-speaking colleagues chose to leave for greener pastures after making their contribution.

Trudeau never pressured anyone to stay by making promises. He may have been too sensitive about losing his freedom to manoeuvre; he may have been able to be more forceful if he could ask people to stay in the service of their country; but he never felt that anyone was indispensable, including himself, and he was reluctant to get on his knees to anyone about anything.

In the case of Turner's resignation in 1975, for example, I think Trudeau recognized the difficulties. Turner had been making a personal sacrifice for many years in terms of what he could have been earning in the private sector. He and his wife had grown up accustomed to a certain lifestyle; they had four children to be educated; and it was obvious that Trudeau intended to stay as Prime Minister for a while longer. There were no mysteries or complications about why he quit. When I heard the news I spoke to Turner on the phone, and asked, "Damn it, John, what the hell are you doing? Don't quit now. The Liberals are ahead in the provincial election campaign in Ontario. Wait a couple of weeks at least."

"It's over," he said.

"You've probably just had a misunderstanding with the boss," I said. "Let me talk to him. Will you meet with him again?"

He agreed, so I went to see Trudeau, who told me that Turner had quit to look after his family. But Trudeau also agreed to another meeting with Turner, so I thought I might be able to swing something. I tried to enlist the help of Macdonald, but he was furious at Turner. "He can go to hell," he said. That's when I wondered what I was doing running back and forth between two grown men. I felt like a busybody, though I still believe Turner might have been persuaded to stay.

The next day I saw him in his office and we talked over a cup of coffee. He told me he didn't want his ambitions to deprive his children of all that he had received in life, so he wanted to make some money. It was as simple as that. The rumours on Bay Street that he had resigned because we hadn't agreed to his demand for a $2-billion cut in spending couldn't have been spread by him, because he would have known they weren't true.

I almost quit myself in 1973, though for slightly different reasons. I had had some problems with my health then, and the doctors thought I might have had a heart attack. I had a wife, three small children, a meagre pension, and a house with a mortgage; and I didn't want to leave my family in financial difficulty if I suddenly died. I knew what it was like to be poor, so I was very conscious of security. I didn't want my children to experience misery after the comfortable milieu I had given them while a minister. So I asked Trudeau to make me a judge. "If I was good enough to be a minister," I joked, "I should be good enough to be a judge somewhere." He agreed. But by the time the election was called in 1974, my health had returned and I decided to stay in government. When I am asked why so many French-speaking ministers became powerful under Trudeau, I am tempted to think it's because we stayed despite the risks and disadvantages, unlike many of our English-speaking colleagues. Nevertheless, after my own scare I can't criticize them for their choices.

Perhaps no time is easy to be a politician. There are always economic problems of some sort and social tensions. But Trudeau's popularity began to plunge in the early 1970s because the expectations about him had been so high. People had thought he was a miracle man, but nobody can be, so there was a sense of let-down. His greatest test had come during the Quebec crisis in October 1970, when the terrorist FLQ kidnapped and held to ransom the British Trade Commissioner, James Cross, and the Quebec Minister of Labour, Pierre Laporte, who was eventually murdered. Trudeau responded forcefully with the War Measures Act.

In theory I was opposed to the imposition of the act and thought we should try to compromise, but Trudeau destroyed my logic in a minute. "If you compromise today," he asked, "what next and what next and what after that?" I conceded that he was right. Besides, both Robert Bourassa, the Premier of Quebec, and Jean Drapeau, the Mayor of Montreal, had sent letters requesting the armed forces, because the populace was afraid. The police seemed unable to handle the job, and the situation threatened to get out of control. I was travelling in the North when I heard that Pierre Laporte had been murdered, and I remember the shock on the faces of the people around me. We were thousands of miles from the scene, yet we felt that the peace and stability we had always taken for granted had suddenly disappeared. Even our democratic institutions seemed threatened by non-elected people prepared to replace the Quebec government.

We had a hell of a dilemma. Since there was no law that covered precisely this type of national emergency we were left with the terrible-sounding and extensive War Measures Act. I used to describe the dilemma this way: you want to transport a refrigerator, and you only have a bicycle and a van. You won't get very far with the refrigerator on a bicycle, but using a big van for such a little object will look silly. That problem still hasn't been resolved in our books. The police asked to round up only seventy people, and they may not have had to arrest the several hundred people they picked up ultimately, but a democracy must use what is at hand to defend itself against violence. In retrospect, the scope of the law may look excessive and unnecessary; but there are many Monday morning quarterbacks in politics.

Personally, I was less afraid of being kidnapped than I was embarrassed by having soldiers trailing me everywhere and camping in my garage. But the atmosphere was tense. One night in October I was late returning to Ottawa from a visit to the Eastern Townships in Quebec, and I had neglected to call home. My wife was waiting with a group of friends, and they got very agitated when I hadn't arrived by midnight. "If someone's killed him, I'll kill someone, too," one of my friends said. That was the kind of craziness people felt at the time.

Trudeau handled the crisis brilliantly. He went along with a compromise worked out by Sharp, who was then Secretary of State for External Affairs. It saved the life of the British Trade Commissioner by allowing the FLQ manifesto to be read on television and letting the terrorists leave for Cuba; but it destroyed political blackmail for a long, long time in Canada, because Trudeau did not bend farther. He was a hero across the country, yet two years later no one remembered that. The people only saw the downturn in the economy and the flashy guy with the long hair and a beautiful young wife, the intellectuals turned on him and said he was ruthless and undemocratic, and the press seemed to want to repent for having created Trudeaumania in 1968.

During the 1972 election campaign he came to a rally in Shawinigan. It was a great evening, the hall was packed, and the crowd was lively. To crank up the mood before the Prime Minister's arrival, I gave a peppy, entertaining speech, full of French slang, and Trudeau must have heard part of it when he entered because he used the same tone when he spoke. He was very excited by a new parks program I was developing called "Byways and Special Places." Modelled on the Blue Ridge Parkway south of Washington, D.C., it was to create a scenic route from Quebec City to Toronto, heritage trails, and wilderness parks. Trudeau tried to express his joy at the idea: "When I think about it, it's just like we were kids and were given candies at Christmas." He used the English word "candies" as French slang to show his delight. The press, however, jumped on it and for the rest of the campaign Trudeau was accused of trying to bribe the voters with goodies.

Though his government barely survived that election, the period from 1972 to 1974 was an exciting and productive term. It was a good test for Trudeau, because it taught him the flexibility and ability to compromise that I saw in cabinet and in caucus. At least he seemed to have grown and changed, and in politics perception is everything. What saved him in the long run was the pride of David Lewis, the leader of the NDP. The Liberals could only stay in office with the support of the NDP because we were in a minority position, so Lewis was forced to vote with us in the House of Commons in order to prevent an election that no one wanted. He did that for two years, but he was a rather proud and doctrinaire man, and he couldn't stand being accused of keeping Trudeau in power. Finally he decided to side with the Tories in a non-confidence vote and force an election.

Immediately after Lewis's announcement, Réal Caouette jumped to his feet and said, "The NDP will drop from thirty seats to fifteen and Lewis will be defeated in his own riding, because he has failed in his responsibility to the Canadian people to maintain the government." That proved to be correct.

If Lewis had held on and made the minority government work, Trudeau probably would have gone to the polls in 1976 and won another minority. But when the people saw that the minority didn't work, they wanted a majority government and gave it to Trudeau over Robert Stanfield. It was part of the luck that gave Pierre Trudeau nine lives.

CHAPTER FOUR

THE POLITICS OF BUSINESS

A FTER THE 1974 VICTORY Trudeau decided to make a major shift in his cabinet, and among other changes he replaced Bud Drury as President of the Treasury Board with a younger man, Jean Chrétien. That surprised a lot of people who thought of me as a social-oriented minister because of my high profile in Indian Affairs; but I had wanted to be an economic minister since the day Pearson suggested that I might become the first French-Canadian Minister of Finance. That's why I had insisted on staying on the Treasury Board under Drury, of course — to show interest and to gain experience.

I grabbed my new job with great enthusiasm, determined to make a name for myself in the economic field. As my arrival coincided with a time of restraint, my reputation as a spender was soon gone. In fact, my nickname became "Dr. No."

The Minister of Finance was John Turner. He had been elected for the first time in 1962, and I had been elected in 1963; both of us were seen as "young contenders," so we were quite close friends. Before he accepted the Finance portfolio we talked about it, and I told him it was a good move. I figured that his ambition was to succeed Trudeau, which made some sense in view of the Liberal Party's tradition of alternating between anglophone and francophone leaders, and he must have felt that I would support him when the time came. In one of our first meetings after my appointment to the Treasury Board, he said that he wanted to cut the deficit. Together we went to see Trudeau, and Turner asked for a cut of $500 million, which seemed massive because the total budget was so much less than it is today. The politics of it would be rough.

"Do it, Jean," Trudeau said. "We'll back you."

I went to my Deputy Minister, Gordon Osbaldeston, who later became the senior public servant as Clerk of the Privy Council. I said, "You know, Gordon, politically it wouldn't be much worse if we cut a billion dollars. Is that possible?" Eventually we cut $1,070,000,000.

Perhaps I was a bit too tough. I had terrible arguments with my colleagues, and our decision to cut the subsidy to dairy producers caused my good friend, Eugene Whelan, the Minister of Agriculture, to have milk poured over his head by a bunch of angry farmers. Trudeau could feel the tension I had caused in the cabinet, but he supported me, as did John Turner, who I think appreciated that he had someone to share the fighting with.

In some ways I was a happy warrior. I had power, and I felt I was doing the right things. In order to keep control, I worked closely with the good group of ministers on my committee, which included Bud Drury, Robert Andras, Ron Basford, Jean Pierre Goyer, and Dan Mac Donald from Prince Edward Island. We made a lot of political judgments by ourselves, and many decisions were reached in conversations in the corridors of Parliament. I insisted that everyone come well-briefed to the meetings, and I didn't permit a lot of questions, in order to move rapidly through the submissions.

This system gave me a lot of clout, but it couldn't go on forever. My number was called one evening at a dinner at the Prime Minister's residence. The occasion was the retirement of Gordon Robertson as Clerk of the Privy Council. Robertson was a great public servant who had developed a system of cabinet committees that were a step forward in public administration. All the senior officials were there, and after the dinner and the testimonials there was an informal discussion of the strengths and weaknesses of the system.

Then someone put the cat among the pigeons. "I have just done a study," he said. "Of all the papers sent to a cabinet committee for a decision, ninety-five per cent are approved subject to financing from the Treasury Board. Yet only fifty percent of the papers sent to the Treasury Board are approved." Soon everyone started complaining about the power of the Treasury Board. It looked more powerful than the cabinet.

Trudeau leaned over to me and joked, "Perhaps we should change jobs, Jean."

"Not a bad idea," I said.

That was the beginning of the end. In time the Treasury Board's authority to decide the allocation of available money was severely diminished. In its place there arose the "envelope" system, in which all the ministers of the "social" departments got together to divide up their pie and all the ministers of the "economic" departments did the same. That was probably a good idea in that it allowed everyone to see what was happening and to participate in making the decisions. In 1980 I became chairman of the social envelope as Minister of State for Social Development, and while that was a powerful position, I knew it was only half of what I had had in Treasury Board.

The committee reforms initiated by Gordon Robertson and carried on by Michael Pitfield were both complex and controversial. They took up too much of the ministers' time and energy; they produced too much paper work; and they resulted in weaker decisions, because even the strong ministers had to submit to collective judgments. But the intentions were good.

The first was to modernize the government by planning. If you used the word "planning" in front of Trudeau in the morning, you had his attention for the rest of the day. At 24 Sussex he had a huge wall-hanging by Joyce Wieland that read "Reason over Passion." Sometimes people played to what he wanted to hear, and sometimes they went overboard with all their plans and rationalizations, but generally the reforms made sense and were needed.

Their second intention was to take the preponderance of power from the bureaucratic mandarins and give it back to the ministers. The committees were to enable the ministers to know what was going on in all the departments, to take part in all the decisions, and to make the political decisions predominate over the bureaucratic decisions. In the old days most ministers had no idea what the government as a whole was doing. Under the new system they could know if they took the trouble to find out, and they could take part in the discussions.

Of course, all this discussion required a lot of patience — sometimes too much — and ministerial participation is not the same as making the final decision. In some ways the more input ministers have, the more frustrated they become because the decisions are never exactly as they want or think right. Instead of feeling more powerful, they feel more left out. Very often it is the prime minister who decides, or he may delegate some of his power to senior ministers. There are always some ministers with more responsibility for calling the shots; and the others always feel they weren't listened to if the decisions go against them. That's not to say they had no power; it's simply that someone else had more. The minister of finance is always powerful and the chairmen of the committees can be powerful. Some ministers are powerful because they have long experience or good administrative skills or wide connections or deep knowledge of the system. Others have strong political constituencies or a talent for pretending they have the ear of the prime minister on everything.

To stay strong a minister must show compromise and agility. He may have great authority within his department, but within the cabinet he is merely part of a collectivity, just another adviser to the prime minister. He can be told what to do, and on important matters his only choice is to do it or resign. So survival and success become a matter of judgment. You have the sense of skating on thin ice all the time and you never know when there will be a hole that will swallow you up. That's why politicians develop a lot of adrenalin, because they live a very dangerous life in the sense that they can lose everything they've built over years in a single day.

Not only do you have to worry about the prime minister and your cabinet colleagues; the Prime Minister's Office and the Privy Council Office are powerful players, too. The PMO draws its strength from being close to the boss, so you never know if it is him or only his advisers talking. The PCO gains power from using its information-gathering system for real influence. Coordination becomes more important than the action. Compromise, the way to protect everyone's interests, becomes more important than a good solution; and the quickness, the responsiveness, and the freshness of departments are lost to empire-building. Even important ministers came to fear the PCO because it was so influential after Michael Pitfield became its chief. He was a mysterious and intimidating person, very intelligent, close to Trudeau, somewhat aloof, and with the Westmount background that made people think he was talking down to them. When you got to know him better, you realized he wasn't, but his manner made a lot of people uncomfortable.

Suppose, however, that your deputy minister is told by the Department of Finance or the Privy Council Office not to do something that you want him to do. Suppose that the wording of a decision made by your committee is changed in the Privy Council Office or in the Prime Minister's Office. You don't know whether it is an error in good faith, someone's shenanigans, or the wish of the prime minister. Suppose you get a phone call from the Prime Minister's Office asking you to do something you don't want to do? Is it an order from the boss or someone dropping his name in a power play? Do you resist or give in? Can you defy the order, cross this particular person? Would you risk a showdown with the prime minister? Obviously you can't call the prime minister every time and ask, "Is it really you behind all this?"

This is when the experience, intelligence, skill, and weight of a minister come to the fore. Like football players moving for a hole in a fraction of a second, you have to rely on your intuition and luck. If you decide to resist, and if it's someone playing a game, you won't hear any more about it; but if you resist and cross the prime minister, you'll probably know very quickly. If you never resist, if you say "yes" to every memo from Finance or the Privy Council Office or the Prime Minister's Office, then you'll always be weak and you'll have no one to blame but yourself. It's a constant gamble. If you lose all your gambles, you'll be kicked out or pushed out or demoted and you'll be a nobody. If you never gamble, you'll always be a nobody. If you win, you survive for one more day.

My career is full of examples. When I was being very tough as President of the Treasury Board, I made it a point not to cut the arts or foreign aid. I knew that pleased Trudeau, and it also pleased me. At one point Trudeau mentioned to me that the National Gallery wanted to buy a masterpiece by the great Italian painter, Lotto, and it needed a million dollars from the Treasury Board. "Is that Lotto-Québec or Lotto-Canada?" I joked, but I got the message, and the National Gallery got the painting. At other times, however, people told me that Trudeau wanted this or that and I didn't pay any attention. He might have said to himself, "That bloody Chrétien is doing his own thing again," but he never got on to me about it, so I was safe.

I had a more serious problem when I was Minister of State for Social Development between 1980 and 1983. There, the allocation of money was done in the open. We developed a banking system in which all the departments put their money on the table and then we divided it up. I was accused of being rude and insensitive during that process, but the real trouble was the presence of the bureaucrats. They had found an excuse to be there, popping up to protect their empires and to defend their interests, and then reporting to their superiors everything that had been said. As a result, the meetings lacked candour. The bureaucrats challenged their ministers, saying, in effect, "If you're good, you'll get what we're asking for."

If the ministers succeeded, then the bureaucrats would say, "Oh, my minister is so powerful, he got this and he got that." Then the press would say the minister was powerful, and the bureaucrats would expect to get even more. It was a question of power, not of substance, so one day I announced, "The banking will be done by me and the ministers. Everyone else, out!" I even excluded my own deputy minister for a while.

Then I said to my colleagues, "On the one hand, we have $300 million in demands. On the other hand, we have $100 million to spend. Let's vote. Be candid. If your bureaucrats are demanding something that isn't your priority, give me your political priority. If you get less than you came for, don't be worried, just blame me. I will take the heat."

They loved it. They could all go out saying, "That damn Chrétien! I asked for four things and he only gave me one!" The bureaucrats, of course, were furious.

Trudeau called me in. "You can't do this," he said.

"But it works," I replied, and I didn't budge.

A classic case of walking the thin line in politics was adjusting the National Energy Program to the changing realities after I was made Minister of Energy in 1982. The NEP was introduced in 1980 to secure Canada's supply of energy, encourage self-sufficiency, and increase the Canadian ownership of the sector. It was based on a worldwide forecast that the price of oil would rise to $80 a barrel. Instead it plunged to under $30. For that reason alone, the program needed modification after three years, but there were powerful forces resisting any serious adjustments.

Trudeau was known to be strong on the NEP. Finance Minister Marc Lalonde, who had introduced it when he was Minister of Energy, was leery about what I might do to his brainchild. Some senior officials in my department who had been involved in the inception of the NEP considered any tampering with it an insult to their wisdom. Indeed, though most of the key people connected with the program had moved on to other jobs, and though the bureaucrats who stayed recognized that changes were necessary, the department was deeply committed to the NEP, and elements within it resisted when I wanted to do anything that Lalonde would not have done.

That became a problem, for example, during my negotiations with Newfoundland concerning offshore oil. Some of my bureaucrats disagreed with the deal I was prepared to offer because they felt I had gone too far in my concessions. Newfoundland used our disagreement as an excuse to walk away from the table, claiming that I wouldn't be able to deliver what I was promising. They didn't know me or Trudeau. At one point a senior official, probably acting on a complaint from Finance or the Privy Council Office, told me he had had to report my offer to Trudeau, who was travelling abroad. Later in the day I received word of Trudeau's response: "If it's good enough for Jean, it's good enough for me." So I had freedom, but I could not sell the store and I didn't want to. I believed in the principles and goals of the NEP and merely wished to adapt the details.

After a couple of years I was moved out of the Treasury Board. Trudeau and Pitfield had realized how powerful the committee could become, and I guess they thought they couldn't dismantle its clout if that son-of-a-gun Chrétien were still in charge. I protested being moved, naturally.

Trudeau used to say I was the most difficult minister to move, because I always got comfortable and happy where I was. He offered me Industry, Trade and Commerce; when I said no, he sent Gordon Osbaldeston to try to persuade me. Before being my deputy minister at the Treasury Board, Osbaldeston had been a Trade Commissioner and he was about to take a leave from the government for a while.

"So you really think it's important that I go to trade and commerce?" I asked him. "You're completely convinced that this is what I should do?"

"Yes," he said.

"Okay, I'll do it, but only on the condition that you come with me as my Deputy Minister."

Poor Osbaldeston was trapped, and the two of us went to Industry, Trade and Commerce in September 1976. I was with the department just a year, but I followed my usual pattern of acting quickly on a number of controversial issues to establish my presence. Within days I flew to Venezuela to help land a Canadian contract to build and supply equipment for a new railway in that country. We managed to get half the contract, though in the end the project was cancelled.

A second issue concerned quotas on imported textiles and clothing. At that time the business was about sixty per cent imports and forty per cent domestic production. The situation was deteriorating for our manufacturers. I was willing to keep the border open to help consumers and to make our industry efficient, but there were pressures to protect the industry until it could improve its productivity. Besides, our trading partners had fewer imports than we did. (While the Americans accused Canada of being protectionist for wanting to have half the business, for example, they imported only twenty per cent of their textiles and clothing.) My solution was to make a deal with the Canadian industry, both the companies and the unions.

"Okay, you guys," I said. "I'll impose quotas for a certain period, but you have to improve productivity. And your prices cannot increase faster than the average rate of inflation in that period. Make your profits and your wage increases out of producing more items. If you don't do that, my friends, I will open the gates as fast as I have closed them."

The industry kept its side of the bargain. In fact, its prices rose less than the average rate of inflation, and its productivity improved noticeably, although there was a drop in employment as automation cut the number of worker-years necessary to manufacture the goods. I think the industry may have kept to the deal because it had seen how tough I had been with my bureaucrats at the meeting. They kept telling me that no minister had ever imposed quotas without checking with the cabinet.

"But have I the authority?" I asked them.

"Yes, but it's never been done before."

"But have I the authority?"

"Yes, but . . ."

"Then I'm doing it."

The thorniest and most pressing decision I had to make in Industry, Trade and Commerce was whether to give financial support to the development of Canadair's Challenger aircraft. The question had been sitting on my predecessor's desk for months, and I had only a few weeks before the option to develop the aircraft expired. I had to act. My senior officials were divided on it, but I felt the project was worth the gamble. Whether that was a good or bad decision may be debatable with hindsight, because the Challenger hit the market during a bad period in the world economy. At the time, however, it made sense and promised a great deal for Canada's aviation industry. At the time I made my decision, Osbaldeston had not yet left the Treasury Board and my successor, Bob Andras, had not fully established himself there, so I was able to get more than $100 million for the Challenger within thirty days.

It was in Industry, Trade and Commerce that I came to know members of the business community, though I had made a lot of contacts in the mining industry and the oil companies while Minister of Northern Development. But knowing them is not the same as having them as pals. Most of my pals are lawyers, bureaucrats, people in my riding or other politicians. Politicians usually stick with politicians, and they certainly run into more journalists than tycoons. Because Ottawa isn't a financial centre, businessmen tend to come and go, so they aren't seen socially very often. Perhaps that's why I have never felt pressured by them.

It might have been more difficult for a politician to keep his independence in the days when the major parties were financed almost exclusively by businessmen, but since the reform of party funding few, if any, MPs rely on large contributions. In my own case ninety-five per cent of my campaign expenses are met by donations from the people of my constituency. Even the $100-a-plate dinners have a good mix of local businessmen and blue-collar workers. It is my experience that the days of the powerful party bagmen collecting huge sums from a few rich guys, are over, thank God.

Of course, Canada has some influential business leaders and some old, moneyed families, but they don't seem to be as visible or as powerful in public affairs as their equivalents in Europe or the United States. Nor do they seem as entrenched or closed. The turnover is greater and therefore the power base is weaker. (In fact, the labour movement seems to have a more stable élite than the business community. Decades pass and the same union leaders keep showing up at meetings!)

I learned early that business is business and politics is politics. The proof is how few important businessmen have made good politicians. They may think they are very smart about everything because they made millions of dollars by digging a hole in the ground and finding oil, but the talent and luck needed to become rich are not the same talent and luck needed to succeed on Parliament Hill. Someone may be a fantastic baseball player, but that doesn't mean he'll be able to stand up on the ice if you put him on a hockey team. Most businessmen have very limited, specialized knowledge, which often gives them a narrow view. Great bankers may know everything about banking but not much about farming or social work, so it's no more reasonable to assume that a great banker would make a great minister of finance than that a great heart surgeon would make a great minister of health and welfare. It's only the lawyers who always manage to get a lawyer as minister of justice.

Much of Canada's business community has to change its outlook and broaden its knowledge. Time after time I have heard businessmen complain about the government's deficit or the government's intervention; and time after time I have been cornered by the same businessmen and asked, "What about my government grant? Where is the government subsidy for research and development? Will you restrict imports into Canada that compete with me?"

The contradictions are everywhere. The people who want deregulation when world oil prices go up want protection when world oil prices go down. The people who shout slogans about free competition in the marketplace want a monopoly in their sectors because they're worried about fragmenting the market. The people who praise risk and the survival of the fittest want guarantees and bail-outs from the taxpayers. I'm not saying they shouldn't try, but they can't have things both ways all the time.

Take regulation. If the government decides there are special cases in which monopolies or near-monopolies should be allowed in order to create viable companies — whether in pipelines or communications or any other field — isn't it reasonable that the prices these companies charge for their services should be regulated in order to protect the Canadian people? Should Canadians give these businesses the right to print money?

Take crown corporations. It's one thing for a courier service to transport letters and documents from one city to another at a cost that only big businesses can afford; but it's another thing to take a letter from an Indian boy studying at the University of Ottawa to his mother in Old Crow. Yet if the private sector were given the best of the business and the public sector were given the worst, these same businessmen would criticize the post office for losing money, for being mismanaged, for being a typical example of government incompetence.

Take the banks. At one point Ottawa moved to prevent an American takeover of the Mercantile Bank by limiting the ownership of any bank to ten per cent. The Canadian bankers used that limit to avoid being taken over or challenged by Canadians, too, and the result was a small clique of extremely powerful banks whose officers were more or less entrenched regardless of what they did or didn't do. Yet bankers continued to go to their clubs and rant against government intervention over expensive lunches. Eventually the Canadian government had to open up the system to foreign banks to some degree in order to foster a competitive spirit.

When I was Minister of Energy in 1983, the Liberal government came to the rescue of Dome Petroleum, which was in danger of bankruptcy. The world price of oil had dropped and Dome had made expensive acquisitions at the wrong time. Rescuing Dome was one of the last things I wanted to do. I felt my department's mandate was to bring peace to the energy sector after the controversies of the National Energy Program. Part of the controversy was whether the government had become too involved in the oil business. Some people were advising me to let Dome go bankrupt, to let the market decide if Dome should survive, but the cost would have been a traumatic shock to Canada's oil industry. It would have resulted in losses to hundreds of subcontractors and serious consequences for the financial institutions that had lent billions of dollars to the company. In the end I negotiated a deal with the banks and Dome; it saved them and didn't cost the government a dime. We bailed out the banks, in effect, but they never gave us much credit for that.

One of the bankers I had to negotiate with was Russell Harrison, chairman of the Canadian Imperial Bank of Commerce. He could hardly be called a Liberal sympathizer. I had had a couple of arguments with him when I was Minister of Finance; and when I went into opposition during the Joe Clark government, he didn't even return my phone calls. When we signed the Dome deal, I said, "Now that we are partners, I hope you will return my calls."

What made him even more unhappy, despite the fact that I had just saved his skin, was that I asked for a photograph to be taken to mark this happy collaboration between the public and private sectors. The night before, Harvie Andre of the Progressive Conservatives had said on television that the "Communists" were about to take control of another oil company, and I wanted to have evidence of myself with four smiling "comrades." I was in a good mood, although none of them wanted to sit next to me. What I should have done was get the bankers to autograph the picture and write "Thanks a billion," too.

Intelligent businessmen recognize that they shouldn't be doctrinaire about economic problems. In reality very little has been built in Canada without some kind of government intervention. The CPR was built with the help of a Conservative government, and even the Lougheed government of Alberta has bought an airline and controlled natural gas prices.

Canadians have always helped one another. With a population of only twenty-five million, things can't be done on a strictly competitive basis. If rates weren't controlled on the railways, there would be no railways. If there were no marketing boards, our agricultural production would decline. If there were no quotas on imports, our clothing and textile industries would vanish overnight. Companies in Atlantic Canada, for example, need transportation subsidies to get their products to market at a competitive price, and companies across Canada are helped by special financing for exports and federal trade commissioners overseas. Every economy needs the same sort of intervention, and every country has it, including the United States. If any Canadian crown corporation had the setbacks and cost overruns that plague the defence contracts to the American private sector, there would be cries of scandal.

The private sector should be allowed to do as much as it can by itself, but there are few businessmen who will refuse useful government assistance on principle. Most of them know in their hearts that it is needed. If the executives of the Sun Life Assurance Company can make their own decisions and set their own pensions and pass their own jobs from one member of the club to another, it is because the government of Canada prevented an American takeover and allowed Sun Life to turn itself into a mutual company, in which the policy-holders became the shareholders.

94

I thought they would remember that when, as Minister of Finance, I asked Sun Life to delay moving its head office from Montreal to Toronto until after the referendum, because the move would be ammunition for the Quebec separatists. But I was told, "No, we're the private sector, we'll make our own decision." These "private servants," more narrow-minded than any bureaucrat, weren't in power by divine right. They were in power because of a government action. But, still, they wouldn't accede to a reasonable request from an elected cabinet minister during a time of national crisis. They still look down on politicians.

There are two particular areas where the Canadian government must provide incentives. The first is regional development. Without incentives everything will tend to become concentrated in the industrial heartland of central Canada. Already the stretch from Oshawa to Hamilton in Ontario is one big town, and it won't be long before Torontonians will have to decide whether to drive or fly when they are invited out for cocktails. It's a modern trend that depresses me.

I don't know why everybody has to live in Toronto or Montreal when there are so many beautiful under-utilized small towns with good services, inexpensive housing, access to nature, and people eager to work. Because of the high demand for accommodation in the cities, an ordinary family has to pay an exorbitant price for a small home, while houses twice as large are available for half the price in other places. Perhaps those big houses are empty because people had to leave for work in the cities after an "uneconomical" plant was closed down due to the lack of a government grant; yet millions of additional tax dollars have to be spent to build the roads, sewage plants, water-treatment centres, and so on to service the new factories, office towers, and suburbs full of urban immigrants.

Part of this trend is human nature: people want to be near the boss, and they want to be where the action is. You can argue that they are more likely to see—and impress—the boss on a regional inspection tour than in a skyscraper full of other employees, but most people don't see it that way.

There is the quality of life to consider. Some people, however, would rather be a somebody in a small town than a number in an apartment block, and many more would like to live a decent life where they can go to a lake or a golf course or an ocean after work instead of into an overcrowded subway car. There are economic benefits, too. A person who makes $35,000 a year in a small town, lives in a big house that cost $50,000, and shops in a local farmers' market is much better off than a person who earns the same amount yet pays $1,000 a month for a medium-size apartment and shops in a supermarket.

When I was President of the Treasury Board, we decentralized 10,000 jobs out of Ottawa. Some were to Matane, Quebec, a town on the south shore of the St. Lawrence River. The bureaucrats warned that we would never find enough competent people willing to move there. In fact, three dozen overqualified people applied for one of the top managerial posts.

Similarly, when new technologies and communication systems allowed us to place government data centres in towns across the country, we found that they had a particularly high productivity rate — in some cases they were producing so quickly the system couldn't keep up. The employees were delighted to have a good job in their home towns; industrial towns such as Sudbury and Shawinigan diversified into the service sector; and regions of high unemployment received more of a boost than would have been felt in Ottawa, which didn't even feel the loss.

Those who insist that regional development is uneconomical should take a broader view. What are the costs of building new urban infrastructures? Do the regions ease the inflationary pressures caused by the cities? What about the quality of life? Canada is the envy of the world for its cleanliness, its safety, its space. If it were measured only in terms of a bottom line, we would probably have to close down the country and move to the sun belt of the United States. Yet we choose to stay here; and, for the same reason, regional development has to remain key to our economic policy.

The second area that will always require government assistance is in helping Canadian companies export their products. World competition is extremely tough, and our companies often find themselves competing against firms whose governments give them subsidies, benefits, or tied-aid advantages; in many cases Canada has to do the same. And that's just one of the many difficulties of international trade. Tremendous effort and persistence are needed, methods of doing business and even standards of business morality vary dramatically from country to country.

On the whole, however, I think Canadians have been too modest about their successes overseas. We highlight our failures, as if we are more comfortable talking about our flops than about our achievements. But I could see, in my travels as Minister of Industry, Trade and Commerce, that many Canadian companies in the international market are aggressive, efficient, and competitive in selling everything from raw materials to high technology.

Many Canadians are bothered by the enormous amount of American investment in Canada. On the whole, I think it is a good thing, but there are problems. Some American multinationals are good corporate citizens, others are not, and the differences usually depend on such variables as the attitude of the head office in New York or the personality of the Canadian chief executive officer. Certainly, most American corporations have enough experience in enough foreign countries to know how to survive, and there are obvious positive benefits in their presence. They bring capital, the latest technology and competition. When I was Minister of Industry, Trade and Commerce, I was even considered soft on the issue of foreign ownership because I felt positively about it, even though there were problems, such as the time the Americans didn't want Ford Canada to sell its cars to Cuba. The most dramatic problem in recent years has been in the oil and gas business.

Basically, American businessmen have always objected to answering any questions or meeting any conditions when they want to buy something in Canada. They assume there should be no questions or conditions. The Tories changed the name of the Foreign Investment Review Agency to Investment Canada so that they could please the Americans by telling them FIRA had been abolished, but foreign investors will still be unhappy to discover they must hire lawyers, file forms, and get approval. Whatever the name, there is still a law, and the law is what the

Americans don't like. However, all countries have laws that control foreigners. It might not be a major problem in the United States now, but you can imagine the American reaction if the Arabs tried to take over General Motors or Boeing. Already there have been stiff reactions in certain states to large Canadian investments, which don't approach the degree of American investment in our provinces. In one incident, a Canadian trying to take over a Canadian company in Canada met opposition from the state of Florida because the company had some businesses there.

The essential problem is that many Americans look on Canada as if it were just another state, not very different from Texas or Ohio. They're surprised when we take the action of an independent country, but what's our choice? If we were part of the American union, we could take our complaints and voice our interests to our senators and representatives in Washington; but we aren't a part of the union and we don't want to be. On the other hand, we are the biggest customer for American goods in the world. That should give us some special consideration. Usually it doesn't. When the American government introduced a tax bill that discouraged Americans from holding conventions abroad, Canada wasn't exempted even though Canadians spend more money—with a tenth of the population—on tourism in the United States than the Americans spend in Canada. No other country was in the same position.

I put Canada's case to Walter Mondale, President Jimmy Carter's Vice-President, and he agreed that we were right. But he said there was nothing the administration could do because any move to exempt Canada from the legislation would be blocked by two senators who were angry at Canada for something else. It is often extremely frustrating to deal with the Americans because the separation of power between the President and the Congress in their constitution complicates our negotiations and drags us into American domestic politics. Sometimes that gives the American government an opportunity to say nice things but do little.

Some people say that the only way for Canada to avoid being hurt by American protectionism is to guarantee Canadian access to the U.S. market by free trade. My concern is whether Canada could survive politically or whether the logical result wouldn't be the integration of the two countries. Even in the European Common Market with a diversity of nations, each with its own strong identity and cultural history, there is a hesitation to give up too much control for fear that national sovereignty would be threatened. Not only would Canada be threatened by the sheer power and numbers of the United States, but it would be vulnerable to the same economic forces that are pulling industries and people from the American northeast to the southwest sun belt. We are even colder, more traditional, and more distant than New England, and there is no guarantee in a free-trade deal that we won't be left to export our natural resources south of the border while all the new jobs will be created there. Without safeguards or defences we probably would be clobbered, because the Americans would be able to do whatever they want. Those who argue that free trade is our only hope and perhaps inevitable have either given up on the idea of a unique and independent Canada or haven't thought about the consequences, including the effect on our economic relations with countries such as Japan. The challenge for Canadian politicians in the next decade will be to find the proper balance that welcomes American investment, encourages fair bilateral trade, and maintains Canada's identity.

There is another, perhaps even more important aspect to the problem of closer ties with the Americans, and that is the whole question of peace and security. Canada is a member of NATO, the free world's military alliance, and it is a member of NORAD, the North American defence system. Our commitment to them will continue, because we believe in them, but there is a lot of controversy on the issue. The Trudeau government tried to examine Canada's role in a realistic light. It saw that we were a minor player by necessity and that our defence expenditures, though a sizeable chunk of our budgets, were marginal in the broad scheme of things. Given this, the debate centred on how much money Canada should spend on its military. Eventually we agreed to increase our defence spending by three per cent a year above inflation, a tough decision to make in a time of increased deficits. Our allies, the Minister of National Defence and his officials, the Canadian military, and the defence lobby all said, "That's fine, that's an appropriate indication of Canada's commitment," but soon many of them began to press for six per cent, nine per cent, and so on. Obviously they have their own interests to advance, just like everyone else, but the federal government has to weigh their demands against the other demands in the society and judge the real rather than the symbolic benefits.

Not only does the United States have a greater role in the world and more money than Canada, its defence spending is more closely linked with its economic growth. The American military supports huge corporations, underwrites a lot of research and development, and spins off the technological advances into the private sector. The magnitude of their spending makes that possible. What is marginal for them, however, would be overwhelming for us. Our defence spending can't have the same spin-off benefits, so to compare it to that of the Americans is really pointless.

Once committed to our allies, we have an obligation to play a role, however small. That's why the Liberal government agreed to let the Americans test its cruise missile over Canada. It was a difficult decision. We all loved peace, as Trudeau's global initiatives showed, and we all supported Trudeau's theory that the simplest way to halt the arms race was to suffocate the research and development of new weapons. But that was the dream toward which we strived. In the meantime, the Russians were increasing the deployment of their SS-20 missiles while the Americans had virtually stopped deployment. NATO decided that a balance no longer existed, so the European partners agreed to accept more American missiles on their soil and Canada agreed to let the cruise be tested to show the Soviet Union that we were not indifferent to its moves.

Now the argument is going the other way. Though it is always hard to know if there is a balance or who has superiority in the confusion of warheads and launchers and submarines and so on, there is a sense that the time has come to control the race. It's like the old problem of needing a bit more bread to soak up the gravy, then needing a bit more gravy to finish off the bread. Both sides are in a position to destroy the world many times over, and the danger of doing so is becoming more and more real. People are beginning to realize the stupidity of the arms race and

100

there is a growing pressure, as there was with biological warfare, to ban the use of nuclear weapons.

That makes it all the more important that Canada think hard before getting involved in the American "Star Wars" research. It may be a destabilizing force that will trigger another escalation, this time into space. Though Canada is an ally and a relatively small player, it's ridiculous to assume our only role is to applaud every action of the United States government. Canada should develop its own positions after careful study and feel free, if necessary, to disagree with the Americans in the same way we would disagree with the British or the Germans or even the Russians. That is a sign of a mature nation. Of course, the United States is our best friend, but that should allow it to receive the truth as we see it without reacting with shock or anger. Certainly that type of honesty is what I expect from my friends, and there's no reason why Canada should deny itself the same reservations about the "Star Wars" system that are being voiced loudly by millions of Americans, even by some within the Reagan administration.

I did not stay in the Department of Industry, Trade and Commerce long, because the political scene changed rapidly. René Lévesque and the Parti Québécois had come to power in Quebec; Robert Bourassa had resigned as head of the Quebec Liberal Party; and there was a lot of pressure on me to take Bourassa's place in provincial politics. At the same time Donald Macdonald, who had succeeded John Turner as federal Minister of Finance in 1975, was thinking of resigning from public life. He had been a member of Parliament since 1962, he wanted to spend more time with his wife and children and return to the practice of law, and he said he didn't have the "royal jelly" to fight to become prime minister after Trudeau. Inadvertently I may have hastened his decision to resign.

Macdonald and his wife Ruth came to visit Aline and me at our summer cottage on Lac des Piles near Shawinigan in the summer of 1977. The four of us had a wonderful weekend, swimming, playing golf, going to parties, and visiting an old friend of mine who had hundreds of Quebec paintings in his house and a large collection of music. We sang songs and told stories, and I retain an image of the Macdonalds doing Scottish dances sometime near dawn.

During a walk with Macdonald I said to him, "You know, your future is very much in my hands and my future is very much in yours."

"How's that?" he asked.

"I have to make up my mind about going into provincial politics. If I go, you will be trapped in Ottawa because I don't think the government can afford to lose two senior ministers at the same time. If you stay, I will probably be forced to go to Quebec City, because the pressure is great. If you resign, I will probably stay in federal politics because I would expect Trudeau to name me Minister of Finance." (That was the press speculation at the time and I thought I would beat out any other candidates.)

I don't know if our conversation was a factor in his decision, but Macdonald resigned in September.

Trudeau was always meticulous about his cabinet appointments. He interviewed ministers about what they wanted to do and he noted their wishes in a book. Certainly he had known my great desire to become Minister of Finance since the days of Mike Pearson; and I had assumed, once I had been named President of the Treasury Board, that I would get the job sooner or later. I knew it was often a political graveyard, but I still wanted it. In September 1977, I got my wish. Trudeau and I were walking up a staircase in the Parliament Buildings when he stopped and said, "Jean, I will name you Minister of Finance."

"I'm very happy," I replied.

CHAPTER FIVE

A BALANCING ACT

I'M A GUY who likes to take risks and to move quickly. If that has often allowed me to be an effective politician, it has occasionally caused me trouble. The most dramatic example of political brinkmanship in my career happened in the spring of 1978 when I presented my first budget as Minister of Finance. I can't say I wasn't warned by some of my colleagues and officials; but if I didn't listen to their good advice, it was because I wanted to try something that I thought was right and important for the country.

It was an economic requirement at that time to stimulate consumer demand as a means of maintaining economic growth. One obvious way was to make goods cheaper by reducing the sales tax. The federal sales tax was a hidden tax: it was levied on the making and distributing of products and showed up in the final price. Reducing it would not necessarily result in lower prices, because the reduction could end up in the pockets of the manufacturers or distributors. On the other hand, the provincial sales tax was added to the retail price at the time of purchase, so a reduction in it would be certain to stay in the pockets of consumers.

My plan was to consult with all the provinces before the budget and get them to agree to lower their sales taxes in return for financial compensation from Ottawa. There could be an additional advantage if the

103

federal and provincial budgets could be coordinated enough to avoid effects that were at cross-purposes. Brian Mulroney didn't invent either consultation or federal-provincial cooperation, as he often implies.

The problem was that because of the traditional secrecy that surrounds the budget, I could not get iron-clad agreements from the provinces. I could only say, "If I did this, would you do that?" Everyone agreed. The most complicated discussions were with the government of Quebec, and I knew I had to be cautious with the Parti Québécois.

With that in mind I approached Jacques Parizeau, the province's Minister of Finance, in the company of his Ontario counterpart, Darcy McKeough, an intelligent, no-nonsense politician whom I always liked. The three of us shared a particularly good dinner at the Hotel Bonaventure in Montreal in order to put Parizeau in a happy mood. A large man whose privileged background had given him a taste for the finer things of life, he had the manner of an English lord and no apparent acquaintance with humility.

I remember being with Parizeau at a meeting of ministers of finance. The subject being discussed was why inflation and unemployment were rising at the same time, contrary to the traditional theories of economics.

"Gentlemen," Parizeau said, with his thumbs in the pockets of his vest and condescension in his voice, "we must forget everything that we learned at university."

"Mr. Parizeau," I piped up, "I don't have to forget, because I never learned it in the first place!"

Deferring to Parizeau's self-esteem was always the best method of getting your own way, so I ate humble pie at that fancy dinner in Montreal. "I don't know what to do," I said. "What would you do in my place?" Clearly he loved being consulted. "Gee, you're good, Jacques," I said. "If you weren't a separatist I'd name you Governor of the Bank of Canada."

That played right to his weakness. "I'm so conservative," he said, "I would have been a good Minister of Finance for Sir John A. Macdonald." It didn't take long to suck him in by appealing to his ego, and to lead him to suggest what at the end of the evening he was willing to take credit for: an agreement to lower the provincial sales tax. Nothing was put in writing, of course, but I assumed that the word of a minister of finance was worth more than a piece of paper, anyway. Certainly I would have been crazy to raise the issue of the sales tax in my budget if I hadn't been convinced that I had a deal with all the provinces.

The budget was presented in April 1978. Nine provinces announced they would be lowering their sales taxes; Parizeau said he needed time to think about what Quebec would do. "Don't worry," I said to my cabinet colleagues. "I have his word. He is a gentleman, and he will deliver, just like everyone else."

Some people said I was naive; but I thought I had been innovative and straightforward, and as a result the Parti Québécois wouldn't try to destroy me by playing politics. "You'll be screwed," people said, but I defended Parizeau's honour.

He turned out to be less honourable than I would have supposed, from his upbringing; and Quebec didn't lower its sales tax generally. Instead it abolished some taxes on selected products, but it still wanted the financial compensation I had offered the provinces to make up most of their revenue losses.

I can only guess that Parizeau had to backtrack because his Quebec cabinet colleagues wouldn't go along with him and hadn't authorized him to make a deal with Chrétien. But a minister of finance who has lost the support of his cabinet and can't deliver on his word has no choice but to resign. If Parizeau had even threatened to resign, he might have won his cabinet over. Instead, he went along with the others to score a few political points. He denied he had made an agreement and demanded money from Ottawa.

"No way," I said. "A deal's a deal, and if there's no deal, there's no money."

It developed into a terrible controversy. The Quebec nationalists, the press, most of the caucus from Quebec, even most of the cabinet thought I should give in. I felt extremely isolated. Every day the Quebec television reports and the newspapers were full of my opponents. I had few defenders and little opportunity to state my case. Old friends

105

and supporters from my riding used to call my home and ask Aline, "Why is Jean being so stubborn about this? He's not usually so rigid."

"He will never give in," my wife answered. "I will not let him. He's right, because he had Parizeau's word."

I knew that, she knew that, and my bureaucrats knew that: but no one else seemed to believe it or think it mattered. I could have called Darcy McKeough to be my witness, but that would have put him in a difficult position: he was an Ontario Tory, and the federal Tories were making so much hay out of my discomfort. Though he didn't volunteer to intervene publicly, I was told that he informed both Joe Clark and René Lévesque that Chrétien was right, that Parizeau had shaken hands on a deal.

It wasn't a matter of me being stubborn; it was a question of honour. After all, I had given my word to the provinces, and I could hardly make a special arrangement with Quebec after the fact, particularly as it had taken a lot of persuasion to convince the West and Atlantic Canada that a reduction in sales taxes wasn't for the sole benefit of the industries of Quebec and Ontario. Yet the pressure on me to cave in was unbelievable.

I said to Trudeau, "If you force me to change my policy, I will. And after that I will see what is left of your Minister of Finance, and then I will decide."

Trudeau supported me. "Do whatever you want," he said.

I remembered that when Diefenbaker became prime minister, he sent a small amount of money to every farmer in the West. It had been accompanied by a letter from him, and it had helped bind them to him forever. This inspired me as a way out of my problem. Instead of giving financial compensation to the Quebec government for a proposed cut in sales tax, I decided to send the cash equivalent directly to the people of the province — $85 for each Quebec taxpayer.

The impact took a while to be felt, but I remember my first glimmer of hope. One afternoon I was being interviewed by a reporter beside Ottawa's Rideau Canal. A sightseeing boat went by and a guy on board shouted, "Hey, Jean! When are you sending me my eighty-five bucks?" As the cheques began to arrive, there were special $85 sales in

Quebec stores, and I even met a Parti Québécois MNA who admitted to cashing his cheque rather than sending it on to the provincial treasury as his government was urging people to do.

One day I was on a radio hot-line show, and a woman phoned to give me hell about infringing on provincial rights and bullying the PQ. Nothing I said convinced her. Finally I asked her, "By the way, Madame, what did you do with your cheque?"

"Oh, I cashed it," she said.

"That just proves one thing, Madame," I said. "Your nationalism isn't worth my eighty-five bucks."

She slammed down the phone.

Still the storm raged on. One day I told my wife that I thought I would have to quit. "I've had a good crack at Finance, I guess," I said. I was completely discouraged.

She brought me breakfast in bed and said, "You have a good breakfast, then you get up and go fight again."

When I was driving to Parliament Hill, I heard a news report: Liberals were up three or four points in the Gallup Poll. So when I arrived at the meeting of the Quebec caucus, which was still giving me hell, I said in a serious tone, "You know, you guys are right. I've made a hell of a mistake and the party will never recover from it. Why, just this morning I heard that we're only up three or four points in the Gallup." After that, for some reason, the great principles that everyone had been defending seemed to fade into the background, and eventually the Quebec government announced a truce.

The incident was a good example of Trudeau's relationship with his ministers of finance. He almost always supported them in what they wanted to do. While he let them know his views, he listened more than he argued; and he never argued in public and rarely in front of the other ministers.

This was clear the day he called me to his office to discuss lifting the wage and price controls that I had inherited as Finance Minister. I wanted to lift them earlier than expected because I was worried about the "bubble" effect, the building-up of pressure for higher wages and higher prices that would explode the moment the controls ended. My notion was that a quick and surprising end would avoid the pressure of a lengthy anticipation.

Trudeau and many of his senior advisers wanted to keep the controls longer, because the program was working well and it was politically popular. When I refused to change my mind, Trudeau said, "We can only take the camel to the water; we can't make it drink."

So I was able to do what I thought best. I set a rather arbitrary date for lifting the controls, and they came off with a smoothness that startled even many of the economists in my department.

Economics has been called the dismal science. Once you get to understand it, you may not find it so dismal, but you don't find it much of a science either. At a reception I held after presenting one of my budgets, I invited the specialists and the other guests to bet what effect the budget would have on the Canadian dollar. The Governor of the Bank of Canada was wise enough not to participate, but everyone else put a quarter on the table. All but three people guessed that the dollar would go up. In fact it went down.

Of the three who had guessed correctly, two were not economists — me and my assistant, Eddie Goldenberg. The third, Sid Rubinoff from the Finance department, was an economist, but he explained his prediction this way: "The textbooks tell the market that the dollar should go up. But the market is crazy, so the dollar will go down."

I learned my economics not from textbooks but from listening over the years to the intelligent, practical views of public servants such as Bob Bryce, Simon Reisman, Louis Rasminsky, Gerald Bouey, Tommy Shoyama and Bill Hood. I followed their discussions in Mitchell Sharp's office, I read their submissions to the Treasury Board, and I heard their arguments in front of cabinet. I believe that made me as well qualified for the Finance portfolio as anyone from Harvard or Bay Street.

Like all departments, Finance is a joint venture of the minister and the bureaucrats. They brief him daily on the economic situation, on interest rates, on inflation, on the dollar, on the reserves, on production and on growth, and all these elements become the basis of his decisions. He sees the problems and the trends; the technicians explain why this is happening or what will be the effect of that.

Often the options are extremely clear, so the decisions are easy to make. Sometimes instinct overrules technicalities; other times political realities are more important than economic ones. For example, plugging a tax loophole may have a financial benefit but be a political disaster: what minister of finance would put an end to the popular retirement savings plans even though he was convinced that Canadian savings are too high?

Above the economic and political details there are usually larger debates taking place within the department. It is the nature of economists to divide and sub-divide into schools of thought. After all, if there were never any doubt about the solutions, everyone would be rich. Before my budgets I encouraged my officials to have a good discussion about their differences. The Galbraithians took on the Friedmanites, and those who thought it was time to stimulate the economy debated with those who thought it was time to cut the deficit. Everyone struggled with the definitions of full employment, reasonable inflation, and fair taxation. Is full employment when everyone has a job or when the economy is working at full capacity? Is there room for growth or will growth create inflation? Should we balance the books by cuts in expenditures or by increases in taxes?

Ultimately, of course, the minister can't spend hundreds of days pondering theories, however interesting or important. Reality hits and decisions have to be made. But that doesn't mean he is locked into a particular course forever. As things change, different methods are required and priorities must be reassessed. Inflation may be the most serious problem for a while. When action is taken to combat it, it fades as the major preoccupation, and unemployment takes its place. Then the deficit becomes a worry, and so on. More than anyone else in the government, including the prime minister, the minister of finance must decide what needs to be done; and he decides how to do it after consulting with his colleagues, his department, and the community at large.

On one occasion I got into a long battle with my officials, who wanted to cut taxes. It was really my way of forcing them to argue their position so I could learn to defend myself in public later on. Suddenly I stopped and said, "This must be the first time in the history of the department that the minister has opposed cutting taxes. Normally it is the politician who wants to cut and the bureaucrats who resist."

"There must have been some politician in history who didn't want to cut taxes," I said.

"Yes," came the reply of Tommy Shoyama. "Herbert Hoover!" So we cut.

Being minister of finance demands flexibility, so I have always argued that a government can't be doctrinaire about issues such as the deficit. The Reagan administration in the United States may have been elected on its promise to balance the books in Washington; yet after four years of hard work it took the deficit from $50 billion to $220 billion. Not that that has prevented the Republicans from using the same old rhetoric, which its supporters love and which has rubbed off on a lot of Canadian businessmen (including those who make a fortune selling Canada Savings Bonds every year). In fact, the United States, which has become paradise for many Canadian Tories, has only had eight or nine balanced budgets since 1931, and most of them were created by stubborn Democrats.

Obviously no country wants a burdensome deficit, because taxes have to be used to pay the interest on the debt and other services suffer as a result. It was my concern about the deficit that earned me the nickname "Dr. No" when I was at the Treasury Board, and there were very small increases in the deficit in my two budgets as Minister of Finance — in fact, the deficit was reduced in relation to the GNP and the budget. The national debt must be a factor that every minister of finance considers, but it cannot be the single, overriding consideration regardless of all the other factors at work.

Japan, which is often praised for its economic success, has a larger per capita deficit than Canada. In meetings with Japanese officials, including a minister of finance, I asked why. The reason was interesting: the Japanese people save a hell of a lot of money — almost a quarter of their income — so the government has to run large deficits in order to recycle money through the economy. Canadians also save a great deal, some fourteen per cent of their income, more than twice the U.S. rate.

Indeed the government encourages them to save by offering tax advantages, which make capital available for development. Over time the accumulation of capital has been immense.

One of the things many, many Canadians do to save is buy government savings bonds. They may not be the greatest investment, but people feel secure with bonds. Even my Dad put his hard-earned savings into bonds. By the time he died and my share came to me, they were worth probably a third of their original value because of inflation, and I wished he had spent the money and had more fun himself. But I, too, will probably put some of my savings into bonds for my own security or to pass on to my children and grandchildren. It's almost human nature.

The point is that after inflation and taxing back as income a sizeable portion of the interest paid out, the government has spent relatively little in servicing much of its debt. Clearly there comes a limit when a nation's credit isn't good any more and no one will lend it money or buy its bonds, but Canada's deficit is nowhere near that big. Canadians in vast numbers still prefer government bonds over those of the private sector. I used to ask Tory bankers who loved to hate the Liberals, "Are you putting your personal savings into Canada Savings Bonds or into the bonds of your friends at Chrysler and Massey-Ferguson?"

Such contradictions make sense only when you realize that political doctrine is as important as economics in the arguments about the deficit. Republican businessmen worship Ronald Reagan despite what he has done to the American national debt. Tory businessmen howled when Allan MacEachen, the Liberal Minister of Finance, tried to raise revenues by discontinuing tax incentives that had served their purpose or were being abused. In other words, the business community wanted cuts, but it didn't want to be cut itself. At least, it didn't want to be cut by the Liberals. But when the Tories cut the generous research-and-development incentives that the Liberals had introduced without getting a word of thanks, there wasn't a squeak.

When executives look at the deficit and say, "If we ran our companies like that, we'd be bankrupt," they are only stating the obvious. It is not the government's purpose to make a profit the way a company does, because a company doesn't have to give a damn about the unemployed poor or provide services that are non-commercial by definition. Of course a government must be managed as efficiently and as economically as possible, and I think it withstands the test of constant public scrutiny better than most corporations would if they were forced to open up. But, fundamentally, comparing the public and private sectors is like comparing apples and oranges.

In spite of all the differences and all the complaints, the rapport between government and business has not been as bad as it seemed to the public. Under the Liberals there were countless instances of cooperation and consultation. I have probably consulted more with the business community than with any other sector during my career, and I never prepared a budget without seeking out the opinions of the Business Council on National Issues, the Canadian Chamber of Commerce, the small-business associations, and the trade organizations.

Their lobbies are well-organized, well-financed, well-presented, and persistent; and many of their leaders are powerful, intelligent, and knowledgeable people who are a pleasure to talk to. Very often the complaint of business is not that it wasn't consulted; the real complaint is that government didn't do what business wanted it to do all the time. If businessmen want to make the decisions, the solution is simple: they should get themselves elected to Parliament.

The same is true for the union leaders. They also can't say they aren't consulted regularly. Certainly they were a part of my budget-making process, and there wasn't a Liberal minister who wouldn't have met the leader of a union about a problem. At times I found labour less persistent than business and more emotional in the presentation of its position. But it seems to me that its real handicap was its association with the NDP. Because union leaders can never be seen to be getting too close to the government, they are caught between making an effective and candid case for their members and judging the impact on their ability to deliver votes to the NDP.

In my opinon that made them less effective representatives and demonstrated the problem of having a national party as the spokesman for a particular interest group. It's as if the unions are cautious about getting from the government any benefit that might weaken the political rhetoric of the New Democratic Party. Even when the NDP gets into power in the provinces, the unions seem to remain on the outside. Maybe it's because they've been in opposition too long and by nature feel uncomfortable on the side of government.

A second difficulty is the structure of the Canadian Labour Congress, a highly decentralized federation of unions. Each leader has his own little empire with its own pension fund and strike fund and jurisdiction. As a result, labour often has trouble delivering on the deals it might have made with government. The forces vary from time to time in different sectors and different regions — the postal workers of Nova Scotia may be ready for peace while the steelworkers of British Columbia may be about to strike—so general agreement is rare and it isn't possible to knock everyone into line. That's basically why the Liberals couldn't get voluntary restraint on wages in the 1970s and had to introduce controls.

Many businessmen feel that the Liberals were soft on labour because we knew that workers have more votes than bankers. Certainly Trudeau, Marchand and Pelletier had worked closely with the Quebec unions in the 1950s; I had been a labour lawyer in Shawinigan a bit later; and no doubt there are more Liberals than Tories with union support in their ridings. But I don't think that biased us as a government. After all, we had to fight the NDP, too.

Even in Shawinigan I met a strong NDP challenge in the 1965 election. The NDP candidate was a popular doctor, and despite my populist roots and style I could feel the pressure. I had to counter with a forceful appeal to the union members. "Your leaders are using your money," I said, "they're using your offices, and they're using your printing presses to try to elect a rich doctor!" It was tough, but it was true. Although I enjoy the company of working people and went out of my way when I was a minister to drop in on union headquarters and elicit union views, I knew the leadership would always be opposed to what the government did.

So while the business community felt the Liberals were in the pocket of the unions, the union leadership accused us of being in the pocket of the businessmen. It was the price we had to pay to be in the centre. Although ministers saw and heard the business sector more than the other sectors, that was largely because the very nature of business requires more contact.

As well as being politicians, ministers are the administrators of their departments, and every department has responsibilities that affect business. So businessmen frequently show up in Ottawa to discuss a specific problem about a tariff or a tax or a research program. Labour doesn't have the same need or desire to concern itself with the details of a particular piece of legislation, although occasionally it will lobby for or against a matter that directly touches its members. When I was Minister of Industry, Trade and Commerce, for example, both labour and management showed up to discuss the quotas on textile and clothing imports. Generally speaking, however, I found myself meeting with more executives from Toronto, Montreal or Calgary than the union leaders, who were headquartered in Ottawa. Any minister who likes to tackle the thorniest problems will spend a lot of time with businessmen.

The great issue that divides business and labour these days is the same one that divides economists: lowering the deficit versus creating employment, restraint versus stimulation. There is no simple solution. Unemployment is a social and human tragedy, even though its causes and effects have changed over the years. Unemployment insurance and welfare have taken away some of the miseries that existed in the past, more members of a family are in the workplace full- or part-time, families are smaller, and there are more opportunities to pick up extra money in the so-called "underground economy." In Shawinigan, for example, the jobless statistics look frightening; but the houses are in better repair than they were twenty years ago, there are more shops, and everyone has a TV and a car. Some say that just proves that the social "safety net" undermines incentive and is abused, but I say it's a sign of progress and civilization. Of course, welfare means idle hands and lost pride, and it must never be an alternative to work, but the nature of work has changed, too.

In the old days work meant building and producing things. A man went into the woods, chopped down a tree, got it to a mill, and turned it into paper or housing. Now the work that took the man months is done in minutes by machines or robots. More is produced with fewer people, so thousands of manufacturing jobs have been lost. But new types of work have sprung up — in education, in hospitals, in information services, in financial institutions, in computers and in sales. Unfortunately the new jobs have not been created in regions first developed for their natural resources as quickly as the old jobs have been lost.

Shawinigan was developed because it had a waterfall. Paper mills and other industries were attracted by the cheap electricity. But now that is less of an advantage, modernization has taken other tolls, and more than 2,500 industrial jobs have disappeared in my riding. The service sector, the public sectors, and some decentralization programs have helped offset the losses to some degree, but the structural problem remains. It is a problem seen throughout the country.

Many people speak of high technology or an industrial strategy as if it were the easy, all-encompassing solution. But high technology requires more risk capital and skilled workers than natural resources and mass labour, and an industrial strategy is harder to put into practice than it looks on paper. The country, the economy and the pressures are too diversified for a grand scheme to succeed.

For example, what strategy can the Canadian government develop for copper or paper or oil when there is no control over the price in the world market? The National Energy Program was a good strategy for oil, based on high oil prices. Exploration was to take place, jobs were to be created, the spin-off benefits for the West were to be terrific, and everything was to have been wonderful — except the market collapsed in spite of all the predictions. World supply exceeded world demand, and there was nothing that any government could do about it.

People say, "Oh, Chrétien, you're too practical. You don't like long-term planning." That's not true. Canada needs long-term planning, and I've done a lot of it. I'm willing to discuss and work with those who think they know precisely how many microchips and dentists the society will need in five years. Their forecasts are useful and if they are accurate, so much the better; but my experience doesn't allow

115

me to be fooled about the chances of success. There are simply too many decisions to be made by too many people in Canada and around the world that can affect any strategy. Even in the great planning societies, where prices and inputs and outputs are rigidly controlled, five-year plans never turn out as expected.

When I was Minister of Finance I came up with a great plan. I even got it approved by the Prime Minister, the cabinet, and all the provincial premiers, Tories and New Democrats alike. Everyone smiled because it was such a beautiful plan. Within five years there was going to be a shortage of manpower because of all the jobs that would be created. The federal and provincial treasuries would be filled to overflowing and all the deficits would be eliminated. Everyone agreed that my plan was practical, everyone praised it and everyone was happy.

The economists assumed that growth would be six per cent a year for the five years. I never considered myself a great economist, but that seemed rather high. After a fight with some of my officials, I reduced it to five per cent, which still would bring most of the plan to fruition. Unfortunately, reality didn't cooperate: the growth turned out to be a recession, and the whole plan turned to ashes. The critics said that we had no strategy, but that was easy to say after the fact. We had one, but it didn't work out as we had hoped.

Strategies for the various sectors need to be thought out and articulated, but always with the understanding that they need flexibility once they hit the real world. I imposed quotas on textile and clothing imports to deal with a temporary problem in a particular sector. It was easy for others to say that a genuine strategy would have been to replace all the textile jobs with high-tech jobs, but what was the reality? Time after time I said to the industrialists, "Okay, I will close all the textile mills in my riding, if you can guarantee that for two jobs lost in textiles, there will be one new job in high technology."

For the realities of life are quickly forgotten in all the theories. Shutting down the domestic textile industry would have made Canadian consumers captive to foreign producers, which could have cost more than keeping that domestic industry competitive; it would also have had an intolerable social and political effect. Politicians are accountable to their constituents, after all, and they are not elected to close down their own towns.

Canada must adjust to the modern world; but those who call for futuristic industrial strategy are often the same people who demand less intervention from the state. That's why I often find their arguments unacceptable.

In 1978, Trudeau uncharacteristically intervened in Finance and almost destroyed my career in the process. It was a time of high inflation throughout the western world: prices were mounting, wage settlements were getting more expensive, profits were soaring and there was pressure on governments to do something. Inflation was the main item at an economic summit in Bonn, West Germany, which Trudeau and I attended that August. I had already had months of discussions with my officials about the situation, and I talked about possible solutions with Trudeau on the way to Bonn.

After our return I went on holiday to my cottage outside Shawinigan while Trudeau prepared a speech to the nation about the Bonn summit and the Canadian economy in general. The polls had shown uncertainty about Liberal economic policies following the resig nations of John Turner and Donald Macdonald; part of the insecurity was based on a perception that Trudeau didn't take enough interest in economic affairs. Trudeau's advisers wanted to correct that impression in the televised speech by announcing some new restraint initiatives. However, instead of sticking to generalities, Trudeau announced that $2 billion would be cut from federal expenditures. Since this came as a surprise to me, the press jumped on the idea that the Prime Minister had pulled the rug out from under his Minister of Finance. The people who had criticized Trudeau for not being concerned with the economy now abused him for interfering with Chrétien's territory, and I was made to look like a fool.

I've never quite decided whether it was a breakdown in communications or a power play by the PMO. Trudeau phoned me to apologize and said that Jim Coutts, his principal secretary, had tried to contact me in advance, but I still felt like resigning. Certainly the Prime Minister had the right to do what he did—he left the details of the cut to me as he should have, and we had discussed the matter generally — but normally a minister of finance would resign in such an embarrassing situation. I decided not to mainly because I was worried about the effect of a French-Canadian senior minister resigning when a separatist government was in power in Quebec.

I had been in politics long enough to know about power games. The art of politics is learning to walk with your back to the wall, your elbows high, and a smile on your face. It's a survival game played under the glare of lights. If you don't learn that, you're quickly finished. It's damn tough and you can't complain; you just have to take it and give it back. The press wants to get you. The opposition wants to get you. Even some of the bureaucrats want to get you. They all may have an interest in making you look bad and they all have ambitions of their own. So even if those who weren't happy with me in Finance didn't create the situation, I knew they would try to take advantage of it. Naturally I had to make a few counter-moves in my own defence.

Trudeau knew that this incident had been damaging to me and to the government. I went to talk to him in the course of preparing another budget for November. "I want this one to be my own," I said. "Let it make me or break me."

"There won't be any interference," he promised.

Then I had to gain back the confidence of my officials. If they sense you're losing control in the cabinet, they tend to make life difficult. "Okay, boys," I said. "We're going to make a budget, my budget. It's going to be a good one, and no one is going to tell us what to do." I could see them smiling at the thought of going into a big fight and winning it.

Since an election was due, everyone thought the November budget would be a political one. But I had already paid a price over the sales-tax controversy for trying to be innovative in my first budget, and the August fiasco had sown confusion in the markets and in the public mind. So I opted for a rather conservative, stabilizing approach, which was generally well received. Some of my colleagues later argued that it cost us the 1979 election, but I figured we had already lost that because

118

of the popular wish for a change. My hope was the Liberals could salvage some support by appearing to be fiscally responsible. In the long run that was the right choice, but for a while it looked like more evidence that good economics don't always make good politics.

Clark didn't win that election so much as we lost it. The Liberals had been in power since 1963. People were tired of Trudeau after more than a decade, and there was no immediate crisis to make them rally back to him. If he had called an election in 1977, following the victory of the Parti Québécois, the Liberals would have obtained an overwhelming majority; but by 1979 many Canadians had been lulled into a false sense that the threat of separation wasn't real.

Indeed, the more often Lévesque called English Canadians a bunch of fools and oppressors, the more they applauded him. Because he appealed to some kind of masochistic guilt, he was often portrayed as the best thing since sliced bread instead of a national menace. So Canadians didn't hesitate about replacing Trudeau with Clark; then they brought Trudeau back at the first opportunity.

I remember an argument I had with some women in Winnipeg during the 1979 campaign. I was canvassing there for Lloyd Axworthy when I ran into an intelligent, articulate, but hostile group of voters. "Madame," I asked one of them, "who would make the better member of Parliament for this riding, Lloyd Axworthy or his opponent?"

"Lloyd Axworthy," she replied.

"And who would you prefer as Minister of Finance, Jean Chrétien or Sinclair Stevens?" (Stevens, the right-wing Tory, had been rumoured to replace me if the Tories won the election.)

"Jean Chrétien," she replied.

"And who is the best man to be Prime Minister, Pierre Trudeau or Joe Clark?" I asked.

"Pierre Trudeau," she answered.

"So your logic must tell you to vote Liberal."

"No," she said. "I'm protesting and I want a change."

CHAPTER SIX

FIGHTING FOR CANADA

THE ELECTION of a separatist government in Quebec in 1976 came as a surprise to me. I knew that the provincial Liberals under Robert Bourassa were not popular, but I assumed that the notion of independence would be a crippling handicap for René Lévesque and the Parti Québécois. They were elected in spite of independence and not because of it, as Lévesque himself recognized on election night, when he cautioned his followers not to get too excited. The people of Quebec had simply wanted a change of government. Nevertheless I sensed danger. The separatist movement had momentum. It had caught the imagination of the young, and its leader had a lot of political ability. Meanwhile, Trudeau was in his third term as prime minister and no one knew if he would stay on or what the effect of his leaving would be. I felt Canada was facing a hell of a struggle that would last for years to come, and I was discouraged.

It was particularly discouraging to see how popular Lévesque was in the French and English press. He was forgiven for actions and language that wouldn't have been tolerated from any other politician. Even journalists who didn't support independence found excuses for him. "He's not really a separatist," they said. "He's a moderate, trustworthy fellow." They said that in 1976, and they were still saying it in 1985, despite all the evidence to the contrary.

If he backed away from the separatist option from time to time, it was only because he had hit a brick wall and needed to save his skin politically. But those were only temporary retreats. The moment a crack appeared in the wall he tried to advance again. There has never been any doubt in my mind that Lévesque was a dedicated separatist since the day he tried to lure me into provincial politics in 1964. "Jean, forget about Ottawa. In five years it won't exist for us."

He had said it with such sincerity that I wondered if he weren't using his position as a cabinet minister in Jean Lesage's Liberal government to advance a cause that might have been stirring within him since he was a boy growing up in a village dominated by the English. Lesage was a federalist, but he was sensitive to accusations of being "Ottawa's valet," and that made him susceptible to the advice of those who saw the Quiet Revolution as a process of gaining independence in bits by taking more and more powers from Ottawa. I believe that Lévesque and some of his colleagues, such as Jacques Parizeau and Claude Morin, were already on the road to separation then and have never left it.

Funnily enough, although Lévesque wasn't able to get me into provincial politics by direct means in 1964, he almost succeeded indirectly thirteen years later. Robert Bourassa resigned as leader of the Quebec Liberal Party after losing the 1976 election, and my name began to be mentioned as his replacement. Strangers as well as friends phoned asking me to run. They said it was my duty, because the situation was serious and the provincial party was discouraged and lifeless. Although I wanted desperately to see Lévesque defeated and thought I could do it, I wasn't very interested in leaving Ottawa, even to become premier of Quebec. However, I didn't rule out the possibility.

In June 1977, I called on Claude Ryan at the editorial offices of *Le Devoir* in Montreal to discuss the Quebec scene. I didn't visit him very often, and his austere and intellectual personality wasn't similar to my own style, but I always found him knowledgeable and impressive. At the beginning of this particular meeting he was somewhat defensive because he had supported the Parti Québécois in his pre-election editorials — not because he was a separatist, he explained, but because he had felt it was time to throw out the Bourassa government. Soon, however, we went on to discuss the future of the Quebec Liberal Party. In his judgment there were only three qualified people available for the leadership: Claude Castonguay, Jean Chrétien, and Claude Ryan.

Unfortunately, either because he had mumbled his own name out of shyness or because of the deafness in my right ear, I missed the third name. I launched into a consideration of the relative merits of Castonguay, who had been Minister of Social Affairs under Bourassa, and Chrétien. After the meeting Eddie Goldenberg asked me, "Why didn't you reply to Ryan's suggestion of himself as leader?"

"He suggested himself?" I was doubly surprised. Not only had I not heard it, but I had never imagined that Ryan harboured personal political ambitions. It is normal that someone who wants to serve his society should want to serve in the most important job available; but I hadn't visualized Ryan involved in politics in that way. I pondered the prospect for a while and then went back to see him.

"Everyone is best doing what he does well," I said. "My life is politics, and I have some talent for it. If you asked me to be the editor of *Le Devoir*, it would be a joke. You are a writer. That is your life, and you are very good at it. Your talent is to be the editor of *Le Devoir*. If I were you, I would not run for public office." I tried to be nice about it, but perhaps I shouldn't have said anything.

Ryan concluded from my remarks that I was intending to run for the leadership of the Quebec Liberals, and he published that as a fact in his newspaper the next day. I thought our conversation had been confidential and I certainly hadn't made up my mind about my future; but his indiscretion forced me to make a decision.

The first step was to assess my chances of winning. To do that I needed to know my support among the Liberal members of the National Assembly. In my experience the acceptance of your peers is an important indication of general acceptance, because it shows that they believe they can win with you. My supporters, principally Michel Gratton and John Ciaccia, did a quick check and found at least fourteen sympathizers among the MNAs, a good base for an outside candidate; and they assumed we could keep the majority of the caucus by the time of the convention.

122

My second stop was 24 Sussex, for a discussion with Trudeau. I knew he was worried about Lévesque's victory, but I also knew he wouldn't tell me what I should do. He rarely pushed anybody to do anything. So he didn't say, "Jean, you have to go to Quebec," but that was more or less the conclusion of our conversation. As the sun set on the beautiful summer panorama of Quebec across the Ottawa River, the decision seemed made in both our minds.

The decision still wasn't certain, however. My future really depended on whether I became Minister of Finance in the event Donald Macdonald quit politics. In September 1977 that happened. The press speculated that Trudeau named me Finance Minister in order to keep me in Ottawa; and some Quebec papers suggested that it was because he didn't have any confidence in me as premier of Quebec.

In fact, however, the opposite was true. He said, "I hesitated to name you Minister of Finance because I was afraid you will refuse to go to Quebec. If you're needed in Quebec, I don't want you to tell me that you don't want to go because you're Minister of Finance."

"Prime Minister," I said, "I guarantee you that if I'm needed in Quebec I will not hesitate to resign my post." But the appointment did cause many people to think that I was no longer available.

Meanwhile a movement had begun behind Claude Ryan, largely on the grounds that an intellectual was needed to combat the intellectuals in the Parti Québécois and that Ryan had nothing to do with the discredited Bourassa government. Other people were working for Raymond Garneau, the very able former Liberal Minister of Finance who had been a good friend of mine since university days. So the pressure was lifted from me and, frankly, I was relieved. But summer passed into winter without anything being settled.

Then Ryan announced that he would not be a candidate, and the spotlight came back to me. I heard the news of Ryan's retreat from Brian Mulroney, of all people. I barely knew him, but I knew of his work on the Cliche Commission, the highly publicized investigation into Quebec's labour problems. He phoned me out of the blue, told me about Ryan, and said, "Jean, you have no choice. You have to be in the race."

"If I have to, I will be," I said.

Then I phoned Raymond Garneau. "Raymond," I said, "I have to tell you there's a lot of pressure on me to run. What are your plans?"

Garneau's name had been unfairly dragged into the political mud and there were doubts about whether he would run while under investigation. In his mind, however, his candidacy would be proof that he had nothing to hide. But by the time I phoned him the investigation had absolved him of any wrongdoing. "So now that I've been cleared," he said, "I don't have to run, and I may not. If I don't and if you do, you can use the organization I've put in place."

As 1977 passed into 1978 I was on the verge of declaring my candidacy, but I decided to hold off until after the First Ministers' Conference on the Economy in February. By the end of January, however, Garneau had jumped into the race and Ryan had changed his mind and followed; I was off the hook. Claude Ryan went on to win the convention and become leader of the Quebec Liberal Party. I remained Minister of Finance until the federal Liberals were defeated by the Progressive Conservatives under Joe Clark in May 1979.

Nobody could have guessed that within a year Clark would be defeated by a vote in the House of Commons, Trudeau would resign and then return as leader, the federal Liberals would win a majority government in the ensuing election, and I would go to Quebec to fight at Ryan's side in the dramatic referendum on Quebec's future in Canada.

When the Liberal Party returned to office in February 1980, Trudeau asked me to become Minister of Justice with special responsibility to lead the federal forces in the upcoming referendum campaign. Accepting that responsibility was the most difficult decision of my life. Normally I leap with pleasure at new challenges — the bigger the better — but this one frightened me. The consequences of failing were so enormous, not just for me or my party, but for the entire country. Moreover, it had become clear that Ryan and I would always have trouble working together because of the differences in our personalities.

While in the opposition I had attended a pre-referendum organization meeting, at which he clearly indicated that he didn't want to have anything to do with me. Perhaps he had never forgiven me for telling him he didn't have the talent to be a politician. Anyway, he had been so unpleasant that Marc Lalonde and André Ouellet said to me afterwards, "I wouldn't have taken the abuse that you took."

I told this to Trudeau and suggested I might be better to take the alternative he had offered, Secretary of State for External Affairs. "I don't understand you, Jean," Trudeau said. "Home is burning and you want to be in Paris, London, Tokyo and Washington?"

Still I couldn't make up my mind, and there was division among my closest advisers about what I should do. Finally I said to Trudeau, "Pierre, why don't you do for me what a big brother would do for his little brother?"

"Okay, Jean," he said. "You're Minister of Justice, you're Attorney General of Canada. You're Minister of State for Social Development, you're in charge of the referendum and the constitution. I hope my little brother will not say that his big brother has no confidence in him."

So I became Trudeau's firefighter.

Under provincial legislation on the referendum all the "Yes" and "No" forces had to group themselves under umbrella organizations. Ryan was in charge of the "No" side. While Joe Clark had been prime minister, the federal government didn't get involved; it had no role to play, because Clark and his advisers saw the referendum as a family feud to be fought out by Quebeckers. He even halted federal advertising in the province, while the Parti Québécois government was plastering every village with Quebec flags and turning departmental messages into subliminal nationalist slogans. (For example, a billboard campaign for seat belts became "Fasten yourself to Quebec.") Even the MPs from Quebec were virtually excluded from participating. I don't doubt Clark's sincerity; but I did question his judgment on this matter and wonder what would have happened had he stayed in power. As it turned out, Clark gave speeches in Shawinigan and Rimouski during the campaign, and I was proud to share the stage with him. He was one of the host of public figures and private individuals, including some provincial premiers and federal MPs, who came to Quebec to help as part of the "No" strategy. Even with the federal counter-attack, money and publicity, even with all the Quebec MPs waging all-out campaigns in their ridings, even with the great speeches by Trudeau, the "No" side only won sixty-forty. Ten per cent the other way would have rewritten history.

Yet Ryan didn't welcome the federal contingent after the re-election of Trudeau. He was concerned that his authority might be weakened, and he believed he could win the battle by himself. He wanted to win it by himself, that was the problem. In his view, the MPs might be marginally useful, talking to their brothers or sisters, but he didn't see the importance of their making speeches and organizing rallies and putting their pride on the line. For him the referendum was an intellectual debate; but while he was winning the arguments, the separatists were winning the hearts of the people. The analysis of his ideas was logical and correct, but it didn't catch an audience like Lévesque's emotional pitches for an independent country, a proud and free people, and a bold and courageous break with the past.

Ryan eventually came to accept the inevitability or advantages of having a federal presence on the team, but he never fully accepted that he couldn't deal with Trudeau on a direct, daily basis and that he had to deal with me instead. At first he wanted me to be a vice-president of a large council. I refused, because the position didn't give me the authority appropriate to the people and power I represented. Instead I got a place on the executive committee. Because the committee was small and the federal representation limited, the work was extremely heavy. I lost about fifteen pounds during the campaign, and I never was a fat guy.

Every morning I met in Ottawa with MPs, ministers, advisers from the Canadian Unity Information Office or senior bureaucrats to get their advice and give them reports. Once a week, after question period in the House of Commons, I drove to Montreal for an afternoon meeting of Ryan's executive committee. Every night I gave a speech or two in various ridings. Then I returned to Ottawa to start again the next morning.

The polls looked bad, nerves were frayed, and it was understandable that differences of opinion turned into tension. On one occasion Trudeau complained publicly about how the "No" campaign was developing. His complaint was based on information from some advisers who weren't as close to the situation as I was, so both he and they had exaggerated the problems. I had to contradict him openly, but he took my response in good grace, and I even rose a bit in Ryan's esteem for having criticized the boss.

We did have some problems, of course. Our first public meeting was a disaster. It was held in the hockey arena in Chicoutimi. Plywood was thrown over the ice, and the place was freezing. There was a good crowd, about 3,000 people, but the organizers had said they expected 6,000, so the press said we had flopped. We had six times as many people as Lévesque got out in Portneuf, but that was overlooked because he squashed his 500 people into a small room and the press said it was a great success.

The real problem with our meeting was that we arranged for almost two dozen people to speak. Each was supposed to speak for two minutes; but no one can say much in two minutes, so everyone went on and on. By the time I got up to speak people were fleeing from hunger and fatigue. I was so furious that I gave one of the worst speeches of my career, full of shouting and frustration.

We learned from our mistake, however, and after that, meetings had only five speakers: a master of ceremonies who was a well-known local personality, the interim leader of the Union Nationale named Michel Lemoignan, Camille Samson from the Créditistes, Claude Ryan and myself. Samson and I were born on the same street, and although he was a very conservative person, he was extremely funny; and we shared the populist speaking style for which the Mauricie is renowned.

"Who will be the ambassadors after independence?" I used to ask. "Who will be in the king-size Cadillacs with the chauffeurs and the flags on the hood? It will not be you, and it will not be me. It will not be the little people. It will be the bourgeois from the Grande-Allée and Outremont. They will be enjoying themselves, but what will be in it for you?"

My speeches were peppered with the slang of Main Street; they included a few English words, such as *"le* flag *sur le* hood." These words are common in the everyday language of French Canadians, and the crowds loved to hear a politician who didn't talk down to them; but I had to take a great deal of abuse from the intellectuals. Many of them were separatists, of course. Lévesque himself was a master of slang, but he was forgiven and I was not. There were howls of protest in the newspapers when I compared separatism to gangrene, yet no one protested when Claude Morin described federalism as a cancer.

The people understood me, however. They too disliked the double standards of those who behave one way in private and another way in public, like all the socialist professors who know the best restaurants and the best wines and who wear their protest buttons while eating filet mignon. The more I attacked them, the more they insulted me by saying that I lacked education and sophistication; but long after I stopped attacking them in my speeches, their insults persisted. When I ran for the leadership of the Liberal Party in 1984, one magazine erroneously quoted a guy from Shawinigan as saying that Chrétien couldn't be taken as a serious candidate because he speaks French badly. Yet the guy in whose mouth this canard was wrongly put is a very close friend of mine who speaks exactly the same French I do.

It is my impression that the intellectuals have less influence in Quebec now than they did in the 1950s and 1960s. Perhaps that's partly because I have been in government too long to be impressed by editorials and abstract theories. When I entered politics, the opinions of *Le Devoir* or *The Globe and Mail* seemed crucial. Now I enjoy them when they're good and dismiss them when they're bad, knowing that life will go on undisturbed. But I trace part of this significant change to the fact that the vast majority of Quebec's intellectuals moved from non-partisan study to support for the separatist option.

Like the poets and the singers, the intellectuals were carried away by the romance of independence. That was understandable in poets and singers: the idea of creating a new country was an exciting dream that lent itself to beautiful poems and beautiful songs. Unfortunately, it also meant that the heroes of Quebec were the losers, the failures.

Wellie Chrétien and Marie Boisvert in 1909, after their marriage in La Baie Shawinigan. He was 21 and she was 17 when they married; she would have 19 children, 9 of whom survived infancy.

With some of my family, in front of the duplex in La Baie Shawinigan where I was born: my mother and father are standing beside my sister Carmen and her husband Charles Martel. My brother Guy (*right*) and I are in front.

My mother Marie in 1952 not long before she died. I always regretted that she did not live to see what her children became.

My father Wellie in 1980 when he was nearly 93. He said to me in his last year: "I can die now, the Liberals are back in power and Quebec will remain in Canada."

With Maurice Duplessis in 1955. Second from the right is Jean Pelletier, now mayor of Quebec City. Premier Duplessis was meeting with the graduating class from his *alma mater*, the Collège des Trois-Rivières.

When I opened my campaign in 1963 in La Baie Shawinigan, with my father (*left*) and his friend J.A. Richard, my Liberal predecessor.

With my wife Aline the night of my first victory, April 8, 1963.

With Lester Pearson on April 4, 1967, when I was appointed to cabinet
as Minister of State attached to Finance. Pierre Trudeau was the new
Minister of Justice and John Turner, the new Registrar General.

With Minister of Finance Mitchell Sharp in my riding, April 1967.
Left, Hormidas Prud'homme, mayor of Grand'Mère, far right, Maurice
Bruneau, mayor of Shawinigan, and Dr. L.P. Lacoursière, mayor of
Shawinigan South.

Talking to a group of Montreal students visiting Parliament Hill in 1967.

With John Rae, my first assistant, when I was Minister of Indian and
Northern Affairs.

With Governor General Roland Michener, on being sworn in as Minister of National Revenue in January 1968. We are now both counsel in the law firm of Lang Michener.

At the Bonn Summit in 1978, with Pierre Trudeau, French President Giscard D'Estaing and Roy Jenkins from Great Britain.

With Queen Elizabeth and Princess Anne in Resolute Bay, July 1970.

Having fought the referendum campaign successfully, I began an
immediate tour of the provincial capitals on May 21, 1980 to discuss
constitutional change with the premiers.

Receiving congratulations in the House during the final phase of the constitutional debate from Pierre Trudeau (*left*), John Munro (*right*), and fellow Liberal MPs behind (*left to right*), Charlie Turner, Robert Gourd, René Cousineau and Francis Fox.

The "kitchen cabinet" revisited on November 5, 1980. Roy Romanow, Attorney General of Saskatchewan (*left*) and Roy McMurtry, Attorney General, Ontario (*right*).

Signing the constitution in the presence of Queen Elizabeth, April 1982. Trudeau had somehow managed to break the tip of the pen and my off-the-record comment was quite amusing to the Queen.

Acknowledging the applause from delegates at the leadership convention in 1984.

With my family the day my first grandson Olivier was baptized. Left to right, my sons Hubert and Michel and my daughter France. Beside me is my wife Aline and my son-in-law André.

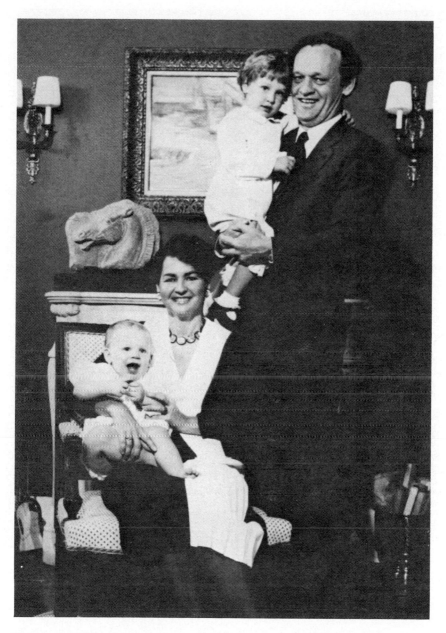

Christmas 1984 with another new grandson, Maximilien.

In opposition for the second time. The boy scout salute seemed an appropriate gesture to the Conservatives.

Louis-Joseph Papineau and Henri Bourassa were seen as flamboyant, inspirational figures, while the great achievers, such as George-Etienne Cartier and Wilfrid Laurier were unappreciated or ignored. It's like the Irish phenomenon: all the great men are the martyrs, those who didn't succeed.

But if that phenomenon makes good art, it makes lousy thought. Once the Quebec intellectuals took the side of separatism, they abandoned truth for doctrine and, in so doing, they lost much respect and influence. Criminals who planted bombs were built up as political heroes, while men of ideas, action, and substance, such as Trudeau, Marchand, Lalonde, Pepin and Pelletier, were dismissed as nobodies because they were federalists.

Once the intellectuals entered the fray, many of them lost their freedom as well as their credibility. As they got closer to power, they were absorbed by it and became deputy ministers, heads of commissions, and so on. Moreover, there was no turning back, because as academics and journalists they were tainted by their government work. I sympathize with their situation in some ways. They have families as well as ambitions to support, and there are few Quebec writers or intellectuals who have inherited wealth or the huge market for their books that Americans can rely on. Nevertheless, the overall effect was to weaken their influence on Quebec society over time.

Part of their intense reaction against me came because I had to demystify their great dream. That wasn't an easy thing to accomplish. It was like taking a toy from a child or shattering a hope. It hurts as much to destroy a dream as to have one destroyed, and it particularly hurts when you have to be tough on your own people. Quebeckers have wanted to rewrite history ever since their ancestors lost the tiny battle on the Plains of Abraham because the English troops crept up on them in the night. "I, too, wish I had been able to wake up Montcalm and tell him the English were coming," I used to say in my speeches, "but I was not there." The audiences laughed, but it was my way of making the serious point that we had to face reality.

"You are dreaming of a big party," I said. "But after big parties there are big headaches. Have you thought of the headaches you will get?'' In some ways Quebec was already paying the price for independence without having experienced the euphoria of it, because the uncertainty had caused money and jobs to leave the province. I warned of Quebeckers having to leave if the economic situation deteriorated, just as so many — including my grandfather — had left for work in New England at the turn of the century. How many modern Quebeckers would be as lucky as my grandfather, who returned and avoided assimilation?

I spoke of how the wealth of the West was part of Quebec's heritage, and I compared the price of gas in Quebec with the price of gas in France. I became emotional at the thought that an independent Quebec would deny its children the great North and the Rockies. I became angry at the suggestion that there were ''pure'' and ''impure'' Quebeckers, depending on their background and mother tongue.

''When you start analyzing people's blood,'' I said, ''that's racism, and it frightens me. Parizeau is married to a Polish woman, so what about his children? Claude Morin is married to an American, so how will his children vote? Is it because of troubles in the bedroom that the rest of us have to have a nation?'' Again people laughed, but I knew the point was getting through and I knew I had to be tough.

One day Lévesque was reported to have said that Trudeau wasn't a pure Quebecker, because his mother had been an Elliott. I mentioned this to Trudeau over lunch, and he started fuming. He was proud that he had chosen to remain a French Canadian when it would have been just as easy to let himself be absorbed into the English-speaking community. His fury inspired him to deliver, in my view the best speech of his career. It happened in Montreal on May 14, less than a week before the referendum.

Though many people wanted him to speak every day across the province, he only spoke three times in Quebec during the campaign. He and I had decided that it would be more effective that way, because if he had repeated the same message over and over, nobody would have been listening to him by the end. It was a risky decision, but it turned out well, as was apparent from the dramatic impact of his speech in Montreal.

"Yes, Elliott is my mother's name," he said. "It was borne by the Elliotts who came to Canada two hundred years ago. My name is a Quebec name, but my name is a Canadian name also."

Someone once wrote, "Nationalism is the hatred of others. Patriotism is the love of your own kind." That has been one of my mottoes in politics, and all my speeches in Quebec were positive expressions of my love for Canada in one way or another. Many of them ended with the cry, "Canada is the best!" We feel proud of our achievements and know there are millions and millions of people around the world who would give their last penny to share our so-called miseries; but too often we are shy about celebrating our country and get caught in the historical divisions and self-centred problems that obsess us.

I have always been very proud to be a French Canadian. The source of my pride is the French heritage of my family. I remember how moved I was when I visited the beautiful little village of my ancestors in the Loire valley. That's why I find it ridiculous when the separatists in Quebec call me a "sell-out" for defending Canada. They jump on my use of slang to show I don't respect my heritage, but they never report or reflect on the serious message I convey after I've warmed my audiences with a few colourful phrases or self-deprecating jokes.

"Remember," I have said in every province, "it was the French Canadians who beat back the English and American armies that invaded Lower Canada on more than one crucial occasion. It was the French Canadians — guys from my neck of the woods, in fact, such as Radisson, Groseilliers, and La Vérendrye — who opened up the West, either by themselves or with the English explorers. So this entire country belongs to us as much as to anyone else, even though we aren't distributed in great numbers across it."

I talked about Canada's tradition of sharing its wealth among regions; I talked about Canada's advantage in having a link with two of the greatest languages and cultures in the world; and I talked about the personal satisfaction of being bilingual and bicultural. Because the message was as tough in the West as in Quebec and sometimes hard for people to accept in either place, I learned to use humour, everyday

147

speech and emotion to establish a rapport with my audiences, often with good results.

For example, I like to tell the story of the old gentleman I met in the East Kootenays of British Columbia during the 1968 election campaign. I had been advised before going into the reception that I should be particularly nice to him, because he had decided to vote Liberal for the first time in his life. I spotted him at once: he looked like a retired British army officer, very stiff, very distinguished, with a handsome beard and cane. "Sir," I said in my broken English, "I am told you have decided to vote Liberal for the first time in your life. Would you please tell me the reason?"

"Yes," he barked. "Because that guy Trudeau will put those goddamn frogs in their place once and for all!"

I wasn't quite sure how to answer, so I said, "Thank you very much." I slipped away and just let him vote Liberal.

That story accomplishes two things besides relaxing the audience. It raises a controversial issue without bitterness or condemnation, and it suggests that Canadians have matured since then. Like my father, I prefer to downplay the wrongs of the past and concentrate on the hopes for the future. I sense in both English Canada and French Canada that the hatreds and prejudices have eroded. There is more effort to understand, more communication and more tolerance. Canada's diversity has become part of our patriotism.

Historically our devotion to our country was impeded by our loyalties to other places, whether France or England. These loyalties divided us and made us measure ourselves against the wealth or culture of ancient regimes. We never celebrated our own riches: our lakes and forests, our space, our freedom, our generosity, our uniqueness. Think about how much time it took and how much agony it caused to get our own flag, yet we were one of the seven powers of the western world, not some little colony. And that was only twenty years ago.

The night before the referendum my wife asked me, "Do you think we will still be Canadians tomorrow night?"

It was a startling question, but I said, "Yes, we'll win." While the polls were showing us neck-and-neck, I felt that we had the momentum and could rely on most of the undecided votes to come our way. It was not fashionable or comfortable to support the "No" side in many Quebec families: brothers were arguing with brothers, children were fighting with their parents and many grandchildren were begging their grandparents to vote "Yes." So it was easier for the federalists to keep quiet until they got into the voting booth. I was hopeful that in the moment of truth most Quebeckers would choose Canada, just as the people had done when they rejected the call to join the American Revolution and repelled the invading soldiers at Châteauguay.

Happily, I was right. On May 20, 1980, for the first time, the voice of the majority was louder than the voices of the élite, and it said "No" to separation. The "No" side won a majority in almost every riding in the province, and I was both delighted and relieved that we had won in my own riding of St-Maurice. Lévesque had made my riding a symbol, campaigning there himself three times. (He knew it was more vulnerable than the ridings of either Trudeau or Ryan, in which there were sizeable anglophone communities.)

It was a great day for Canada, but I can't say I was swept up in the victory celebration. Instead of the euphoria that usually follows an election win, I felt only the sadness that comes when you destroy some one's dream. I walked into the Radio-Canada studios in Montreal for an interview, and I was greeted by bitter silence, except from a security guard, who said, "I'm happy to see you. There are a lot of long faces here tonight." Someone even disappeared so he wouldn't have to shake my hand. I wasn't surprised, of course. On an earlier visit to Radio-Canada I had met a friend who worked there as a technician. I knew him to be a federalist, but he was wearing a Parti Québécois button. "It's like my union card," he explained. Perhaps he was too sensitive, but he didn't want to be singled out as unfaithful to the cause.

Many English-speaking Canadians don't know how strong the pressure had been, particularly from the media. At the time I was angry, but now I can see that they were probably just reflecting the pain that existed in the society. Even in the moment of victory I felt sorry for those who had fought so hard for what they truly believed in. There were many Quebeckers who had invested their emotions in their dream and were crying that night.

I wanted to be with my people in Shawinigan, but I drove to Montreal for the final rally with Ryan, who wouldn't let me speak because he felt I had stolen enough of the show. Then I dropped in on a small party, and finally I joined a dozen or so friends at my hotel. We were like firefighters after a fire, too exhausted to celebrate, too relieved to be exuberant. My happiest moment came the next day: I returned to Ottawa and received a standing ovation from the House of Commons.

Before the vote Trudeau had clearly set out the implications of a loss. "Our heads are on the block," he had said. I took that to mean that all the Quebec Liberal MPs would have to resign because we had lost the confidence of the people. Many Canadians still don't realize how close or how significant the referendum result was.

Sometimes these emotional situations are seen more clearly from the outside. On a trip to Washington in April 1982, I met Joseph Kraft, the distinguished American newspaperman. "What Trudeau did was unprecedented," Kraft said. "It's the first time that a movement of a revolutionary nature that had its roots in language or colour or religion evolved without violence. You bet on democracy and you won."

Certainly violence could have broken out. Emotions were so high that just one argument in a Montreal tavern could have led to bloodshed.

At a town meeting in Alma, Quebec, in the early 1970s, a very intelligent Liberal got up and said, "Chrétien, when will you tell the separatists that there will never be independence, that the federal government will never allow it to happen? If the people of Texas were to propose independence from the United States, the Marines would be there within hours and that would be that." All the federalists applauded him wildly.

But I didn't agree. "We'll put our faith in democracy," I said. "We'll convince the people that they should stay in Canada and we'll win. If we don't win, I'll respect the wishes of Quebeckers and let them separate." It was a strange feeling to have all the separatists on my side; but that was what I believed, and that was what we achieved despite the handicaps.

In retrospect, the referendum was the biggest mistake made by the Parti Québécois. Until then its strategy had been extremely effective for Quebec and highly dangerous for Canada. It was described to me by Claude Morin.

"We'll separate from Canada the same way that Canada separated from England," he said. "We'll sever the links one by one, a little concession here and a little concession here and a little concession there, a move here and a move there, and eventually there will be nothing left."

That's exactly what the Quebec government did. It asked for a new power here and an international presence there, and because each demand looked reasonable and in the best interests of the province, the people went along. In time Quebec would have been independent in all but name and there would have been no turning back. But the referendum focused the issue, even though the question was fuzzy. The people had to make a choice, and the separatists lost.

By 1985, a few months before his resignation, Lévesque had admitted that the idea of independence had hit a brick wall. It gives me great pride to think that the federal Liberal Party laid some of the bricks and added some cement to make the wall strong. But I am not under the illusion that separatism is dead forever. There will always be Quebeckers who want to turn back the clock and awaken Montcalm. Nor can anyone guess what pressures for cultural survival will appear or what forms they might take as the global village gets smaller under the impact of direct-broadcast satellites and high technology.

Perhaps the whole notion of cultural survival will become as obsolete in the next fifty years as religious authority did in the last fifty years, or perhaps it will become the major challenge of the twenty-first century. Whatever happens, I am personally convinced that it is possible to be a proud Quebecker and a proud Canadian at the same time. Far from being exclusive, they are complementary, for without Canada Quebec cannot survive. The proof is the Quebeckers who went to the United States to earn their living and vanished into the mainstream within a generation.

Of course, it has not always been easy for French Canadians to keep their language and their culture across the country, but that is changing. English Canadians are beginning to relate their own identity to the presence in their midst of a large and dynamic francophone population, and more and more anglophones are learning French. Both cultures are discovering the advantages of knowing a second language, not in terms of rights or duties, but for personal satisfaction and intellectual gratification. Eventually speaking both languages should become a common experience in Canada. That has been a consistent theme in my career.

One of the first speeches I gave as a minister was to the chamber of commerce in Kelowna, British Columbia. "It's tough to learn another language when you're thirty," I said in my poor English, "but my kids won't have the problem I have had. They will grow up in both languages. Your kids should do the same. Let them learn French here, not for the sake of the few French-speaking people in Kelowna, but as an asset to their own lives."

Two-thirds of the audience gave me an ovation; the other third sat on its hands. Since then I have seen an increase in effort and good will, and all levels of government have created institutions and programs that will ensure that the brick wall against separatism remains strong.

The referendum campaign taught all Canadians about the fragility and the magnificence of their country. It was a battle that we fought together and won together. Because it was difficult and traumatic, people wanted to put it behind them, to forget about confrontation, and to dream of a more peaceful time of harmony and consensus. Like the English rejecting Churchill after the Second World War, Canadians turned on Trudeau, despite the extraordinary victory he had achieved. They wanted to turn that page of history and begin again. That's human nature — we all want fresh starts and new hopes. But we must take care not to turn the page so roughly that the courage of the people and the lessons of the past are torn from our memories.

CHAPTER SEVEN

A PROMISE TO THE COUNTRY

A T NINE O'CLOCK the morning after the referendum Trudeau and I met in his office. "Where do we go from here?" he asked me. During the campaign he had promised that a "No" victory would not mean a victory for the status quo. It would be a call for a renewed federalism. Now it was time to act on that promise. We were meeting in Trudeau's office to discuss what the renewal would be and how it could be achieved. Two basic proposals emerged: to patriate the constitution and to introduce a charter of rights.

The first sounded simple enough, but it hadn't been possible in fifty-four years of effort. Canada had been created in 1867 by the British North America Act, an act of the British Parliament that established the rules and the institutions by which we govern ourselves. With time Britain's authority over Canada diminished in practice, and in 1926 Canada was offered absolute control of its founding document: Canadians would no longer have to go through the formality of asking Westminster to make changes in the BNA Act for us. Even if that formality didn't cause the average citizen to wake up in the middle of the night with worry or shame, it was a national humiliation, for, legally, Canada was still a colony of Great Britain. When people understood that, they wanted it ended.

The problem was that Ottawa and the provinces couldn't agree on who could change the document once it was home. Could Ottawa alone change it? If not, did all the provinces have to approve each change, or just the majority of the provinces, or perhaps the majority of the population? Until they came up with an amending formula, Canada's pride suffered, and the formality remained.

Trudeau almost got an agreement at a conference in Victoria in 1970, but at the last minute Quebec Premier Robert Bourassa backed away. That agreement would have been a good deal, because Quebec would have received the right to veto any amendment, a right that neither it nor any other province ever had in law, although there was a custom that Great Britain wouldn't change anything unless everyone substantially agreed. However, Bourassa chose to hold out for more powers as his condition for signing, so the whole thing bogged down. Time after time the difficulty wasn't finding an acceptable formula; it was that acceptance of the formula was used as a bargaining tool to get additional powers.

Trudeau's second proposal, for a charter of rights, had been a wish of his since the 1950s and a goal for many people since John Diefenbaker introduced a bill of rights in the early 1960s. However worthy in intention, Diefenbaker's bill was merely a piece of federal legislation. This meant it applied only to federal matters and it didn't have the overriding legal authority of a constitutional bill of rights. The provinces could ignore it, and the courts weren't sure what to do with it. Ultimately it didn't guarantee many freedoms at all. Entrenching a charter in the constitution would overcome those limitations.

My particular interest was to guarantee minority language rights across the country — for the francophones outside Quebec and the anglophones within Quebec. I saw a rare chance to undo the historical error that was made when French Canadians lost the right to their schools in the West. That increased their assimilation and prevented many Quebeckers from moving to different parts of Canada. Manitoba, Saskatchewan, and even Alberta might have been francophone provinces in other circumstances. In practical terms I knew that the re-introduction of French schools wouldn't change history or the character of the West, but I felt it was important as an assertion of national unity.

Given the long series of failures in constitutional reform, neither Trudeau nor I was deluded about the chances of success. Some advisers and colleagues were saying that Ottawa should act unilaterally and go at once to England to get patriation, an amending formula, and a somewhat limited charter. But we believed that it was better to try another round of negotiations with the provinces, using the goodwill and sense of purpose that developed from the referendum result.

That very afternoon I flew to visit all the premiers at Trudeau's request, even though I was near exhaustion from the election and referendum campaigns. In fact, I was due to leave for a holiday in Florida, and my wife wasn't happy about the new delay. "Tell Mr. Chrétien," she said to the driver who arrived to collect the clothes I would need for my trip to the provincial capitals, "that if we don't leave for Florida by Sunday, he will get sovereignty-association." It was a joke on the Parti Québécois euphemism for separation, but the driver didn't laugh. "She's really angry," he told me.

My first stop was Toronto, where I met Tory Premier William Davis and his advisers at the Albany Club. Davis impressed me a great deal. He had narrowly won his party's leadership in 1971 and had had close calls with two minority governments in three elections, but he had persevered and survived, and he emerged an extremely skilful politician. Though he was a bit too prudent at times for my taste, he developed a moderate stance that earned him admiration, even from the NDP.

During the referendum campaign he had asked me if he should make a speech in Quebec. I encouraged him because I felt too few English Canadians were speaking up. In some ways he wasn't very well received, because his government hadn't guaranteed official bilingualism in Ontario; but his speech was useful nevertheless.

Davis really rose in my esteem during the constitutional debate. He never played petty politics, and his contributions were always of the highest calibre. From our first meeting he was straightforward and firm, and he stuck to his word even when Joe Clark and most of the Tory premiers opposed him. "It's not a partisan issue," he said. "It's not a question of Liberals versus Conservatives. Canada can't go on forever having its constitution amended in a foreign parliament, and a charter of rights and freedoms is a sign of our maturity as a society." I was delighted for him when he won a majority government in 1981 after taking that forceful stand. It allowed him to leave politics at the top of his form three years later.

I would have preferred Davis to have covered Ontario by Section 133 of the constitution, giving the francophones of Ontario the same rights as the anglophones in Quebec, before he left office. I think he came close a couple of times, but he chose to take a more gradual approach in order to avoid a negative reaction in his province. The federal government always felt it would be an abuse of his support on the constitution to force him to accept something that we were not forcing on every other province. But I liked to keep the pressure on him, nevertheless.

He had a close adviser named Hugh Segal whose wife's grandmother, Madame Cossette, lived in Shawinigan. I knew her quite well, and one day I got the idea to use her to keep the heat on Davis. I phoned her, explained the situation in Ontario, and asked her to phone her granddaughter's husband. Madame Cossette agreed and I briefed her on what to say. She gave Segal a long, made-up story about being with a group of old folks who were talking about Bill Davis and wondering why such a nice man wouldn't give the francophones in Ontario the same rights that the anglophones in Quebec had. Her account was so dramatic that apparently Segal couldn't sleep that night, and the next morning he arranged a special meeting with Davis and his top advisers to discuss the issue. It was only months later that he discovered that I was behind the call.

After seeing Davis for dinner I flew that night to Manitoba for breakfast the next morning with Conservative Premier Sterling Lyon, and then to Saskatchewan for lunch with NDP Premier Allan Blakeney, to Alberta for tea with Conservative Premier Peter Lougheed, and to British Columbia for dinner with Social Credit Premier William Bennett. They all were pleased that we had won the referendum and seemed more receptive to reopening the constitutional debate than I had expected, but each had his reservations about the amending formula and the charter.

Although all the Western premiers had their good qualities and made useful contributions, I tended to see Lougheed as the leading Western voice. He was strong and articulate, and he seemed to wield great influence over his colleagues. Often his silence was as eloquent as his words, and I could see the others studying his look to read his mind. Even Allan Blakeney, the brainy socialist, seemed afraid to cross Lougheed. Much of Lougheed's strength came from his fervent, single-minded defence of Alberta's interests. It sometimes made it difficult for him to appreciate the national picture, but it gave him a power that had to be respected.

He could be very tough; but oddly enough I don't think he was ever as tough with the federal Liberals as he was with Joe Clark's Conservative government. He was needlessly tough with Clark in public, in my opinion, and many people accuse him of contributing to Clark's downfall. Personally, I can't complain—he was always pleasant to me, even though he preferred to deal with the Prime Minister than with an ordinary minister who might have been beneath his lofty status.

There was a rumour after the 1980 election that he wanted me as federal Minister of Energy. Our rapport was established when I was Minister of Indian Affairs and Northern Development; we negotiated a lot of business in the West concerning the Indians and the parks, and so on. Later, as president of the Treasury Board, I helped him rescue the Syncrude mega-project, a billion-dollar oil sands consortium deal in which both Ontario and Alberta were to participate. Donald Macdonald, then federal Minister of Energy, had invited me to the meeting in Winnipeg, and it quickly became apparent that the deal was going nowhere. Some partners were withdrawing, Ontario and Alberta were at each other's throats, and the discussions had deteriorated into confrontations. Since I was a neutral outsider, I was able to go back and forth among the players, particularly Lougheed and Davis, to work out an agreement. We got one by the end of the day, and I think my efforts on behalf of the West were noticed.

My interest in the West and knowledge of its problems went back a long way before that. In 1907 my mother's family had moved from Shawinigan to St. Paul, Alberta. According to the family legend, my grandfather Boisvert had been a very jolly innkeeper who probably drank as much as he sold. His wife was very religious and in her mind fun was not the way to Heaven, fun went with Hell. She felt he should go through Hell on earth to get to Heaven, so to speak, so she persuaded him to sell his assets and emigrate to Alberta, where they broke land in Therrien, outside St. Paul, three days by buggy north of Edmonton. "After I got there," my grandfather used to say, "I drank twice as much!" It was in letters from the West that I learned about combines and sections and the agricultural situation, and I learned even more during my grandfather's occasional visits home.

In my own way I suffered through the bad times and rejoiced in the good times through the experiences of my Western relatives, who now total more than 250 people. As I often say to them, "Too bad for the Liberals that you all aren't in one riding. We'd have a chance for one seat in Alberta." Many of them showed up at a rally in Edmonton during my leadership race, and I was very proud to see them in the front rows with T-shirts that read "Chrétien for the West." They are now in their fourth generation in the West, and despite the difficulties in getting a French-language education, half of them have managed to maintain their heritage. I hope that our efforts for constitutional reform will make it easier for the next generation.

Over the years I grew closer to Westerners because I sensed we shared the same perception of the powerful Ottawa-Toronto-Montreal triangle. It seemed to hold all the wealth and power, all the financial institutions, all the industrial activities; and we seemed to be outsiders unable to penetrate it. Even though I became an important cabinet minister and have lived in Ottawa for many years, I never lost the sense that the power establishment looked down on me because I was from rural Quebec. I vividly remember feeling out of place when I was guest speaker at a nomination meeting for Bud Drury in Westmount, where the élite of Montreal live.

My feeling was probably no different from that experienced by Calgary oil men when they first enter one of the forbidding towers of the Toronto-based banks for an important loan. The feeling may be irrational and petty, but it is as strong among people from the Mauricie or Cape Breton or northern Ontario as it is among Westerners. All of us are made to feel that we lack sophistication and culture because we are still close to our rural roots compared to those who have made it in the cities for several generations.

No one is to blame really. The fault lies with human nature and the problem is the same for Texans in New York or French provincials in Paris. Sometimes I think it is a chip on the shoulder that I must overcome; at other times I am proud that I have been near power for so many years and still remain critical of the establishment. Either way it has given me an empathy with ordinary people in all regions of the country, even in the West, where French-Canadian Liberals aren't exactly worshipped.

In fact, whenever the West didn't give the Liberal Party enough MPs to permit strong Western representation in the cabinet, I liked to champion Western causes and to express Western views—"on behalf of my family," I used to joke. The problem was often a problem of perception rather than of fact. I probably had more deputy ministers from the West than from Ontario or Quebec. Most Westerners weren't aware of how many people from the West, such as Tommy Shoyama, Basil Robinson, Gerald Bouey, Al Johnson and Gordon Robertson, became extremely powerful in the public service.

But the lack of political representation was a problem, a vicious circle that we didn't know how to break. The less the West was represented, the more alienated it felt. The more alienated it felt, the less it chose to vote Liberal, and the less it was represented. That was Trudeau's greatest frustration. He tried extremely hard to overcome it and did a great deal for the West, but he never made a breakthrough and rarely received any credit. The few Western Liberal MPs, such as Otto Lang and Lloyd Axworthy, always became very powerful ministers, as did the Western Liberal senators such as Bud Olson and Jack Austin, who were put in the cabinet to bolster Western influence despite protests against non-elected officials being given so much authority.

159

If I had obtained for rural Quebec the money and advantages that Otto Lang obtained for Saskatchewan, my Commons seat would have become more secure than one in the Senate. But no matter how many subsidies we gave to prairie farmers or how many thousands of railway cars we built to transport their grain, it seemed to make no difference. To an extent the problem wasn't money — money can't buy a rich person and money can't compensate for the feeling of not belonging. In fact, we might have lost some respect in the West by assuming that money was the answer.

One day, as Minister of Finance, I met with a group of businessmen in Vancouver. They were complaining and giving me hell about how tough things were under the Liberal government in Ottawa. It was the usual stuff that businessmen say just before they ask for their grants and their tax write-offs.

"Gee, you guys, I understand your problems," I replied. "This morning when I woke up in my hotel and opened the curtains, I saw all your big yachts in the harbour. And I thought, 'It must cost a hell of a lot to put gas in those huge machines. It must be terrible.' Then I went for a stroll around town. When I first came to Vancouver in 1967 the tallest building was the Hotel Vancouver. But so many tall office buildings have been put up during the years of *terrible* Liberal administration that I couldn't find the bloody hotel again. So I can understand that it's getting tough for you guys, real tough to make your third million."

The fact is that the greatest expansion in Vancouver, Calgary, and throughout Western Canada occurred when the federal Liberals were in power; but nobody wanted to admit that. Even in the good times, those who made money never felt it was enough. It is one of the sadder characteristics of capitalism that people must always want more and more. Expectations rise with income, and there is little encouragement to be happy with what you have. Some mornings I wake up and say, "I must be crazy to stay in politics when I could earn so much more in the private sector." But my wife reminds me, "We don't need more. We're happy, we have a nice house and a nice cottage, and we can give our children everything they need."

Yet it is difficult to limit expectations. When the West grew rich

160

under the Liberals, it thought it could have grown richer faster under the Tories. When the economy slumped, the West found it easier to blame the Liberals than the collapse in the demand and world price for oil. It's probably good for Western Canada to experience a Tory government in Ottawa for a little while. It will learn that there are limits to growth, and neither the limits nor the growth have much to do with what party is in power. The Tories may say that they'll let Western oil prices go to world level instead of being fixed, for example, but that won't be much of a promise as long as the world price stays low or drops.

The West might also learn that the influence of Ontario and Quebec isn't confined to the Liberal Party. Any national government will feel it, as many Western Tories discovered to their frustration when Brian Mulroney came to power with large debts to Ontario's election machine and his new Quebec supporters. Central Canada can't be pushed aside easily. It has the population, the industries, the financial houses, and the ridings to assert its strength. Ontario has been the main beneficiary of Confederation, and as a result there will always be some tension between it and the West.

As the West becomes wealthier and economically more mature, it will press for a greater manufacturing sector, which will probably be developed at Ontario's expense and in spite of Ontario's resistance. The perpetual challenge as a minister was to make changes that benefitted the West without hurting central Canada or vice versa. That wasn't always possible, but when it was managed by an adjustment here and a deal there, no one ever gave Trudeau the credit he deserved. Whenever I struck an agreement that helped the West, he made a point of congratulating me. But I knew that nothing would have been possible without his support and encouragement.

The best example was his government's tackling in 1982 of the age-old problem of the Crowsnest Pass freight rate. In essence, it was a huge subsidy to Western farmers for the transportation of their grain to the ports. The price of moving a bushel of wheat had been fixed by Wilfrid Laurier; and no one had dared tamper with it since, because the farmers had come to see it as their birthright. As a result there was a serious distortion in the economics of transportation. It became cheaper to send a bushel of wheat than a letter from Moose Jaw to Vancouver. It therefore became more expensive to transport other commodities because the railways had to make up for their losses on moving grain. That deterred the development of a manufacturing base in the West because it increased the costs of moving finished goods to the market.

Of course, the farmers weren't happy about losing a portion of their subsidy in the Liberal reforms, but much of the extra money collected from them went into double-tracking the railway. That was necessary and served everyone by allowing more goods, including grain, to be carried with fewer bottlenecks in the system. As controversial as these changes were at the time, opposition to them died down quickly, and almost no revisions were proposed by the Tories. Yet, instead of being praised for his courage in doing something positive and important for the development of the West, Trudeau received nothing but abuse.

The same thing happened with the National Energy Program in 1980. Some Westerners, in their time of success, had forgotten the concept of sharing on which Canada had been built. They argued that their resources belonged to them and were not to be shared with the less fortunate parts of the country. Alberta accumulated an enormous trust fund for its citizens and howled when Ottawa tried to get some of the wealth for the rest of the nation. The most vehement critics seemed to forget that federal money had poured into the West to alleviate the hard times of the 1930s, nor did they remember that the Liberals were defeated in 1957 for trying to build a pipeline to bring natural gas from the West to the Ontario market in order to generate Western prosperity.

They also forgot that wealth hasn't always rested in central Canada. At the time of Confederation the Maritimes had been the rich partners. Indeed, in 1869 Joseph Howe had called for separation because he felt Nova Scotia had to provide too much for central Canada. Then circumstances changed. Wealth shifted from Halifax to Montreal to Toronto to Calgary, and as it did, it became the turn of others to help those who once helped them. That is Canada. Perhaps the Maritimes will become rich again in fifty years or sooner. Perhaps Alberta will become poor again in a hundred years. Nobody knows what will happen, and that's why nobody must forget the principle of sharing. To forget is short-sighted as well as selfish.

The real problem with the NEP was not the selfishness of the producing provinces. It was not even Canadianization, or Canadian prices for oil and gas, or Canadian self-sufficiency in energy. The real problem was that Ottawa, the oil companies, the banks, the industry experts and practically the entire world made a bad bet in 1980. Everyone assumed that the demand for a finite and essential resource would push up the price. In fact, overproduction and a decrease in consumption pushed it down. The opposition liked to blame the Liberals publicly for misreading the play, which we certainly did. But we were in excellent company with the private sector, and privately no one really faulted us. By the time I became Minister of Energy in 1982, the price of oil had already stabilized and begun to decline, so I had to reassess the NEP. The Energy portfolio was new, complex, and politically challenging for me, and that's why I had asked Trudeau specifically for it once I was finished with the constitution.

Energy is so vital to the economy, so strategic, and so lucrative that many Canadians wondered if it should be so overwhelmingly in the hands of the American multinationals. There was a scare during the OPEC crisis in 1973, when some Exxon tankers destined for Canada with oil were diverted to the United States by order of the American head office. Whether the scare was justified or exaggerated, people realized how completely dependent we were on foreign decisions and foreign information. That realization prompted the Liberal government to create a national oil company, Petro-Canada, which enjoyed tremendous public support. Petro-Canada was to keep the government informed of what was happening in the industry, stimulate high-risk activity in frontier exploration and expensive mega-projects and guarantee Canadian supply by dealing directly with foreign producers, most of whom have their own national oil companies.

After the second OPEC crisis in 1979, when the Iranian Revolution forced a dramatic hike in world oil prices, we moved to increase Canadian ownership in the energy sector through incentives and regulations in

163

the National Energy Program. Canadian ownership moved up to forty per cent and the smaller Canadian companies benefitted from additional grants and other advantages. Despite the attacks on Petro-Canada and Canadianization, they remain popular, and even the Tories have come to accept their basic purposes.

The Americans were unhappy, of course. Their government and multinationals zeroed in on the aspect of the NEP that gave the federal government a twenty-five per cent interest in any oil and gas discovered on crown land. They said this "back-in" clause was retroactive expropriation. It wasn't, but the Americans became obsessed with their own slogan and refused to accept the arguments I put to their delegations when I became Minister of Energy.

I understood the truth of the matter because its roots went back to the period when I was Minister of Indian Affairs and Northern Development responsible for the crown lands in the North. In those days the federal government could take up to half of any oil or gas field discovered on its land without having to pay any compensation. The industry thought the rule was unfair, so I repealed it and began to negotiate a new arrangement. Because the issue wasn't urgent and because the industry dragged its heels hoping for a better deal from another minister who would be less tough than I seemed, the negotiations went nowhere. Meanwhile, the multinationals kept drilling on crown land without knowing what the regulatory régime would be. It was as if you built a house on property you didn't own: you can't protest that you've been expropriated if the asking price for the property turns out to be more than you expected. But that's exactly what the Americans did. I told them, "You guys would have done ten times better if you had made a deal with me in 1970. I was a real softie then." But they hadn't made a deal. They had continued drilling anyway because they needed the oil and were relying on Canada's reasonable nature, and now they had to pay up.

Paying up was the real source of their unhappiness, but I don't think the "back-in" clause was an unreasonable price. Canada could have gone back to its old rule. Every producing nation from Norway to Indonesia has a royalty formula and most of their formulas are infinitely more severe than that of the NEP. In the United States itself the right to drill on federal lands is sold by auction and the oil companies sometimes have to pay hundreds of millions of dollars without knowing if they'll find oil. In Canada they only have to pay after the fact, the federal share is not unjust, and Ottawa compensates the companies for a quarter of the drilling costs. Nevertheless, the Tories bought the arguments of the multinationals and promised to get rid of the "back-in" clause without getting anything in return.

I made concessions when they were useful and logical, but the main problem was to get beyond the emotions, fabrications and suspicions that the NEP had unleashed. I worked hard to establish a rapport with my provincial counterparts, and I consulted widely in the industry. It took some months before I could feel the mood improve and a sense of reality return, but I used to joke in the West, "Don't praise me too much or I'll be hurt in the East." The constant trick was to appease the Western interests without creating problems in the East.

For example, suddenly some assets of BP Canada became available for purchase on good terms, and Petro-Canada wanted to buy it. I wasn't opposed for any doctrinaire reason, but my mandate was to bring peace to the Oil Patch. The last thing I wanted was another controversy such as the one over Petro-Canada's acquisition of Petrofina in 1981. The Petrofina takeover had been financed by a special tax on gas. It had taken Petro-Canada into the retail business; its gas stations competed directly with the multinationals, much to their anger. BP Canada would give Petro-Canada even more stations in even more parts of the country, particularly Ontario. That was a good thing as far as I was concerned, since Canadians wanted to be able to put their money where their hearts were; but I didn't want to impose another special tax to pay for the new purchase. "Okay, you can buy BP," I told Petro-Canada, "but you'll have to finance it in the market as a commercial venture." It was a compromise that satisfied both the industry and my colleagues.

Compromise and sharing were on my mind during my cross-country visit to the premiers. I flew directly from the Western capitals to Atlan-

165

tic Canada, with only a brief stop in Ottawa to refuel the jet and to say hello to my wife in order to preserve my marriage.

I had breakfast in Victoria, arrived in time for tea in Charlottetown with Conservative Premier Angus MacLean, and had a relaxed dinner with Conservative Premier John Buchanan in Halifax. Early the next morning I flew to St. John's for my first encounter with Conservative Premier Brian Peckford. It was a good meeting, but Peckford was an enigma to me. I found him a mysterious guy, not easy to get along with, and hard to read. A far more likeable though unconventional personality was Conservative Premier Richard Hatfield, whom I visited in Fredericton after leaving Newfoundland. He was willing and eager to help with the constitution. However, I couldn't say the same for René Lévesque, the only premier who refused to see me on my quick pilgrimage.

I returned to Ottawa and reported to Trudeau before leaving immediately for Florida with my wife. What began at five o'clock in Halifax didn't end until twenty-four hours later in Boca Raton. We got to Miami after midnight and rented a car, which broke down on the highway. Armed with only a credit card (because I hadn't had time to get to a bank in all the rushing around), the Minister of Justice of Canada and Madame Chrétien were seen hitchhiking in the middle of the night somewhere in Florida. It had been a long, long trip.

I had told Trudeau that the mood among the premiers was good, and although I had met resistance on some points, there was general agreement to make one more attempt at a major constitutional reform. In June the Prime Minister and the premiers met and set the agenda for a series of ministerial conferences during the summer of 1980: one week in Montreal, one week in Toronto, one week in Vancouver, and one week in Ottawa. The purpose was detailed discussion of patriation, the amending formula, the charter of rights, and any possible revision of the powers of Ottawa and the provinces, in order to establish common ground for the autumn meeting of the Prime Minister and the premiers.

To avoid the usual problem of the amending formula becoming a bargaining tool, most of the discussions passed over the "shopping list" of demands for more powers and concentrated on the "people's package" of rights and freedoms. Since I don't like failing, I become extremely stubborn when I want something. So I threw myself into these debates with an energy and dedication that were increased by the intellectual stimulation of the exercise. As a lawyer in Shawinigan I had been more interested in making a living than in pondering great academic puzzles, but now the intricacies of constitutional law caught my imagination.

Day after day the federal and provincial delegations assembled and worked their way through the agenda. Should any province have a veto on constitutional amendments? What are the implications of entrenching freedom of speech? What is the meaning of aboriginal rights? What, if any, changes should be made to the Senate or to the Supreme Court? Which level of government should control communications or offshore resources or family law?

We made a bit of progress on some things, we returned again and again to more difficult matters, and gradually we discovered everyone's hard-line positions. After each session, which usually began early and lasted into the night, the bureaucrats and lawyers worked the ideas of the ministers into texts that were brought back for approval or further debate. It was a fascinating education in law and politics, and since I was co-chairing the meetings with Roy Romanow, Saskatchewan's Attorney General, I was constantly in the middle of the fray.

Many times I found myself the only spokesman for the federal government while trying to create the impression that I was the provinces' best friend in Ottawa. "I'll try to get this for you from the cabinet," I would say, "but I know I can't get that from Trudeau." Everyone assumed that I was just an agent for my boss as the provincial ministers were for theirs. In fact, I felt I had more leeway than my counterparts. It was not unusual for them to interrupt a discussion in order to phone their premiers for advice or authority. I virtually never called Trudeau. Instead I relied on my own judgment and my reading of his mind. Nor did he ever call me to ask what the hell I was doing.

Of course, I knew what he wanted, I reported to him and the cabinet regularly, and I assumed his advisers were briefing him from the field; but on the whole I was amazed by his flexibility and generous confidence. His attitude was completely contrary to his public image, which was that his ministers were puppets who wouldn't introduce a comma without his permission. Trudeau let his ministers work on their own and only pulled them back in line when they were in serious error.

The biggest difference between Trudeau and me in federal-provincial affairs was that he wanted to win the arguments but was willing to let the provinces run off with the cash, while I was happy to concede the arguments but wanted to keep the cash. The Trudeau years were a period of significant decentralization. If you compare the portion of the Gross National Product spent by the federal government when Trudeau took office and when he left, you will discover that the importance of Ottawa in the Canadian economy diminished considerably. Through transfer payments, equalization payments, and unconditional payments the provinces obtained the lion's share of national spending. In fact, so much federal money had to be passed on automatically under the federal-provincial arrangements that Ottawa lost effective control over its deficit.

Ottawa also gave up most of its influence on how that money would be spent. Instead of tying the payments to conditions that would ensure national standards in health services or higher education, for example, the federal government bowed to the provinces' complaints that that would be an intrusion into their jurisdictions.

The result was that many provinces took the unconditional payments and used them for other purposes. When Ottawa committed itself to paying the equivalent of fifty per cent of the cost of higher education plus complete indexation, for example, the provinces started to cut back on their own share after the fact in order to save or redirect the money. The federal portion grew greater and greater until it reached ridiculous dimensions. There were instances of Ottawa paying 120 per cent of the costs of post-secondary education, and even though it knew that at least twenty per cent was going into asphalt somewhere, it couldn't do anything.

Not only did no one admit that the federal government was making such an enormous contribution, no one was willing to return the favour by giving Ottawa a say in what training might fit the medium-term employment outlook or what standards should be available to every Canadian student. So provinces produced a glut of barbers when everyone had long hair, and they produced more anthropologists than high-tech specialists because it was cheaper to do so. Yet Ottawa was seen as failing in its national responsibilities.

Despite this decentralization, Trudeau never received any thanks. Because his major weakness was his love of winning arguments, the public thought he was unable to concede anything; and when he did concede something, everyone thought that he was probably doing so for devious reasons. He was perceived as an expert chess player: why did he give up that piece? how will he trap me later if I take this small advantage now?

People focused on his personality rather on what he did, so he looked stronger than other prime ministers who gave away much less. Similarly, although he held more federal-provincial conferences than any other prime minister, he wasn't seen as a conciliator or consensus-seeker because he wrestled in an honest and rational way with real problems instead of creating a soothing atmosphere of happy slogans that solve nothing in the end. His strength made everyone presume that he didn't need moral support, so it was easy and satisfying for the press, the public and even for the party and the cabinet, not to rally to his side the way many had rallied around Pearson when he was in trouble. Though Canadians depended on Trudeau in times of crisis, they rarely rushed to his defence when he was in a jam. It was assumed he would hold his own ground.

The side-effect was a tendency to sympathize with the provinces that tried to take him on. It was like a sport in which the cheers and advantages are given to the underdogs, except that the provinces were no longer the underdogs. Canada was at risk, but to support the national interest would be to support Trudeau. Since it didn't seem to matter whether he gave in to the provinces, since they only demanded more and more, and nothing earned him any thanks, he chose to do what he thought was best for Canada.

169

Maintaining good relations with the provinces is considered a positive thing in Canada's political game, but it can't be achieved all the time. It is the nature of provincial governments to demand more money and more powers, but rarely if ever do they offer Ottawa money or powers in return. Many times they take federal funds to build useful projects or provide beneficial services without even acknowledging the national contribution, yet it was usually torture for me to get them to hand over some territory for national parks that would benefit primarily their own citizens and economies.

The problem was that the rich provinces were getting richer and the poor provinces were getting poorer. Provincial power for the sake of provincial power was diminishing the federal government's ability to transfer funds to where they were needed. The provincial case was usually put by the strong, rich provinces or by poor provinces that expected to become rich. It was the poorer provinces, such as New Brunswick and Nova Scotia, whose premiers fought most eloquently to have equalization payments inscribed in the constitution. That was a major reason why Ottawa resisted giving many more powers to the provinces. When Trudeau and I received the "shopping list" of demands from the premiers, we burst out laughing; there would have been nothing left of Canada if those demands were met.

At the opening of the constitutional debate I presented my provincial colleagues with a document I had commissioned on Canada's economic union. Anticipating the outcome of the Quebec referendum, I wanted to know what were the minimum powers Ottawa needed to manage a viable and prosperous Canada, and I asked Tommy Shoyama, the retired Deputy Minister of Finance, to lead a high-level group of officials in finding out the answers. What were the powers that really mattered? What non-essential powers had been turned into political issues or matters of principle over time? In a world of satellite television and video cassettes, did it matter whether communications were a national or provincial responsibility? Did it matter whether family law fell under federal or provincial jurisdiction? Ultimately, however, the discussion ran into trouble because Ottawa was willing to give up what wasn't necessary, but the provinces weren't willing to give up what was necessary.

Many of the premiers seemed shocked at the idea that Ottawa should dare ask for more power in order to make the economic union work. They thought they had us on the run, ready to agree to anything to get patriation and the charter: but we turned the tables on them. Since most of them couldn't argue against the logic of the document, they resorted to shouting slogans. They ignored the decentralizing aspects, however, and focused on Ottawa's concern with the mobility of manpower and capital and restrictions on the purchasing policies of the provincial governments. Many premiers were more concerned with their provinces than with the nation. They wanted to remain the big shots, more powerful and prestigious than the governors of American states.

As a result, Canada hasn't been able to achieve its own common market. I have always been puzzled that few of the individuals and associations who call so loudly for a common market with the United States have spoken up as vocally for a genuine common market within Canada. We don't have one, in fact. There are scores of barriers that affect trade among the provinces: from preferential hiring to preferential buying, from provincial licences to provincial regulations. Yet when Ottawa moved to reduce those barriers, the provinces screamed that we were trying to grab some of their powers, and they were backed by their businessmen, who wanted to protect their little empires. Everyone is in favour of the free movement of goods and people until affected by it; everyone is against protectionism in principle but fights for its practical benefits. In my opinion, we should break down our inter-provincial trade barriers before we try to negotiate a common market with the United States.

Because the press and the public have long seen the struggle as the poor little provinces trying to wrest some minor concession from big mean Ottawa, they are shocked when the federal government makes demands or resists those of the provinces. In the United States the bias is in favour of the national government. In Canada, the provinces get the benefit of the doubt. That is an important difference, and it means federal politicians have to sell the merits of their case directly to the people. If you get into a confrontation with the provinces and you can't convince the people that you're right, then forget it — it won't wash.

This inherent tension in federalism is also its inherent beauty. Because there is constant competition between the two levels of government to shine in the eyes of the electorate, no social problem will fester long without one government moving to deal with it or, at least, to use it to club the other government. In unitary states such as France or England, it's easier to ignore or overlook the discontents of regions remote from the capital, because they have no institutionalized champions who can get headlines and mobilize power the way Canadian premiers can. Even when a provincial premier and a federal prime minister are of the same party, political pressures will demand that they try to score points off each other, for the dynamic of federalism is a perpetual struggle for the esteem of the people.

At different times and for different reasons one level will emerge with the momentum, but the practical political struggle to change the balance always makes the public the ultimate winner. That was the situation with the national parks, for example. There was conflict between Ottawa and the provinces until the federal government managed to convince the population of the rightness of its position; then the public will was expressed. Once that happened, the provinces had to concede and the conflict was over.

A politician in a federation ought to develop as much credibility as possible. Candour, trust and sincerity keep confrontations to a minimum. Your opponents will know that when you finally resist, it means that you really can't move any further, and you can take a hard stance without offending them. For politics is, in essence, a great fraternity. Whatever the party or jurisdiction of politicians, you all are elected officials, and that gives you a community of interest. When you aren't talking business, you tend to talk about your problems as politicians, your successes and your failures, and the partisan element vanishes. The warmth of friendship can do much to thaw the chill of political tensions or the coldness of technical negotiations.

One of Trudeau's greatest weaknesses was that he usually went straight home by himself after the federal-provincial sessions. No matter how nice or civilized he may have been during the day, the lack of an opportunity to unwind with him in the evenings kept the barriers and suspicions high. Despite the combative image I sometimes project, I too like to be liked, and I have worked hard to get to know my provincial colleagues on a friendly basis. At one time the daughter of an Alberta cabinet minister spent a couple of weeks with my family at our cottage in order to improve her French; at another time a Newfoundland cabinet minister told an audience that I was his province's best friend even though there were difficulties between our two governments. At no time did my efforts prove more pleasant or useful than during the summer of 1980. After long sessions working on the constitution, the participants got to know each other well. We had meals together, we went to baseball games and football games together, and we had fun.

Sometimes humour seemed the only thing that kept us going. At one point we got bogged down trying to define freedom of conscience. "So why put it in the charter?" someone asked. It was the end of the day and I was tired, so I said, "Yeah, why? Let's leave it out." Suddenly I felt a hard kick on the back of my chair. It was from Pierre Genest, a hefty and very funny friend who was one of the federal government's best legal advisers. "I guess we leave it in," I said. "Trudeau's spy just kicked me in the ass." He was more effective than my own conscience.

The mix of people was incredibly interesting. The federal team included such strong negotiators as Roger Tassé, Michael Kirby, Gérard Veilleux, Fred Gibson and Barry Strayer, as well as my cabinet colleague John Roberts, Minister of Science and Technology and the Environment, and Eddie Goldenberg. I had asked Trudeau to give me Roberts because I found him articulate, knowledgeable and self-assured. Though that last characteristic struck some people as arrogance, it was valuable to me because it let Roberts assume the tough-guy role; I could appear to be the nice guy always ready with a compromise. Goldenberg's father Carl had been involved in federal-provincial negotiations since the days of Mackenzie King, and his mother Shirley was an economics professor at McGill University; I used to joke that I got three brilliant minds for the price of one.

The provincial teams included ministers and officials of equal quality: Roy McMurtry and Tom Wells from Ontario; Garde Gardom from British Columbia; Dick Johnston from Alberta; Gerry Mercier from Manitoba; Roy Romanow from Saskatchewan; Gerry Ottenheimer from Newfoundland; Horace Carver from P.E.I.; Harry How from Nova Scotia; Premier Richard Hatfield from New Brunswick. Quebec sent Claude Morin and Claude Charron, both intelligent, well-spoken, and dedicated to the cause of independence.

I can't say I ever became friends with Morin. I found him a proud man, who tended to speak down to people and a skilful schemer, whose only goal was to make our work fail. On the other hand, I found it easy to communicate with Charron. I used to argue with him that the Parti Québécois had to honour the meaning of the referendum result and begin to work within Canada. "If you were to make a deal on the constitution now," I said to him, "you could get a lot for Quebec and the people would be pleased." Sometimes I felt he was tempted, but he was always caught by the first purpose of his party. "Jean," he would say, "you know we are separatists. So how can we sign up for a new confederation?"

The dilemma of the separatists was that they were also social democrats. So the minute Ottawa began to talk about rights and freedoms, Quebec had to become involved. How could social democrats such as René Lévesque and Claude Morin tell Quebeckers that they wouldn't support freedom of speech or freedom of religion? They could argue that some freedoms had implications that intruded on provincial matters, but as soon as they accepted one freedom, they were trapped and could be drawn further and further into the process: their ties were caught in the wringer. If they accepted freedom of speech, how could they refuse freedom of association or the right of bail? If they accepted a whole list of freedoms and rights, how could they reject the whole charter with any logic or credibility?

They would have done better to take the tough position of Manitoba's Premier, Sterling Lyon, who supported patriation without an amending formula or a charter of rights. He argued that unanimous consent for any constitutional amendment should be required until a formula was worked out in Canada sometime in the future, and he opposed the charter as incompatible with the British judiciary system. That position may not have been too popular politically, but at least it was honest and more logical than the position the Parti Québécois had to take as social democrats.

Despite all the obstacles and differences, by the end of the summer of 1980 there was a sense that we had made progress in many areas and that some kind of deal might be possible when the premiers and the Prime Minister met in September. Of course, every deal can slip away at the last minute, but everyone was optimistic enough to have a group photograph taken for the record. The rapport was so good, in fact, that I often wonder what might have happened if we had been left to negotiate the conclusion. Instead, as was necessary, everything was passed up to the First Ministers' Conference, which immediately degenerated into a disaster.

Even before it started, the premiers were angry about a federal strategy paper, leaked by a federal civil servant sympathetic to the separatists, which implied that Ottawa was prepared to act without provincial consent on patriation and the charter. That paper was only analyzing the options available should the conference fail, but it provided an excuse to those premiers who wanted to deny Trudeau his crowning achievement. Their damage was great: all the hard-earned goodwill and consensus of the summer were tossed aside.

The premiers ganged up on the Prime Minister during the dinner given by the Governor General in the ninth-floor reception room of the External Affairs building. I've never been to a worse gathering, and I couldn't believe the insults that flew. I was shocked. "Are these the same people who were willing to do anything a few months ago to keep Quebec within Confederation?" I asked myself. "Are these the same people who were praying that Trudeau would succeed in holding the country together?" Now they were arguing that the Prime Minister of Canada should never again preside over the federal-provincial conferences except jointly with one of the premiers. Trudeau was so angry

175

that he wanted to storm out of the room; but, according to protocol, he couldn't leave until after the Governor General. "Finish your dinner and go," he said to Ed Schreyer, who was beside him, "so that I can get out of here."

The next morning at the meeting no one was in a better mood. Brian Peckford said, "I prefer the Canada of René Lévesque to the Canada of Pierre Trudeau," without realizing how deeply offensive that was to those of us who had fought the life-and-death battle of the referendum. Trudeau, who was supposed to have the premiers to lunch at 24 Sussex, said, "I guess I'll have lots of leftover salmon because there's no point in going on negotiating with you people."

The conference led to nothing at all.

"Okay, let's go," the cabinet said. We had a promise to keep to the country. Given no choice after more than fifty years of effort, Ottawa would go unilaterally to Great Britain to bring home the constitution.

CHAPTER EIGHT

A NEW CONSTITUTION

THE FEDERAL government's plan now was to pass a resolution in Parliament approving patriation, the amending formula that had seemed acceptable to all the provinces at the Victoria conference in 1970, and a charter of rights that incorporated the consensus worked out during the summer of 1980. We decided to do what had to be done, do it quickly and cleanly, and live with the consequences.

The federal NDP, Ontario and New Brunswick supported the resolution. That was an extremely brave decision for Ed Broadbent, the NDP leader. He had been under pressure to fight us from his colleagues in the Saskatchewan government and some of his own MPs whose doctrinaire views seemed to make them higher than God. They argued over every comma and accused Broadbent of being in bed with Trudeau. There were days when he looked virtually alone. But two of his predecessors, Tommy Douglas and David Lewis, encouraged him in his position, and Lewis even phoned me on one occasion. "Hang in there, Jean," he said. "Don't give up the fight."

The federal Tories were trapped in the same dilemma as the Parti Québécois. Patriation and the charter were popular measures to an overwhelming percentage of Canadians; to oppose or impede them was unwise. Yet, once the Tories began to fight for a better charter, they were caught, because it was difficult to support some freedoms and rights without having to support them all. I used to tease Flora Mac-

Donald, now Minister of Employment and Immigration in the Mulroney government, saying that by opposing the charter she was opposing the equality of men and women. But that was the type of contradiction all her colleagues faced on many issues. Nonetheless, the Tories fought a strenuous battle in the House of Commons. The government's December deadline was pushed into the new year and further delayed by the lengthy public hearings of the constitutional committee.

The committee was co-chaired by Senator Harry Hays of Alberta and Serge Joyal, the young MP from Quebec. They were an unusual pair but they complemented each other well. Hays was a typical Western cattleman who had some old-fashioned views and a great sense of humour, both of which occasionally got him into hot water. Joyal is a sophisticated, rather serious Montrealer with a reputation as a party maverick. Joyal's hard work kept the discussions on a high level, and Hays's easy manner kept them moving along. The work of the committee took longer than expected because so many people wanted to appear before it. (The committee was a good example of the useful role ordinary MPs can play.) There were more than a thousand submissions, almost all concerned with improving the charter of rights for the people rather than distributing powers among the federal and provincial governments.

I was a witness for more than a hundred hours, explaining the meaning of key words or sections and defending the government's package. It was a hell of a test. Although I had learned a lot about constitutional law since becoming Minister of Justice, it had never been my specialty or my first love, so I always worried about putting my foot in my mouth. I knew that great professors and famous lawyers had studied and written about its intricate details over the decades; I also knew that anything I said in the committee could be used by future courts to guide them in their deliberations on the constitution. No wonder I shook every morning, wondering how I was doing, up against people who had taught and pondered the complex subject all their lives.

Though I occasionally let my officials handle the more technical issues, I answered most of the questions from my study of the briefs and

178

my own experiences during the summer. I even came to enjoy the really good questions and the really tough debates. In the middle of the hearings, however, I was hospitalized after complaining of pains that felt like a heart attack. They turned out to be indigestion, probably from a little too much celebrating at the birthday party my wife organized for me in January; but the doctors realized I was also suffering from exhaustion and ordered me to bed for a week.

While the resolution was making its way through the parliamentary process, the opposing provinces decided to question its legality in the courts of Manitoba, Newfoundland, and Quebec. Only the Newfoundland court concluded that it wasn't legal for Ottawa to act unilaterally, but even its arguments looked weak. In order to settle the legal question and to overcome the disruptive tactics the Tories had adopted in the House of Commons — in spite of the many concessions the government had made in the committee — we decided to delay the resolution until an opinion had been delivered by the Supreme Court. A favourable opinion was expected by June 1981, but the judges kept up the suspense throughout the summer. Besides feeling frustrated, we were concerned that our momentum was in jeopardy and that the popular support we needed would deteriorate as people got fed up with the whole issue, which had now dragged on for over a year.

To make matters worse, in April 1981 the opposing premiers allied themselves into the so-called "Gang of Eight." They agreed to patriation on condition that the charter was dropped and the federal amending formula was replaced by one in which any province could opt out of any constitutional amendment with full financial compensation. The shock was that Quebec joined the gang and gave up its claim to the right to veto any proposed amendment. I had always refused to sacrifice Quebec's veto, even at the cost of alienating other provinces, because I felt it was important as a safeguard and a symbol for Quebeckers; so I was surprised by what Lévesque and Morin would do just to bash Trudeau a little more. Davis and Hatfield had the courage to risk being seen close to Trudeau in order to achieve what they knew was good for Canada. Instead of opposing Trudeau simply for the sake of opposing Trudeau, they understood the national interest and became national figures as a result. Instead of being diminished, their strength at home increased, too.

In my view, the Gang of Eight was motivated by fear: they were afraid of the political effects of making a deal with Trudeau while he was unpopular in their provinces. For example, John Buchanan of Nova Scotia always gave me the impression that he agreed with what we were doing and was close to joining us, but I guess he was even more concerned about his next election.

The same seemed true of Allan Blakeney of Saskatchewan, although his fear seemed as much of the anger of Peter Lougheed as of the opinion of his electorate. "Yes, but what about Alberta?" he said, whenever I thought we were close to prying him away from the gang. For a man of intelligence and principle Blakeney disappointed me. Although he understood every nuance of Ottawa's position and a deal would have helped him make peace with the federal NDP caucus, he never stopped looking over his shoulder. But all his wariness didn't help his career; he was defeated in the next election anyway, so he should have done what he knew to be right in the first place.

One day I read in the newspapers that Romanow said Saskatchewan needed three things before it could join the federal side. I telephoned him and said, "I can't deliver three, but I can deliver two. Do you think your premier will accept two?"

"I think he will," Romanow said.

So I went to Trudeau and said, "I have a deal with Saskatchewan if we give up these two points."

Trudeau answered, "You don't have a deal and you will never have a deal. Blakeney will never sign."

"If you're so certain," I said, "let's offer to meet all three of Romanow's conditions. I'll bet you a dollar. You have nothing to lose."

So we made the offer and the bet. Saskatchewan immediately came back with more demands. I had to pay Trudeau the dollar.

The entire summer of 1981 was maddening. I could feel Trudeau's irritation and impatience at the delay of the Supreme Court decision. He used to ask me, when we were sitting together in the House of

Commons, if I had heard when the decision was coming, and he seemed uncomfortable in having his schedule upset. He was always systematic in everything he did, and he had been hoping to have patriation by Canada Day, July 1, 1981; but there was nothing to do but wait. Unlike Roy McMurtry, who had pleaded Ontario's case before the court, I hadn't appeared on Ottawa's behalf, though I did slip in among the spectators one day to see the federal lawyers, J.J. Robinette and Michel Robert, in action. I think everyone was slightly startled to see the Minister of Justice listening in the audience.

When the decision finally came in September, Trudeau was on a tour of Southeast Asian countries; I was listening to the judgment over the terrible television transmission in my office. The voice of Chief Justice Bora Laskin wasn't the only thing that wasn't clear; the majority judgment itself seemed rather ambiguous. It stated that the unilateral action of the federal government was legal but offensive to the traditional "convention" of getting provincial consent for constitutional amendments. My staff and I jumped on the word "legal" and dismissed the rest.

I tracked down Trudeau in Korea and told him the news. "It's legal. I'm going to call a press conference and claim victory right away." Trudeau agreed; we would go into the details later.

So I went to the press and said we had won and would proceed on our resolution as planned. "The convention is irrelevant," I explained. "There is a convention that we have an election every four years even though the law says one is required every five years. So someone who breaks a convention may be reproached by the electorate but can't be attacked by the law." McMurtry agreed with my interpretation.

I kept in contact with Trudeau, and by the end of the day he told a press conference that, even though Ottawa had won in the Supreme Court, he was willing to have another First Ministers' conference to see if the convention couldn't be satisfied by gaining more provincial support.

That night Romanow and McMurtry came to dinner at my house so Romanow could drop off the bottle of scotch he had bet me on the Supreme Court decision. (Contrary to reports in the Quebec press, we didn't get drunk on it. In fact I still have it at home waiting for an occasion.) We had a couple of beers and talked about what would happen next. Should there be another conference? Would Saskatchewan budge? What modifications could be made to make the charter more acceptable? What about Quebec's veto in the amending formula? And so on. Nothing was decided, of course; I discussed the same questions with my officials during the following weeks, and Romanow and McMurtry did the same in their provinces and across the country. The only new development was that the Prime Minister and the premiers agreed to meet again in November.

The November conference was the last chance for a consensus, and everyone knew it. Sometimes Trudeau met with Davis and Hatfield, alone or with their ministers, to iron out worries that Ottawa was going too far with the charter. Sometimes the Gang of Eight met; sometimes all the premiers met; sometimes everyone met in the Conference Centre. Meanwhile, I had my own meetings with premiers, ministers, and officials. After a couple of days there was some sense of progress, but Trudeau was beginning to believe that the only way out of the impasse was to hold a national referendum on the amending formula and the charter.

The Liberal caucus was receptive to the idea, but I was strongly opposed. I had seen too well the splits the Quebec referendum had made in families and friendships: I never wanted to go through another one. I hadn't taken the idea too seriously. I remember one meeting in which Michael Pitfield was supporting Trudeau's notion that the people should decide in the event that Ottawa and the provinces couldn't agree. He cited some American examples and launched into a learned discourse about democracy in the United States with references to the Hamiltonians and the Jeffersonians and so on. I got impatient. "Tell me, Michael," I interrupted. "Which baseball teams are these guys playing for?" I was willing to talk about a referendum as a strategic threat when negotiating with the provinces, but I never wanted or expected to use it. Now I realized that Trudeau was prepared to use it as more than a fallback position.

On the third day the conference was in danger of breaking up. Sterling Lyon had to return to his election campaign in Manitoba, and René Lévesque was preparing to leave. Then Trudeau dangled his challenge of a referendum, and Lévesque jumped at it: there would be a referendum on the amending formula and another one on the charter of rights. Lévesque got Trudeau to agree that each referendum would have to get a majority in the West, in Ontario, in Quebec, and in Atlantic Canada in order to win.

"But we'll end up with nothing," I protested to Trudeau. "The West will never vote for an amending formula that gives a veto to Quebec; and Quebec will never vote for one that doesn't give it a veto. With the charter we might win easily in English Canada, but Lévesque will be able to fight us on the old war horse of federal encroachment on provincial rights."

But Trudeau was ecstatic when Quebec accepted the idea, because he had broken the solidarity of the Gang of Eight. That had been the essence of the federal strategy, but nothing had worked before. Lévesque was hooked by the fantasy of getting a second chance to win a referendum against the federal government; but his allies didn't like the prospect of fighting Ottawa on the charter in their provinces, and they quickly rejected it. Their faces revealed their feelings when they saw Lévesque siding with Trudeau.

Trudeau exploited their discomfort by announcing to the press that Ottawa and Quebec had a deal. Almost immediately there was an angry reaction among Parti Québécois supporters in Quebec, and the other Gang of Eight premiers gave Lévesque hell over lunch. During the afternoon session he backtracked, claiming that he hadn't understood Trudeau's offer properly. Trudeau was furious and threatened to adjourn the conference. "We're going nowhere," he said. "There'll be no more meetings. Ottawa will act alone."

During the afternoon I circulated among the provincial ministers to pressure them into shifting their positions. "You know, you guys," I said, "there's going to be a referendum. I don't want one and you don't want one. But I'm telling you, I'm going to go into your provinces, and I'm going to say you're opposed to freedom of religion and equality of women and all that. And I'm going to clobber you."

183

That morning I had had breakfast with Romanow and McMurtry. I had written out on a napkin an alternative package that Trudeau might buy as a compromise. Now Romanow asked me if I thought the alternative was still possible. We began to talk about it in detail: who might accept what, and what might have to be adjusted. For privacy and quiet we went into the small kitchen in the Conference Centre. We sketched out a proposal, Romanow took it to try on the others, and he returned with Roy McMurtry to give us some help. The three of us put together a possible deal that came very close to the final one.

Its essence was an exchange: the provinces would accept the charter, modified to alleviate most of their objections, if the federal government accepted their amending formula modified, to alleviate Ottawa's objections. That meant that any province would be able to opt out of a constitutional amendment instead of having a veto, but there would not be guaranteed fiscal compensation. Ottawa could never accept such compensation because in practice the rich provinces would opt out of any amendment that required them to share their wealth with the poorer provinces. A national scheme of unemployment insurance, for example, wouldn't have been possible.

When I left Romanow and McMurtry I wasn't sure I could sell the compromise to Trudeau. I tested it on Serge Joyal and Jim Peterson, my parliamentary secretary, and then went to the Prime Minister. Trudeau listened like a sphinx. To convince him I said, "Why not sample the reaction of a couple of MPs?" and I dragged in Joyal and Peterson, without letting Trudeau know I had already got them on my side. Finally I pleaded with him to try another round in the conference. "Saskatchewan will come up with something," I promised.

So he went back to the session and announced, "Apparently Saskatchewan has a compromise." But Romanow hadn't completed his sales job on Blakeney; so nothing happened, and the meeting was adjourned till the next morning. There was a mood of failure and gloom in the air, but I was feeling a new hope because Trudeau hadn't rejected my deal out of hand.

After a dinner with some of my advisers, I went to a high-level meeting Trudeau had called at 24 Sussex. One of its purposes was to give a number of senior ministers, including Lalonde, MacEachen, Roberts, LeBlanc, Ouellet, Herb Gray and Gerry Regan, an explanation of what was happening. They soon realized that Trudeau seemed in favour of a referendum as the solution and that I was pushing hard for a deal. Obviously Trudeau's view carried a lot of weight, and everyone seemed adamant that there be no more watering-down of the charter of rights. At one point Trudeau left the living room to take a phone call from William Davis, and I grabbed the opportunity to make a strong pitch for a compromise.

"I'm telling you now," I said, "if at the end of this meeting you decide on a referendum, I won't be putting on my running shoes again for you. I've had enough of families divided, villages divided, French divided against English. A national referendum will be worse. You'll get East divided against West, Protestants divided against Catholics — everything." Then I turned to one minister who wasn't known as a great salesman. "You go and sell Ottawa's package. I won't. I will never touch another referendum in my life."

My little speech had some effect, and Trudeau came back to the room to find the group more divided than before. As usual he listened attentively to the discussion that followed and did not do much talking himself. When the meeting broke up, he took me aside and said, "Jean, if you can get the majority of the provinces with a majority of the population to accept your solution, I think I'll be able to accept it. But let me sleep on it."

I drove home feeling pretty good. Earlier in the evening I had received a message from Garde Gardom, the colourful British Columbia Minister of Intergovernmental Affairs, and now I called him. "What's this damn piece of paper Romanow's showing around?" he asked. "Can you really sell it or is this another bluff, you damn Frenchman?"

"It's serious," I said. "I think I can sell it."

"Then you'll have a new constitution," he said, "because British Columbia can buy it and so can Saskatchewan, Ontario, New Brunswick, P.E.I., Nova Scotia and Newfoundland. We don't know about Alberta, Manitoba or Quebec."

185

So I told my wife that Canada had a new constitution and went to bed. But I couldn't sleep. I thought of calling Trudeau, but I knew about his strict habits and guessed he wouldn't appreciate being woken up even for such a monumental piece of news. I tried reaching Roy Romanow but couldn't, so despite reports that I had conspired with the provinces all through the night, I had no part in the wheeling and dealing that went on.

I figured correctly, however, that Quebec would be the odd man out. I remembered the conversation with Claude Charron, who was always more candid and less manipulative than the rest of the Quebec team, to the effect that there would never be a package that the Parti Québécois could buy. That was unfortunate in my opinion, but it couldn't stop our push for a new constitution. At last, around 6:30 in the morning, I reached Romanow, who had deliberately stayed away from his hotel room so that no one could accuse him of dealing with me.

"In half an hour," he said, "Lougheed will be awakened by Dick Johnston and told of the deal. We're expecting Alberta to agree."

"What about Quebec?"

"Quebec will never sign anything," Romanow said. "We'll inform them at seven o'clock of what we've done, and then we'll see how they react."

"In that case," I said, "make sure Manitoba doesn't sign. It will be difficult for Ottawa if Quebec is the only holdout."

"Don't worry," he said. "Lyon will never sign."

But at seven o'clock Romanow called me back to say that Lougheed had agreed and was going to convince Lyon to do the same, probably for the sake of Western unity. Lyon had left Ottawa because he was in the middle of an election campaign, but he obviously realized the political consequences of being alone with Quebec. Still, he was reluctant to go along and wanted to postpone a decision until after his election, so his agreement with his fellow premiers was subject to certain conditions. As it happened, he lost the election, and the succeeding NDP government signed the new constitutional deal. Meanwhile, Lévesque was told that the eight provinces were going to present a new compromise to Trudeau at the morning session and that there was some indication from Chrétien that Ottawa would accept it.

At 7:30 I phoned Trudeau. "Mr. Prime Minister, if you agree now with what you agreed last night, then you have a new constitution," I said, and I listed the majority of the provinces with the majority of the population.

Trudeau rarely got emotional, but he said, "Jean, if you were here, I'd hug you."

He still hadn't seen anything in writing, however; so I went to breakfast at 24 Sussex to explain the deal to him and some of his senior officials, who were probably wondering if Chrétien had given away the store. The mood was relaxed and there was a fine sense of achievement. Later when I drove with Trudeau to the Conference Centre, he said, "To think that Lévesque and Morin believe you're not educated enough!"

"And to think they believe you're *too* educated!" I replied.

It had been agreed among the eight provinces that Premier Brian Peckford of Newfoundland would propose the compromise, apparently because he was the youngest premier. He did so as if it had come spontaneously to mind. Trudeau studied the text while the Quebec delegation watched closely for his reaction. Trudeau the actor frowned and looked unhappy; Lévesque and Morin smiled and looked pleased. But at last Trudeau said, "It makes a lot of sense."

There were still some rough spots to navigate, some clarifications to make, and some details to improve, but everyone was carried away by the excitement of reaching the end. Everyone except Lévesque, of course. He claimed he couldn't accept the deal because of three problems.

"Okay," Trudeau said, "let's see if we can solve them." But Quebec wasn't willing to sign anything. Finally Trudeau said, "If you don't want to sign, we will finish the work among ourselves."

It was one of the saddest moments in my career to see Quebec so isolated, particularly when Lévesque asked, "Won't you please give me back my right of veto?" Personally I felt that was a proper request, not for Quebec as a province but for a minority population with unique concerns in linguistic and cultural matters, but it was too late. Lévesque had given up Quebec's veto when he made his deal with the Gang of Eight and now he had to pay the price. As soon as one province refused to reconsider it, the issue was dead.

During the weeks that followed, I continued to try to overcome Quebec's objections, to the extent of modifying the principle of minority language education and agreeing to fiscal compensation when Quebec opted out of amendments that affected culture and education. That required a hell of a lot of selling to Trudeau, but he went along in the end, as did the nine other premiers, who were willing to reopen their sealed bargain in order to bring in Quebec. Of course, Lévesque could never accept anything; but ultimately Ottawa incorporated these changes anyway, to leave the door open for Quebec to sign in the future. I used to joke that these were the first constitutional amendments in history to have been negotiated over the telephone.

These weren't the only changes we made. To get the consent of the majority of the provinces, the federal government had had to settle for an incomplete guarantee of rights for women and to drop aboriginal rights from the charter. Allan Blakeney opposed the women's rights clause for some sophisticated reason having to do with the authority of the legislative assembly. It might have been an elegant argument, but in politics elegance is usually less important than effect, and he certainly looked bad. He hadn't been opposed to native rights, but he had gone along with the objections of Alberta and British Columbia in order to gain their support on the women's issue. So the three of them forced the rest of us to abandon women and the natives. Our only consolation was that we could come back to those clauses later, and I sensed that we would be back sooner rather than later. "Wait till the women and the natives go after those guys," I said to Bill Davis at the end of the conference.

It didn't take long. Within hours women's groups and native associations realized we had let them down, and within minutes the press had determined who the culprits were. Blakeney quickly found himself singled out as the lone opponent to the entrenchment of women's rights. It was a great humiliation for the NDP across the country, there

188

were demonstrations and pressure campaigns mounted against the Saskatchewan government, and I turned the heat up under Romanow. "Roy," I said, "I'm about to make a speech in the House of Commons. If you give in, I'll say your boss is a great guy. If you don't, I'm going to sock it to him." In addition, I managed to get Alberta and British Columbia to desert their ally. Eventually Saskatchewan buckled.

In the middle of that controversy I ran into Lougheed at the Grey Cup game. "Wasn't it funny to see your socialist neighbour all alone against the women of Canada?" I said, and we had a good laugh. Then I became serious. "Peter," I said, "I hope you will not be all alone against the Indians next week."

"I've thought about it," he said. "Why not try to find a compromise with my guys right away?"

The compromise turned out to be a single word. Alberta was worried about recognizing aboriginal rights when it didn't know what they meant or implied. We debated the meaning again and again, until finally I said to Alberta's Attorney General, "Look, why don't we just talk about the rights that exist, the 'existing rights'?" The inclusion of the word "existing" puzzled some of the constitutional experts and didn't please many of the native leaders, who thought it would put the onus on them to prove that a right did exist. But I was confident that it wouldn't affect anything. In the view of the federal lawyers, a right either existed or it didn't exist. Yet the change was enough to satisfy Alberta, and that was important for me. I've never believed in seeking perfection at the risk of losing everything.

With the amendments and the support of nine provinces, the constitutional package proceeded easily through the House of Commons in December. It was in the form of a resolution to the British Parliament, which debated it for four days in March 1982. There were frustrating delays, as the British government was reluctant to be pressed; but even more frustrating was to listen to the interference of the British MPs who had been lobbied by Quebec and the native leaders. It amused me to think of the separatists begging Britain to keep them dependent, but it also made me angry to see Canadians abusing their own country in a foreign capital. That gave the British MPs the liberty to tell Canadians what they should or shouldn't do, as if we weren't an adult nation.

I watched part of the debate from the gallery, and there were times when I wanted to jump down and put some old-fashioned colonialist in his place or correct some grossly misinformed piece of rhetoric about how Canada had robbed and raped its native people. Trudeau had said that the only role for the British Parliament was "to hold its nose and pass the bill," and he was right.

The last step was to get royal approval. Once more I went to London, this time to see the Queen and bring her the Canadian proclamation. I accompanied the Canadian High Commissioner, Jean Wadds, to Buckingham Palace, but I was ushered into the Queen's office to see her alone.

It wasn't the first time we had met. The first time was in the Northwest Territories in 1970 when my wife and I escorted the Queen, Prince Philip, Prince Charles and Princess Anne on a tour in my capacity as Minister of Indian Affairs and Northern Development. It was an exciting experience for a young French-Canadian couple, and we studied all the books of protocol to make sure we didn't make any mistakes. At the end of the five-day trip we arrived in Fort Providence to unveil a plaque to Alexander Mackenzie, who had discovered the Mackenzie River. There were several thousand people present, television coverage, and lots of press.

Just before the ceremony the president of the Historic Sites and Monuments Board came to me with a problem. According to the program he was supposed to go to the microphone and lead everyone in the national anthem. "But, Mr. Minister," he said, "I have a terrible voice and I haven't the nerve to sing in public." I also have a terrible voice, it's loud and rather rugged, but I've never been shy, so I offered to start "O Canada" in his place. When the time came, I went to the microphone, and I began to sing. Unfortunately I knew only the French words. Since no one else knew them, no one else joined in, and I had to sing the whole thing solo. My wife said she had never been so embarrassed in her entire life.

A few months later I met Prince Charles at a reception in Ottawa. I was surprised when he recognized me by name among the crowd. "But how could I forget you?" he said, "Your singing of 'O Canada' in the North last summer has become part of the royal folklore."

For one reason or another I met the Royal Family five times in less than two years. On one occasion I was in London with my wife and daughter, and the High Commissioner told me that the next day the Queen was hosting a reception at Buckingham Palace for veterans of the First World War. "It would be nice for the Canadian veterans if a minister was with them," he said. "So why don't you and your family go?" Since it would be nice for us too, we accepted with pleasure.

The next day we were with the veterans in a large reception room in the palace. Because I was a member of the Privy Council as a minister, protocol required that the Queen receive me in a private audience. She hadn't been informed of which Canadian minister she was to meet, and when she came into the small room where I was waiting, she exclaimed, "You again?"

"Your Majesty," I said, "I am *the* royalist from Quebec!"

It wasn't long afterwards that I was travelling with my family through Scotland on my way to visit the drilling sites in the North Sea. We passed through Balmoral, where the Royal Family has its summer residence, and we saw from the road the Royal Standard flying over the castle, indicating that the Queen was in residence. We stopped for gas in the next village, and while we were waiting, I noticed someone familiar staring at me from across the street.

He came over. "Aren't you Chrétien from Canada?"

"Yes, and aren't you the Queen's secretary?"

He was. We had met on the royal tour through the North. "Why don't you come and have tea with Her Majesty at Balmoral?" he said. "I'm sure she'll be delighted."

I was sure she would think me some kind of royal nut, so I declined. I don't think my wife and daughter have ever forgiven me.

Now, seated in the Queen's office, I briefed her on the history of the constitutional debate and found her already well-informed. At her invitation our conversation was in French, which would have surprised quite a few people in Shawinigan, and it lasted almost an hour instead of the scheduled twenty minutes.

In April she came to Canada to sign the proclamation and, in a kind gesture by Trudeau, I signed my name just below Her Majesty's, although there was no technical reason for my signature to have been there.

I was proud of what we had achieved. We had patriated the constitution at last. We had an amending formula that had the approval of almost all the provinces even if it wasn't the federal government's preference. And we had a charter of rights and freedoms that, for all its compromises and controversies, is one of the best in the world and which is now changing our legal system for the better. Besides my pride, I felt privileged to fight with Pierre Trudeau for what we believed was right. Watching him under attack from all sides for so long I learned the meaning of leadership.

CHAPTER NINE

MAIN STREET ... BAY STREET

IN EARLY 1982 I travelled to London to get the Canadian constitutional changes approved by the British Parliament for the last time. I was in a great mood. The game was over, I could relax and I felt like a big shot riding in the front of the government plane. I invited some journalists to join me for dinner and, as usual, they asked if I would run for the leadership of the Liberal Party once Trudeau retired.

"I might run if Trudeau goes," I said. It was my standard answer and I thought the discussion was off the record, but this time it made headlines across Canada: "Chrétien to run when Trudeau goes." For the first time people began to take my candidacy seriously.

In fact, the possibility had been in my mind since Trudeau's first resignation as leader in November 1979. That was a mixed-up business. Within weeks of his announcement, the Liberals, the NDP, and the Créditistes ganged up to defeat the Tory minority government on its budget and to force an election. So the Liberals found themselves in the awkward situation of starting a leadership race and an election campaign at the same time.

Some people have argued that the confusion had been orchestrated by Trudeau as a way of undoing what he had done and staying on as leader. I don't think that was true, though I believe he saw an opportunity when it presented itself. I remember how his eyes gleamed with

193

pleasure when he learned that the Créditistes would probably not vote for the Tory budget, almost guaranteeing its defeat. And I also remember the sense of purpose in his voice when he announced that the Liberals would try to bring down the government.

Though he rarely revealed more of his thoughts or emotions than a look in his eye and a hint in his voice, I had the impression that he wanted to stay on, if he could rally the support of the party, in order to get a shot at fighting the Quebec referendum as prime minister. Even so, it took some time and a lot of debate before Trudeau made up his mind about what to do. The party itself was divided between those who were urging him to stay and those who were suggesting he go.

I was of two minds. "Pierre," I said, during a phone conversation, "it's difficult to get into politics and it's difficult to get out of politics. Now you're out, you've been praised for your decision, and you'll finally have time to be with your three boys. It might be better for you if you stay out. But, of course, if you come back, we'll all be behind you. And if you're crazy like me, you will come back."

In my opinion the Liberals could have won the election without Trudeau. A leadership convention would have earned the party and the new leader a lot of good publicity a few weeks before voting day, and Joe Clark was in deep trouble with the electorate, anyway. But Trudeau's judgment may have been better than mine, and his come-back was a real asset to our battle in the referendum. My own view was coloured by my inclination to run for the leadership, even though I didn't think I could win and most of my friends said I was crazy to try.

The major barrier seemed to be the Liberal tradition of alternating between anglophone and francophone leaders. Though a surprising number of English-speaking colleagues said to me, "Oh, no one gives a damn about that," an equally surprising number of my French-speaking colleagues did give a damn. They saw the tradition as a positive custom and they were reluctant to break it: one break now could open the way to a series of anglophone leaders later on.

On the other hand, I encountered a lot of feeling that there should be at least one strong candidate from Quebec. Perhaps if I couldn't be the king, I could be the kingmaker, and as I told Joe Clark when he was thinking of running for the leadership of the Progressive Conservative Party in 1976, "If you don't run, one thing's for sure: you won't win." To my mind losing is always better than never trying, because you can never tell what may happen.

In 1979 I thought I would be running against John Turner and Donald Macdonald. Because both were prominent ex-ministers who had become Bay Street lawyers in Toronto, I figured I had a small advantage in those parts of the party and the country where a populist minister from a rural region might be preferable, even if he spoke with a French accent. As it happened, Turner decided not to enter the contest, so I saw myself in a one-on-one race with my old friend, Donald Macdonald. He assumed he was going to win but urged me to compete against him anyway in order to make the convention exciting. However, both of us had to abandon our ambitions once Trudeau decided to stay.

During the next couple of years I tried to keep my name in the forefront as a potential candidate without running into Trudeau's wrath, although I'm told I came close to having him take me aside and say, "Jean, I'm still here and I'm still the boss." But I felt I had to plan something or else nothing would happen. I have always organized my own campaigns and some of my friends were warning me, "If you want to win, you'll have to start working at it." There were reports that people were travelling back and forth to see John Turner in Toronto; rival ministers were expanding their staffs for unknown purposes; and in spite of my loyalty to Trudeau I didn't want to be left at the starting-gate. So, while I refused to formalize anything, I didn't refuse to initiate or respond to private discussions about the leadership.

The next step was taken by my parliamentary secretary, Ron Irwin, a very pleasant and fiery guy who had been a football player and then mayor of Sault Ste Marie before becoming a member of Parliament. I mentioned to him that I would run if I could get the support of twenty-five MPs. Caucus support is always a handy indication of party support. The MPs usually know the good and bad qualities of the candidates, and their survival as politicians often depends on the leader's popularity in their constituencies. I often said, "Before I dive into the pool, I'd like to know how much water there is in it," and I developed the idea that I needed a layer of French water, a layer of English water, and a layer of money before I'd plunge.

Irwin took up the challenge by himself, though I didn't try to stop him. "Who do you think might be for you?" he asked me. Then he sought out likely people, dragged them in to speak with me, and polled all the Liberal MPs about their preferences. Soon he came back with twenty-eight names for Chrétien. "But Trudeau had thirty-five MPs when he won the leadership in 1968," I said. So Irwin went off again. He enlisted the help of his friends, lobbied, argued and on several occasions got so excited talking to the press that I had to cool him down.

Even Trudeau picked up the signal. "What's going on, Jean?" he asked one day.

"Oh, you know, the boys are just talking a bit."

"Be careful," he said.

Eventually Ron Irwin, his caucus co-chairman Robert Gourd, and my parliamentary secretary David Dingwall developed a group of good MPs, generally progressive and independent. That's when I knew I would be a serious candidate. Most of those who came to me at that time were less concerned about furthering their ambitions than with helping me personally. I had few enemies in the caucus and many friends, because through the years my door was always open, I had tried my best to help them with their problems, I had agreed to speak at fundraisers and so on in their ridings whenever possible, and I had deliberately avoided putting myself in positions where I would have to be unnecessarily tough with them.

That's partly why I turned down Trudeau's offer to be Quebec leader after Jean Marchand in 1975: I didn't want to be trapped in making decisions on patronage, local contracts, and appointments that cause so much friction and bad blood. There's always a heavy price to pay for that kind of influence although I later realized that I would pay a heavy price in Quebec during the leadership campaign for not controlling the party machine. In any event, at this stage my approach had its rewards, as in the case of an Ontario MP who came to me out of the blue to offer his support for the leadership. I had once helped him in his riding, and he was grateful. To those Quebec MPs who were hesitant my friends said, "Come with us. We Quebeckers have to show strength. We have to have a candidate in the race, that candidate has to do well, and no one will blame you for supporting Chrétien." That argument swayed a lot of people and I expected to do quite well in Quebec.

The only other serious contender for the MPs was John Turner, who was seen as a winner in a general election and therefore attracted those preoccupied with staying in power. But I detected that his right-wing image bothered a lot of Liberal MPs, and his caucus support was limited. Moreover, I had had dinner with Turner in Toronto when I was Minister of Finance, and I had been surprised at how out of touch he had become about politics since his resignation. So, all things considered, I assumed he could be overtaken if he decided to run.

In the back of my mind, I figured that Donald Macdonald would enter the race. Knowing the rivalry between him and Turner, I suspected that their contest could become bitter, and that the only compromise acceptable to both camps might be good old Jean Chrétien, provided I placed well. But long before Trudeau resigned I had visited Macdonald at his home in Toronto and he told me that he didn't intend to run and said that if it were a race between Turner and myself, he would support me. To have had his blessing in the middle of the campaign would have been a hell of a boost, but I couldn't have predicted that Macdonald would become the chairman of a royal commission on the economy and therefore be unable to rally behind me. That was a great disappointment, one of several wheels that weren't to function on my wagon, though I understood his situation.

On the last day of February 1984, Trudeau resigned and a leadership convention was called for June. Despite the rumours that he might stay on, I was sure that he would leave. My feeling was that his personal agenda after the 1980 election was very short. When we were waiting for the Supreme Court judgment on the constitutionality of our proposal for unilateral patriation during the summer of 1981, I sensed his impatience and anger with the delay. It was as if he had an important deadline in mind.

I'd say, "But, Pierre, if the judgment doesn't come in June, it'll come in September," but his unease always made me suspect that he had set a date for his departure from politics. I was on my way to Montreal when I heard the news on the radio, and that evening I participated in a CBC television program on Trudeau's career. The panel discussion was accompanied by a lengthy documentary on John Turner.

I still maintain that if the media hadn't gone crazy for Turner that first day, I could have won the convention. I saw the effect immediately when one MP who was on the panel with me declared for Turner as soon as he saw the documentary. (I guess he wanted to be in the cabinet, though as it turned out he even lost his seat in the election.) The same story was repeated again and again. MPs who had urged me to run, saying "Never Turner" or "Anybody but Turner," jumped on the Turner bandwagon before he had even declared his intention to run, all because the press had decided that he was a shoo-in. I lost a few names from my list in the initial hoopla, but it never made sense to me that a candidate would be elected before delegates were selected. I guessed many Liberals would share my view. It was a convention they wanted, not a coronation.

Then Marc Lalonde declared that it wasn't the time for a francophone leader. I hadn't expected him to support me joyfully, but I hadn't expected him to pull the rug from under me on the first day, either. Lalonde is very bright, very knowledgeable, and very good in debates, but he is poor in human relations at times, however pleasant he might appear at a cocktail party. He had a difficult job as Trudeau's tough guy, but he never helped himself by cushioning unpleasant truths in humour or by showing some sensitivity. Although he told me he was going to remain neutral, I know he twisted a lot of arms. I wasn't sure whether his remark about alternation had been planned or not, but I suspected it had been when one of Lalonde's allies in the caucus, Jacques Olivier, said at the same time, "I'm for an anglophone this time."

"So you're for Turner?" he was asked.

"No, there may be a lady running," he said.

I assumed he meant Iona Campagnolo, the president of the Liberal Party; but I had talked to her and she had told me then that she wouldn't run. In fact, her daughter Jennifer was urging me to be a candidate and came on board right away. So I said, "Let them have their fun. Eventually Lalonde will have to come to me because he said he could never go to Turner." That turned out to be rather naive.

At first, however, I was so furious about his statement that I decided not to run. I even dictated a bitter letter to that effect, which said, "It's sad that the one who had worked so hard for the charter of rights should be denied the leadership of the Liberal Party because he was born French." My secretary must have alerted someone, because I got a phone call from Trudeau's former principal secretary, Jim Coutts, urging me not to quit.

Later I met Trudeau and told him, "That's it, I've been shafted on the first day, I'm not running."

He said, "Don't make any announcement just yet." Then he went into the caucus and said, "If alternation is everything, then I don't belong here as prime minister. I thought I was selected because I was good, not because I was French." It was a powerful speech that gave me new hope. I decided to stay in the race.

At that point, though I had more than forty MPs behind me, I had only one declared cabinet minister, Senator Bud Olson. (The former Alberta MP had come to me on his own initiative in 1979 because he felt I was "the best politician on the Hill.") But, Mitchell Sharp advised me, "If you don't have any Quebec ministers, then forget about running. Now is the time to play hardball."

From the outside, many people think that a leadership campaign is a very exciting, high-spirited race in which candidates of rather similar views vie for the support of the party faithful. On the inside, it is not quite so simple. While the competition is certainly exciting, it is also deadly serious, particularly within the caucus. Careers are in jeopardy and for those who must choose, the choices are never easy or perfect. If you believe that a particular candidate will win the convention, you can never be certain he will win the election. If you go with the perceived winner, there are probably many others competing for a place

199

on his bandwagon. There are also old friendships and associations to consider and there is no shortage of people to remind MPs of their conflicting loyalties and interests. Nor is there any safe place to hide: unlike the vote of the ordinary delegate, a member's decision is known, and the people who try to stay on the sidelines in such a battle are often the most resented.

As in all high-pressure contests, leadership conventions bring out the best and the worst in people. With so much at stake and so many people involved, emotions run wild. Fatigue blows the smallest highs and lows out of proportion. And just as in an old-timers' hockey game, it doesn't take long before one or two high sticks or vigorous body checks turn a friendly competition into a more combative game. Once the battles start, they are hard to stop.

At times, discussions can become heated and the language used can be quite forceful. Once, for example, a colleague told me that he wouldn't be able to support me, but I shouldn't worry because he wouldn't work very hard for Turner. "No," I replied, "no, work as hard as possible. Don't double-cross Turner like you've double-crossed me. When you look back on this, you'll be able to say that you only double-crossed one guy, not two."

I had assumed from the start that I had the support of André Ouellet. We were close friends. Several sources had reported that Ouellet was saying, "Jean hasn't got a chance of winning, but he is my friend and I will support him." I had received the same message from him when we went skiing the month before Trudeau resigned. "It will be difficult," he said to me, "but I will be with you." In fact, I even showed him the list of my supporters in the caucus and we discussed some of them in detail. So, though I knew Ouellet was feeling somewhat embarrassed about supporting me, I was sure I could count on him when I went off to meet the rest of the Quebec ministers.

I was tough with them. "There is only one of you who is willing to come with me now," I said. "I don't understand those of you who are supporting a guy who has not done much for us for the last eight years. You guys owe everything to Trudeau. I'm the only one who wasn't made a minister by Trudeau: I was appointed by Pearson. But, I will go and happily defend Trudeau and his policies because I believe in them. When I leave politics I'll leave by the front door. I know what reputation I will have. I'm less sure about yours." Some of the faces were as white as the wall.

Pierre DeBané, Pierre Buissères and Charles Lapointe came to me, giving me one more Quebec minister than Trudeau had had in 1968, when only Jean Marchand and Bryce Mackasey supported him at the beginning. Still, I was waiting for Ouellet and hoping for Francis Fox — I figured that with them I could successfully counter whatever the establishment was up to in Quebec. But Fox was leaning toward Turner for the understandable reason that he assumed Ouellet would be my Quebec kingpin and therefore there would be great opportunities for him in the other camp.

Meanwhile, Ouellet seemed to be slipping away from me. My guess is that Fox had told Ouellet that he was going to Turner and Ouellet had begun to waver. Later I heard that Ouellet had said to Turner, "If you take Fox as your kingpin instead of me, I will organize for Chrétien," so Turner dumped Fox and took Ouellet. I'm told Fox came close to deserting Turner but decided to stay with the perceived winner.

Ouellet came to see me just before Turner entered the race to confirm that he wasn't going to support me. He was followed by Fox, Ed Lumley, the Minister of Regional Industrial Development, and Judd Buchanan, a former senior minister. They all had the same message: "Don't run, Jean. You'll be hurt and humiliated." They probably had decided collectively what they were going to say.

"It's too late, I'm running anyway," I said, "and I will prove you wrong." But it was tough to see four very good friends leaving me.

John Turner entered the race in the middle of March with an opening statement in Ottawa. I never underestimated him as an opponent: he was a new face, he had experience in government, he looked like a winner, and he had all the press attention. He also represented the longing of many Liberals to re-establish the link with the business community that St. Laurent and C.D. Howe had had and Trudeau seemed to have lost.

But when I read his statement I perceived he was vulnerable in three areas: the impression that he wanted nothing to do with Trudeau; the impression that he wanted to move the Liberal Party to the right; and the impression that he wanted to woo the West by being soft on bilingualism. The third point had the most important immediate effect because I had a poll indicating that I was trailing Turner by more than two to one in Quebec. So it was encouraging to have strong grounds on which to challenge him.

In addition, I expected that some time within the twelve weeks of the campaign the press would turn on Turner. The media had been too good to him and would feel guilty. Once that happened, Turner's "winability" would become less certain. There were still important cabinet ministers to be picked up, such as Allan MacEachen, Roméo LeBlanc and Monique Bégin, and there could be surprises along the way to give me momentum. Almost from the first day, for example, Turner had to issue clarifications of statements he had made on bilingualism in Manitoba and Quebec, and each one increased my confidence. One of the best shots I got off in the campaign came when I was asked a question in the House of Commons about something Turner had said in Newfoundland. I answered, "I will wait for the clarification." There was great applause from all sides, and I've never seen Trudeau laugh so hard.

Ultimately I was offering the Liberal Party a real choice as well as an exciting convention. The Liberals hadn't been led by a populist since Wilfrid Laurier. King had been a sober bureaucrat, St. Laurent had been an establishment lawyer, Pearson had been a distinguished diplomat and Trudeau had been a sophisticated intellectual. Suddenly there was a populist on the scene defending the Liberal heritage and appealing to "Main Street, not Bay Street." Because I had stayed in politics, I was in touch with Liberals across the country and I knew their thoughts and concerns well enough to reflect them.

The Liberal Party is basically an alliance of three groups: moderate anglophones, French Canadians and new Canadians who feel comfortable in and grateful to the Liberal Party. In essence, to be a Liberal is to be middle-of-the-road. Liberal roots are in the pragmatic, free-market philosophy of the nineteenth century, but over the course of a hundred years the party also became the guardian of a social vision. I sensed that most Liberals didn't want to depart from the principle of universal social benefits regardless of income, for example, and I agreed with them. Once a government begins to tamper with universality, the whole system is threatened. Social benefits are given to every Canadian citizen as a right. They can be taxed back from the rich, because the rich should pay more taxes than the poor, but to extend the social safety net to some and not to others makes it charity, not a right. Any deviation from the fundamental principle invites further erosion of the benefits themselves.

That's what happened when some provinces began to charge user fees. Free medical care is now a right of every citizen. To charge an additional $2 opens the door to charging $20 or $200 or $2,000 because the principle has been destroyed. Ultimately the rich would have access to medical services and the poor wouldn't. Moreover, those who compare our taxes to taxes in the United States rarely add in the terrifying amounts the average American taxpayer must spend on health insurance and medical care. I sometimes joke about the Canadian who has a heart attack in Miami. When he gets out of the hospital, he gets his bill and has another heart attack. Besides, what price can we put on freeing Canadians from the fear of becoming ill?

In the end, the shock of seeing ambition and opportunism push aside old friendships and life-long principles was tempered by the deep emotions I felt when people came to help me during my leadership race without considering the consequences, because they believed in what I believed: people of the intellectual stature of Jean Marchand, Gérard Pelletier, Donald Macdonald, Tommy Shoyama and David Croll urged me to run. Most of the Liberal MPs who said they were behind me didn't give in to the pressure to desert me, and virtual strangers stepped forward to work hard in the campaign because they shared my vision of Canada. One of my financial backers was a man I had only met once. He said, "Mr. Chrétien, I want to thank you for what you have done for the country, and this is my way of doing so." He really put his money where his mouth was.

I was also being urged on by the other candidates — Donald Johnston, Mark MacGuigan, John Roberts, John Munro and Eugene Whelan. They knew I was the only one who could block a first-ballot victory by Turner. I told each of them, "Okay, if I run and if I have a chance of winning, you'll have to remember that I ran on your advice and you'll owe me something." That was the only deal that was ever made.

Whelan and Munro said, "No problem." They were good friends and strong progressives. In fact, I had offered Whelan the chairmanship of my campaign before he decided to run, and Munro and I shared many friends from our terms as Minister of Indian Affairs and Northern Development.

John Roberts indicated that he would come to me, and he did. He ran because he felt he would make a good prime minister. Certainly he had the intellectual capacity, but he didn't seem to have the proper political image. In the end the result didn't match the quality of his campaign performance, which was consistently high.

I really thought Mark MacGuigan would come to me, but he didn't. He was courageous in some of his policies and he worked hard, but he wasn't very consistent in his performance. I always felt that MacGuigan was too educated for his intelligence; he seemed to stumble over his degrees, and that hurt him as a politician.

Don Johnston ran a good campaign, and as he was third at the convention, he stayed on the ballot. I had the feeling, however, that he would have come to me if he had been fourth. To some extent, we were all running against Turner, but I was the most serious challenger. The rest could only hope that the party would reject both the front runner and the francophone.

"Fasten your seatbelts!" I said in March, when I announced my entry into the race before a large, enthusiastic crowd of MPs, senators, constituents, and supporters in the ornate West Block committee room where the constitution hearings had been held. "It's going to be a hell of a ride!"

So the campaign now had its first requirement, a candidate, and my candidacy already had a clear cause. I was to campaign as a

"Liberal's Liberal" and try my best to remind Liberals across the country not to run away from the record and put expediency before principle.

Two more ingredients would have to be added — a campaign team and the money to finance our effort. My old friend from Toronto, Bob Wright, agreed to serve as my finance chairman, and prior to my announcement he confirmed that we would be able to raise the money to finance a proper campaign.

I had begun to call on old friends and former associates; and, although some of them were unavailable because of work, many volunteered for responsibilities in the campaign organization. The manager was my former assistant, John Rae. His first job was to get a team in place across the country and to build our support in the constituencies where delegates were to be selected. Things were proceeding better than anticipated in English Canada, but I immediately ran into trouble in Quebec. I knew there was a problem when I contacted some of my old colleagues from the referendum fight, such as Jean-Claude Dansereau and Léonce Mercier. They had told me they would be with me, but now they were waffling. Dansereau made excuses and Mercier claimed he couldn't organize for me because, as Director General of the party in Quebec, he had to help arrange the convention.

It was terrible. At one point I had nobody, because everyone who knew the party had been blocked at the top. The machine was turned against me. Mercier, for example, had been told by Lalonde that if he helped me he would have to resign his job. He had already been fired from a similar job with the provincial Liberals for supporting Raymond Garneau against Claude Ryan before being hired to work for the federal party and subsequently for the referendum.

But Mercier was an emotional guy and he was humiliated by the knowledge that I was being nailed by the party establishment in Quebec, which wanted to protect its position with Turner. After many weeks alone I persuaded Mercier to join me, and he did so out of loyalty for what I had done for the party and the country. That changed things, because he's quite a guy. His decision broke the iron grip and created a favourable impression. Turner's statements on bilingualism were

205

beginning to make a lot of Quebec Liberals uneasy, and I was able to take advantage of my closeness to Trudeau and my work on the constitution. Turner's supporters were put on the defensive by their friends, and some of them threatened to quit.

Meanwhile, I was encouraged by what was happening in English Canada. During the first weekend of my campaign I went to a party convention in Toronto and found friendly crowds and a lively Chrétien team. I called myself a "clear Grit," the Ontario equivalent of the *rouges* who had struggled against the Family Compact in the early nineteenth century. The reaction in the corridors and in the press was fantastic.

The next weekend I was in Quebec City. I had a couple of hours to spare, so I sat in my hotel room and started calling the presidents of riding associations across Canada. To my surprise they all were very sympathetic and upbeat, which offset the mixed reception I would get downstairs. Because I knew almost everyone, I could sense their dilemma. On the one hand, they wanted to be with me; on the other were their problems with alternation and the winning image of Turner.

I left Quebec and flew directly to Vancouver, arriving late but dramatically at an all-candidates' forum. I entered the hall in the middle of a speech and apparently stole the show as the television cameras surrounded me, the people pushed forward and everyone stood to applaud, even John Turner.

So the race was on: first, to meet the Liberal associations that would be selecting the delegates for the convention, and then to meet the delegates. I was extremely well-received in the market in Fredericton and a small, last-minute reception in Halifax drew more than 500 people. Support in Newfoundland was growing so fast that everyone on my team there was becoming very excited. In many places in the West we got many more people than Turner's team did. Although a great many people had committed themselves early for Turner, I began to feel some movement away from him, while my own supporters held on despite the arm-twisting by anglophone ministers such as Lloyd Axworthy, Gerry Regan, Herb Gray and Judy Erola. But my people had little to gain and nothing more to lose, in spite of the increased pressure. In all parts of the country, the Chrétien team was up against the local party establishment.

Everywhere I went I attacked the idea that only John Turner was a winner. I felt that the party would feel more comfortable with me, but it was afraid of losing the next election because of the scare tactics of people who said, "If you want to lose the election, you can always vote for Chrétien." I wasn't afraid of the Liberal record, and I wasn't afraid of Brian Mulroney. "Let me beat Turner," I told the delegates, "and Mulroney will be small potatoes. If I beat Turner, the entire nation will see me as a giant killer and a real winner because the public knows that Turner is a better man than Mulroney. Give me Brian Mulroney for seven weeks across the country!"

I always said that Turner is a good man, but I think I'm better — otherwise I wouldn't have run. When I was asked why I was running, I answered, "Because I know Turner," which was a powerful argument because most of the people who jumped to him had never talked to him. I didn't mean this in a disparaging way. I only meant to counter the view that had been created that he was some sort of superman.

Leadership campaigns are not the same as election campaigns. In the Liberal Party they have been infrequent and there is little training for them. They are impossible to organize ahead of time, and there is no public money available for the candidates. Many of the blue-chip party contributors mistakenly don't want to contribute to an internal leadership race within a party. Because of Canada's size, the compressed time and every delegate's desire to be courted individually, there are tremendous scheduling and logistical demands on any candidate. Because I was behind, I wanted to work as hard as physically possible to meet as many delegates as I could. While no stranger to the fatigue of a political campaign, I learned the true meaning of fatigue during my leadership run. But the best tonic for a candidate's fatigue was the warmth of the people and the confirmation that my message was getting through. My team and I worked on adrenalin and instinct, and I was lucky that our campaign grew as steadily as it did with each successive week. By the end I was ahead of Turner in the polls across the country.

Certainly we out-campaigned Turner. If he had two or three meetings a day, I had five or six. While we lost many of the first meetings that tied up delegates early, we did well in the hotly contested battles. We took almost all the youth delegates from Quebec from under the machine's nose, and we took the delegates from Vancouver-Quadra, where one of Turner's key organizers was the riding president. I was told I won more elected delegates than Turner across the country.

By the time I came to Ottawa for the convention in June I was optimistic. I told the press I had 1,000 votes on the first ballot, but I thought I had around 1,200. My estimates were that Turner would get 1,500 votes and all the other candidates would get around 500 votes. The other candidates coming to me with most of their votes in the second ballot would push me over the top. Even during convention week, I maintained my sense of progress. The press was excellent, the campaign tent was a big hit with all the delegates, the party that we held for all the Ottawa taxi drivers was a fantastic success. Everyone was telling me I had a good chance.

But there were some worries, too. One was to prepare my major speech for the night before the vote. I wanted to have a written speech, though I wasn't sure whether I would read it or improvise from it. That was debated all week, and it remained a debate long after the convention. I decided to read the speech, and some people were disappointed, but it probably wasn't a factor in the result either way.

More important was my unfulfilled hope for a dramatic development during the week. I never gave up trying to get Lalonde, LeBlanc or MacEachen to come over to me. Two of them would have damaged Turner and given me the last-minute boost that Trudeau got from Sharp and Drury in 1968. I got Roméo LeBlanc, but it was clear that Lalonde's declared neutrality was turning into active support for Turner, through his network if not directly, and nothing would budge MacEachen. And now I know he was committed to Turner long before he made his famous move on the convention floor.

In fact, most of the party establishment — the sizeable number of ex-officio delegates who got a vote by virtue of being party candidates, senators, party executives and former ministers — had seen the media hype for Turner and run for a place on his wagon the very first week. That was a bloc of votes I couldn't seem to sway very much.

Something almost happened during the campaign to create the momentum I was hoping for. Doug Anguish was an NDP member of Parliament from North Battleford, Saskatchewan. He was approached by a four-man local committee, representing NDPers, Liberals, and dissatisfied Tories, who wanted to prevent a Tory victory in the next election. Their poll showed the Tories at something like fifty per cent, the NDP at thirty per cent, and the Liberals at fifteen per cent. But when the name of Jean Chrétien was put in as Liberal leader, the NDP and Liberals changed places in the poll. These guys concluded that the best way to stop the Tories was to have a Chrétien-Anguish combination, and they urged Anguish to become a Liberal and support me.

I talked with him several times, and I felt he was very close to a deal. When I met him in Saskatoon, I knew how significant his decision would be. It would show I was acceptable in the West and with NDP voters, and it could have been the surprise that changed the entire campaign. However, the story was picked up in the Saskatchewan press, Anguish was lobbied by other people and he worried that he would have to go back to the NDP if Turner won.

"Doug," I said, "you can write history. If you come to me saying that you're joining the Liberals because of Jean Chrétien, you'll make me the leader and you'll prevent the Tories from coming to power. It's the chance of a lifetime. For the rest of your life people might say you were nuts, or for the rest of your life you might be a very important politician."

"I'm not ready," he said. He backed off and was defeated in the September election.

The morning of the convention vote I went to a series of breakfast receptions and on arriving at the Civic Centre I saw a restaurant billboard: "Buy one, get one free." I remembered that Turner's supporters were arguing, "Vote for Turner and you keep Chrétien. Vote for Chrétien and you lose Turner." I was destined to be the one for free. I

209

knew I had lost. An experienced politician feels that sort of thing. The spirit of the previous days was not quite the same. I went home and told Aline, "Get ready, we've lost."

On the first ballot I got 1,067 votes, about 100 short of my estimate. Though the difference had not gone to Turner, the gap was too big for me to pass him. The other candidates had done better than I had expected, and many of their votes would go to Turner on the next ballot because he was so close to the top. But most of the candidates came to me as they had promised, which was very moving considering the consequences to their careers.

First, I reached Whelan on a phone, "Gino, it's Jean, are you coming?"

"I'm humiliated, Jean," he said. "I only have eighty-five votes, and I can't be sure of bringing them all."

"It's you I want, not your votes," I said. "I want the Canadian people to see that Gino from La Rivière aux Canards is going to support his old friend Jean."

So he picked up his green cowboy hat, waved at Turner, and walked all the way over to my box. Then John Munro came, without any hesitation. John Roberts was in a more complicated situation. Some of his advisers were urging him to go to Turner to save his political career. He loved politics and couldn't really envisage life without it. Moreover, he had been convinced that he was going to have at least 500 votes and be third on the first ballot, so he was shattered to have come fourth. But out of friendship and principle he came to me, and I was deeply touched.

MacGuigan went to Turner, but he was not as important a factor as Johnston. I went to see him, but his advisers were divided about what he should do. Johnston seemed determined to stay in the race: he had the idea that some of Turner's votes were going to come to him.

"Are you off your beam, Don?" I said. "You won't gain votes, you'll lose votes. Don't kid yourself. I still have a five per cent chance of winning if you come to me now. Otherwise the game is over."

But he stayed in, and I went to vote for the second ballot. I knew I was finished, of course. I went to my trailer, took a shower, changed my shirt, and had a beer as some people dropped by to show their support. Then I got up and said, "Let's go, let's go down in style," and I went back to the floor where Aline was waiting. My troops were looking discouraged. Soon their spirit returned as I led them in cheers and songs despite what was in my heart.

When the final result came, I was very calm and at peace with myself. I was proud to have been the anti-establishment candidate after more than twenty years in politics, a small-town guy fighting for the ordinary Canadian. Indeed, I like to take some credit for the progressive tone that was struck by all three parties in the election that followed shortly after the convention. Certainly I wonder if the success of my campaign didn't encourage Brian Mulroney to emphasize that he was an electrician's son from Baie Comeau rather than a former president of the Iron Ore Company, and John Turner to stress that his grandfather had been a miner. I knew I had achieved much more than anyone imagined at the beginning. The party decided that John Turner was the better man to form the government and lead us into the election, and I was on the platform to move that the decision be made unanimous.

Every politician must learn to accept the verdict of the people. If you cannot take it, you don't belong in the game. Of course, there will be scars, but the best healing process is to forget and carry on.

"You must have been angry that many of your cabinet colleagues didn't support you," people still say. No, I was not angry, I was disappointed. After all, I had fought the referendum, I had campaigned in their ridings, and many of them had told me that the Liberal Party needed a strong French Canadian and a progressive in the race. But they all had ambitions and careers, and there is nothing more natural than that in politics. After the convention was over I didn't cry, and neither did my wife. We had lost a few illusions, but I made a lot of new friends and accumulated fantastic memories.

Naturally there were some uncomfortable moments. The next day Turner's office phoned to say Mr. Turner wanted to speak to me. I was kept waiting twenty minutes before he came on the line. It felt like an eternity. Though it was a small matter that couldn't have been his fault, the fatigue and disappointment of the convention was setting in and it didn't help my mood during this, our first conversation since his victory. I congratulated him, however, and he generously asked if he might come to see me. "No, no," I said. "You're the boss now, and I should come to see you." So I went.

After a rather awkward start, he handed me a beer and we relaxed. "You will be my partner, Jean," he said. "I'll name you minister of whatever you want and Deputy Prime Minister."

"What about Quebec leader?" I asked.

"That will be more difficult," he said, but he didn't say no, and we agreed to meet again.

Then I received a call from Brian Mulroney, offering sympathy and saying he had a new poll in his hands. "Jean, you lost," he said, "but I know that I will be the next prime minister. According to my polls, if you had been leader, I would win six seats at best in Quebec, but with Turner, I'll win twenty-six seats at least."

"You're bragging, Brian," I said. But it has been established since that he was not.

Then Eugene Whelan came to me, furious because Turner had told him he wouldn't be in the new cabinet. "I don't give a damn," he said. "This guy will lose the election and I'll be in the opposition back-bench with you in a few months, anyway."

"Why do you think that?"

"Because Turner is a carbon copy of Mulroney, and the Canadian people will vote for the real Conservative."

Both these conversations increased the temptation not to stay on, but the real pressure came when Turner told me I couldn't be Quebec leader. "Listen, John," I said, "you have to understand one thing. I have nothing against you. You had the right to run, and you had the right to win. You're a friend of mine and I think you will be a better prime minister than Mulroney. But I can't be number two in Canada and number three in Quebec. I promise you one thing — I'm not a double-crosser. If I shake hands with you, that's it, you can rely on me. I've been faithful to Sharp, faithful to Trudeau, and I'll be faithful to you. But you owe me Quebec."

212

"It's impossible," he said.

So I got up and said, "Okay then, goodbye, John."

He got very agitated. "Wait, give me time and I'll fix it up."

"Look," I said, "I know I'm creating a problem. I'll make it easy for you. I've never wanted to be Quebec leader in the past because I hate to deal with all the lawyers and engineers and architects who want government business. So I'll be happy to delegate that. Give Quebec to a committee of three: myself as chairman, André Ouellet and Charles Lapointe." That would effectively have made me boss in Quebec while solving Turner's problem, and that's what happened eventually.

In the meantime my wife and others were telling me not to run again. Aline showed me an editorial in *La Presse* that said, "We see nothing in politics that won't be frustration for Jean Chrétien." "That's the truth, Jean," Aline said. "Don't listen to anybody, you owe nothing more."

An important argument on the other side was that I had to protect the people who had been loyal to me. That became part of my negotiation with Turner. I couldn't save Whelan's seat in the cabinet because Turner had decided to drop MacGuigan, too; but I kept fighting hard for Munro, Roberts, LeBlanc, Olson, DeBané, Lapointe, Buissères, Charles Caccia and David Collenette. Munro and LeBlanc dropped out because they didn't want to be in Turner's cabinet and, surprisingly, Olson was replaced at the last minute by Allan MacEachen, who had just declared that politics was over for him. Roberts, Caccia and Collenette were reappointed.

The real problem was my three Quebec ministers. Turner didn't want any of them, and he had some strong arguments: he was reducing the size of the cabinet; he had dropped two of the Quebec ministers who had supported him; and he needed room for some new faces. So I told my three guys about the difficulties and they said, "Don't worry about us, Jean. The important thing is that you stay." In the end, Turner kept Lapointe, although that was used against me by those who seemed more bitter and aggressive for having won the convention than I was for having lost it. I know at least six colleagues who were told

213

that they were not a minister because I insisted on keeping Lapointe. The worst was that each of the six believed it.

During this period, in June 1984, I discovered something interesting. Uncharacteristically, I refused to make myself available to the press, and my silence created a lot of nervousness and speculation. People began to speak for me or against me in public. Some said I would stay, others said my appetite was too big and I didn't deserve anything; but everyone was uncertain about what I would do. I met with Turner a few more times, he asked for my advice on various issues, we became friendlier, and eventually I agreed to stay. We shook hands, and I went to tell the caucus of my decision. Everyone was very tense, as no one knew what I was going to say.

It was Trudeau's last caucus meeting and, unfortunately, I spoiled his final moments by arriving at the end of the meeting. All eyes were on me as I went to my seat and fidgeted with a piece of paper, as if I were unhappy. The chairman indicated that I had something to say, and I stood up. "I will not, I will not, I will not . . ." I said, and I could see everyone inching forward — "quit!" Everyone cheered and jumped up and down and rushed over to me. It was a great reconciliation. Even Monique Bégin gave me a kiss.

Immediately after the new Liberal cabinet was sworn in, there was a lot of talk about holding a quick election. The polls looked good and almost everyone was advising Turner to go directly into a new campaign. He asked my advice and I gave him the scenario I would have followed if I had won the convention. "Don't call an election now," I said. "You have to show the people that you are a new prime minister. You'll have the entire summer to make an impact, just like Mulroney did last year after he won the Tory convention. All the attention will be on you. Go to Washington, go to London, go to France and Germany. Stop off in communist countries to revive Trudeau's peace initiative and end up in Japan to talk about trade. Return to Canada in time to meet the Queen and the Pope. Then you can call an election in September to coincide with the American election in November, and since there's no mood for change down there, there'll be less mood for change here."

Turner was very sympathetic, but mine was just one of many voices advising him and one of the very few urging a delay. So an election was called in July for September. It didn't take long for circumstances to change. It soon became apparent that the Liberals were heading for a major defeat, despite all the initial optimism. I campaigned in ninety-five ridings, and I had no doubt that the campaign was going nowhere.

When that kind of mood seizes an electorate, it is useless to cite the facts and reasons why a party that had done so many of the tough jobs necessary for a better future deserved a better hearing. Even the best party organization in the world can't stop a landslide. Despite the myths about the Quebec Liberals' "Big Red Machine," for example, the days when a small clique could deliver votes were long gone. Every party can still draw on traditional support from some people and areas, but most voters have become more sophisticated and party affiliations less predictable. If a party is looking good, it gets a big machine; if it is looking not so good, it gets a small machine. In both cases, the machine is the result rather than the cause of the general attitude. The strong organization of the Ontario Tories couldn't prevent Bill Davis from getting two minority governments in the 1970s or Frank Miller from losing power in 1985, and Brian Mulroney's Tories didn't sweep Quebec in 1984 because they had a better machine than the Liberals. People voted Tory because they did not like the new Liberal Party very much.

They were also influenced by published polls. Polls are a new fact of political life. While it is still debatable whether they reflect instability or cause it, no one can doubt that they have changed the election process. Every time they fluctuate, great careers and important policies go up or down with them. The media distribute them as news items, yet their effect is incredible.

When the Liberals began to fall in the polls during the summer of 1984, it had a snowball effect that nobody could stop: as fewer people came to believe that the Liberals could win, more people decided to go to the winner. I could feel the impact as I crossed the country trying to crank up the faithful. For one reason or another, the Tory wave in Quebec was fantastic, as old traditions and loyalties were swept away overnight.

For the last three days my wife called me back from campaigning for others so that I could concentrate on my own re-election. Even though I was quite sure of winning, there was some uneasiness because of the mood across the province. During those three days, I did a very fast tour of the riding. The Liberals were very pleased to see me back and campaigning hard.

Fortunately for me, I have a large number of loyal supporters, who have worked hard and effectively over the years to help me get elected. They and the people of St-Maurice have always been with me when I needed them, and I never needed them more than on September 4, 1984. Despite the Tory landslide, I lost only 3,000 votes in my riding from the last election, and I was the first candidate to be declared a winner in Quebec. In fact, I received the highest percentage of votes of any Liberal in Canada. That made me both humble and grateful. The support I received from the people of the Mauricie once again gave me the strength I needed to continue along the rocky road of politics.

216

Raising a fist in frustration when the tally is announced at the 1984 leadership convention.

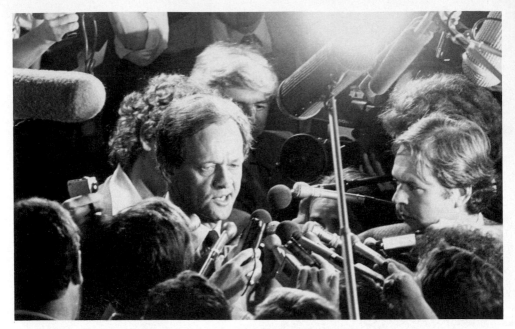

After a meeting with Prime Minister-designate John Turner,
I announced to reporters that I would remain in the cabinet.

I was happy to work with Mr. Turner and took my
responsibilities as Minister for External Affairs seriously.

Former Prime Minister Trudeau was among the hundreds of people who turned out for the launch of *Straight from the Heart* in October 1985.

With Aline, on my way to the Chateau Laurier Hotel in Ottawa to announce my candidacy for the leadership of the Liberal party of Canada, January 1990.

Water-skiing—and putting to rest any doubts about the state of my health—at my cottage in Lac des Piles, Quebec.

Not just promises; we went to the people with policies. The Red Book was central to the 1993 federal election campaign.

Aline and I acknowledging the applause of supporters at party headquarters in Shawinigan on election night, 1993.

Supporters came to meet me when I arrived in Ottawa as Prime
Minister-designate the day after the election.

Being sworn in as Prime Minister by the Clerk of the Privy Council, Glen Shortliffe, at Rideau Hall.

In my office on Parliament Hill.

CHAPTER TEN

TIME OUT

D URING THE 1984 election I showed up on an open-line radio program and a caller said, "Mr. Chrétien, be candid. You have been in the government for years, you have been a powerful minister in every major department, and now you will be in opposition. Will you stay or will you quit?"

In reply, I admitted that the Liberals looked headed for the opposition, but I vowed to work to be an excellent MP.

Certainly I couldn't guarantee that I would stay forever. I was fifty years old, I had given more than two decades to public life, and I was prepared to take on new challenges. I remembered a letter I had received from a friend who had run against me twice, once as a Tory and once as a Créditiste. "Someday we will sit together," he wrote. "We will have grey hair and be in rocking chairs, and I will laugh at my defeats and let you brag about your successes." I was beginning to think that he may have been the real winner, because he had learned at an early age that life is more than having your name in the paper.

Also, with the departure of Pierre Trudeau, I sensed that the national agenda that had led me into politics had been virtually completed. The crucial things, such as the referendum, the constitution, and the Charter of Rights and Freedoms, had been accomplished, and the problems that remained seemed like technicalities in comparison. Trudeau had led us safely through a period in which the very essence of the country was threatened and, in doing so, he had presented many challenges, provoked many controversies, and disturbed many interests. He had stirred us to try to measure ourselves against his intelligence and his vision and all the great issues of his time, and he had tackled the fundamental structures that other politicians had feared to touch. That had cost him and his party a lot of political support, for, in practice, people don't like the significant reforms they're always calling for in theory, and it is understandable that Canadians wanted a return to quieter times.

So when Mr. Turner asked me to serve in his cabinet in June, I told him that I would be happy to work with him, but not to be surprised if I quit politics within two years. He had a good chance of remaining prime minister for a long time, I assumed in those days, and since that meant I had probably missed my only chance to become leader, I had better think about doing something else.

After the defeat of the Liberal government I took my role on the opposition benches in the House of Commons seriously. On parliamentary committees and party committees I was deeply involved in such important matters as free trade with the United States, "Star Wars," South Africa, and the voyage of the *Polar Sea* through Canadian waters. I attended dozens of fund-raising events across the country, and I campaigned for Liberals during the provincial elections in Ontario, Quebec, and Newfoundland. But the more I did, the higher my profile became, and the more I created a problem, because the press argued that I was trying to threaten John Turner's position.

Even the unexpected success of *Straight from the Heart* in October, 1985, was seen as the opening shot of a new leadership campaign. But there was no convention, so how could there have been a campaign? When I gave Turner a copy of my book, I inscribed in it, "Thank you for having won the convention. Because if you had not won, I wouldn't have had the time to write this book." He laughed, and I never heard any negative reaction from him to what I had written. In fact, all my colleagues seemed pleased by my success.

Since that success came on the eve of a Liberal policy convention in Halifax, however, the press began to build up a fight between me and Turner. It wasn't what I wanted, but the book's popularity only highlighted the dilemma I found myself in. If I was out working for the party, I was accused of working for myself. If I wasn't up asking a lot of questions in the House, I was accused of refusing to help the leader. As my position got more and more difficult, I got more and more frustrated.

Finally, on February 27, 1986, rather than show up in Quebec City at a Liberal convention where I was certain to be a lightning rod for tensions within the party, I announced I was leaving public life. At the age of fifty-two, while still enjoying good health and high popularity, I was able to listen to my own eulogies.

Getting out of politics is sometimes more difficult than getting in, but leaving was the best thing I could have done. Far from being a painful separation, I was happy to go and I guess Turner was happy to let me go. By removing myself as a factor in the caucus, I allowed him to stand clearly on his own. And after twenty-three years in politics, I had a new challenge in life.

Whenever I had dealt with the business community as a minister, there always came a point in our discussions (particularly when I was winning an argument) when someone would say, "That's all very well, Mr. Chrétien, but you've never had to meet a payroll out in the real world." And though I had been reasonably successful running a law office in Shawinigan, I knew I didn't have a good reply. I had come to look like a political junkie who could do nothing else in life but make speeches and get elected. So I wanted to find out if I could succeed in private life.

That's largely why I turned down the indirect offer of a public appointment from Mr. Mulroney. I didn't think there would have been anything dishonourable about accepting the offer, but I took some pride and pleasure in being able to say no. I had come to Ottawa with nothing but my willingness to work hard, and I was leaving with nothing else.

After the 1984 election I had begun to work part-time, usually a day a week when it didn't interfere with my parliamentary duties, for the Toronto law firm of Lang Michener Cranston Farquharson and

Wright. In the fall of 1985 we took the bold step of opening a branch in Ottawa, which was already a very competitive market for lawyers. Yet within a couple of years we grew to thirty lawyers. Since two of my colleagues — Roger Tassé, who had been my Deputy Minister in Justice, and Eddie Goldenberg, my former assistant — had been as involved in the constitutional reform process as I, our office was well positioned to handle files arising from the Charter of Rights as well as the whole field of government regulation and organization.

So I had some grounds for optimism on my first morning as a full-time lawyer and private citizen, but like everyone else who hangs out his shingle for the first time, I spent fifteen minutes staring at the telephone and wondering if it would ever ring. Suddenly I got a call from the Shoal Lake Indians from the Lake of the Woods. They needed a lawyer and remembered the work I had done on behalf of the native peoples more than a decade before. After I hung up, I called my wife and told her how moved I was that my first clients should be native people, that they had not forgotten me. After that, other native groups approached me too, and it felt wonderful to work with them again.

At the same time I began working with Gordon Capital Corporation, who had asked me to join them as a special adviser. I didn't want to take a full-time job or move to Montreal, but I did agree to spend a couple of days a week in their Montreal office. That brought me close to the new vitality evident in the Quebec economic scene, and the new generation of French-Canadian entrepreneurs who are both aggressive and internationally oriented. I also became Gordon Capital's representative on the board of B.C. Forest for a while.

Several other companies invited me to join their boards, including the Toronto-Dominion Bank. Shortly after the Mulroney government imposed a special tax on banks, the T-D's chairman, Dick Thomson, asked me to talk to more than fifteen hundred of his employees about the animosity between politicians and the banks. For an hour I really let them have it about the insensitivity of bankers toward the needs of the community and so forth — and I did such a good job, apparently, that Thomson offered me a seat on his board!

220

I was an iconoclast among all those Establishment types, most of them diehard Tories, but I enjoyed being there, and I learned a lot about the internal operations of banking. I used to kid Thomson that he would someday regret having given me that inside look.

I hadn't sold my soul to Bay Street, in other words. My law practice took me among the poorest of the poor. (One winter night, while visiting a native community in northern Manitoba that had neither running water nor indoor toilets, a friend and I got locked outside the tiny airport. We were talking about the cold, for obvious reasons, and I wondered what it would be like to freeze to death. "We'll know in about five minutes," my buddy said.) I was proud, too, to serve as a special counsel to the union at Canadair, a company I had helped save as a minister that is now one of the success stories of Canada's aeronautic industry. And I was happy to do a series of speeches at universities across the country for a speakers' agency. In fact, I was amazed. As a politician, I used to get a couple of hundred students to hear me talk for free. Now, with a fee at the door, I occasionally attracted a couple of thousand. I enjoyed them so much, I answered questions until they got fed up.

I had a great life with all these jobs, and I was finally able to be more generous with my wife and family. Most people don't realize the sacrifices MPs and ministers are required to make. Not just with money, which has never been very important to me, but with time. I particularly savoured the more frequent opportunities I had to be with my three grandsons, the youngest of whom had been born the day before I resigned from public life.

During the 1988 election I visited twenty-three ridings from British Columbia to the Maritimes. It was a complex election. There was such volatility that each of the three national party leaders was in first place at one time or another during the campaign. The Liberals even fell to third place for a while, and there was a rumour that Turner was going to be replaced in mid-stream. I was in Europe at the time, but as soon as I got back, I delivered a major fund-raising speech in Shawinigan. The party of Laurier, King, St. Laurent, and Trudeau was not going to finish last, I said. It was the duty of every Liberal to wake up. Two days later, Turner did extremely well in the televised leaders' debate, and the party pulled ahead. It could not sustain that lead, however, and the Tories ultimately won a second, though much smaller majority.

My phone started ringing almost immediately. People told me that Turner was going soon, I was the one to succeed him, everyone was behind me, blah, blah, blah. And because at least one campaign had already begun for the leadership, they urged me to get moving. Though I couldn't do much until Turner officially quit, I told them I would probably re-enter public life. "If it becomes a question of national survival," I had written at the conclusion of the first edition of *Straight from the Heart*, "to hell with privacy, leisure, and the easy life, I will be there because I owe to Canada all the privileges I have received."

I was not happy with the state of the nation under Brian Mulroney. In 1980 my colleagues and I had gone into Quebec and said to Quebeckers, "Canada is a great country with a magnificent future. Stay in Canada and together we can do great things." For the first time since Confederation the people of Quebec had been consulted directly about their wishes, and they had chosen Canada. For me the Quebec referendum, the patriation of the Constitution, and the Charter of Rights marked the end of Canada's "first phase" as a nation. We were on the threshold of a new era of achievement and unity. But now I was worried again about whether Canada would survive.

International communications, high technology, and the pressures of slow growth after thirty years of rising expectations had caused doubts about the value of national sovereignty and the future of cultural distinctiveness around the world. Not only had the fate of the language and culture of French Canada in North America been put in jeopardy by the American media and the forces of globalization, but English Canada had also become more concentrated on the United States market than ever before. It was no longer impossible to imagine that the French language might decline in strength as quickly as the Roman Catholic Church had declined, or that the entire country might be absorbed by our neighbour to the south.

In the past, Canada had kept pace with the United States because our economic and resource base had made us competitive. But the new technological base threatened to let the Americans shoot ahead of us in the short term, and the traumatic effect of that might tempt some Canadians to give up our institutions, our traditions, and our independence for a short-term gain. Getting through the transition would require a great deal of national will and national vision if Canada was not to succumb to the mirage of the American Dream.

Some people have seen a contradiction between my Canadian patriotism and my opposition to Quebec ultra-nationalism. At times that has bothered me, too. Once I discussed it with Trudeau. We were walking into the Centre Block of Parliament and as he passed through the revolving doors, I said, "Our position isn't logical, Pierre." He froze. Then he pushed the doors around again and came back out. "What did you say?" he asked.

Upon reflection it was apparent that there is no contradiction. I think separation would destroy the French fact in North America, not build it up. As the economy of an independent Quebec deteriorated, more and more francophones would join the exodus that the anglophones had started. Indeed, even the threat of separation has caused that to happen. I've come across scores of French Canadians working in Toronto, the West, and the United States, and the number of Quebeckers living permanently in Florida is unbelievable. A priest in my riding told me during the 1980 referendum campaign that he estimated $4 million had left his small parish alone to be invested in Florida homes and apartments. As was the case when my grandfather emigrated to New Hampshire, if people have to choose between the economy and language, they will choose the economy almost all the time. It is a vision of the destruction of my people that stirs me to fight for Canada. I don't do it, however, in order to see Canada become part of the United States and turn its back on what makes us unique.

Canada is not a single language or culture; in fact, it welcomes diversity. Though it may have proportionally fewer rich people than

223

the United States, it probably has proportionally fewer poor people, too, and it compensates for having fewer opportunities by having cleaner cities, less violence, and more social benefits. Nor can the advantages be assessed simply in financial terms, even if they are clearly proven. Most Canadians have always been willing to pay a price to remain Canadian in order to enjoy a certain quality of life, just as many of them already sacrifice the economic benefits of cities in order to maintain the pleasures they find in their regions and small towns.

It was easy for me to attack the intellectual dishonesty in the claim that Quebeckers would be wealthier in an independent state. It was harder to attack the more honest argument put forward by separatists, such as journalist Pierre Bourgault, who said, "We will be poorer, but we will be happier." That type of argument can have great power. For example, I have a small cottage on a lake near Shawinigan. It isn't grand or expensive, but I love it for its character and the beauty of its location. So I would pay a lot of money and fight to keep it if it were threatened. It's somewhat the same feeling with a country. Personally I'm not prepared to sacrifice anything for an independent Quebec — though I respect and understand those who are — but I am willing to make sacrifices for an independent Canada which includes Quebec.

Brian Mulroney, on the other hand, seemed more upset when Canada was critical of the United States than the United States was. He was a man who knew that one of the great weaknesses of people is flattery, and during his time in office he chose to flatter both Ronald Reagan and George Bush. I didn't like his buddy-buddy approach, because I don't believe that the personal friendship he valued so much has anything to do with international politics.

Americans are very tough negotiators, and they never buy anything from you that they don't need. Sometimes we have to agree to disagree. That doesn't mean we don't have good relations. When I met President Bush in my capacity as Opposition leader, I told him that friendship is friendship, business is business, and the two cannot be mixed.

224

During the Tory leadership campaign in 1983, Mulroney had warned against the effects of free trade on Canadian interests. In office, however, he seized the business community's assertion that Canada needed a free-trade deal. I found it strange that the same businessmen who had come to my office when I was a minister and begged for protection for their industries were now demanding free trade. In private they qualified their stance with nuances and exceptions, but publicly they followed each other with the same set speech, and without asking too many questions.

I am a free trader. I believe in free trade, and I know that Canada is, per capita, the greatest trading nation in the world. Our exports account for 40 per cent of the total output of our private sector, and one in five Canadian jobs is directly dependent on exports. I am proud, for example, of the Auto Pact that the Liberal government negotiated with the United States in the early 1960s. That was a free-trade agreement, but with some guarantees. Brian Mulroney's free-trade deal, on the other hand, didn't have enough guarantees. It also weakened our defences against Americanization by shifting our trade policy from an international orientation toward a continental one.

Nor did it secure our access to the American market, as it was intended to do. There weren't clear definitions of subsidies and dumping, for example, and the mechanism for resolving disputes was often lengthy and costly. Those flaws became evident in the series of ongoing disputes and harassments that continued after the deal's implementation.

Mulroney's continental strategy risked making Canada the fifty-first state of the United States. Link by link, a bit at a time, the cable was threatening to become so long and strong that all the important economic decisions would be made in Washington. And his strategy toward Quebec, while precisely the reverse, was no less a threat to the future of Canada. Indeed, it was the old strategy of the Quebec nationalists who plotted to separate step by step, a bit at a time, until nothing remained to keep Canada together.

I was appalled when he made his compact with the Quebec nationalists and reopened the Constitution. If Mulroney had been wise, he

225

never would have touched it, and might still be prime minister today. It was his biggest mistake, but he had nobody but himself to blame. Before he started talking about the Constitution, the Parti Québécois was down around 18 per cent in the Quebec polls and in a real mess. But, afterwards, with all Mulroney's rhetoric about the humiliation of 1982, how Quebec had been isolated and stabbed in the back, support for the PQ shot up like a rocket.

I still remember a black-tie dinner at the Mount Royal Club in Montreal, before Mulroney entered politics, when he stood up and sang my praises as the saviour of the country for fighting the 1980 referendum and patriating the Constitution. But few people bothered to look behind the myths he was now perpetuating. Mulroney's notion that Lévesque would have signed if we had been nicer to him was the most naive idea I've ever heard. Lévesque was a separatist and wouldn't have signed anything. We were the national government and had to defend the national interest.

The myths were used effectively, however, in selling the Meech Lake Accord. I opposed it because I thought it undermined the Charter of Rights and did not deal with all the constitutional reforms that the other provinces, the territories, and the native groups were still demanding. Better, I argued, to clear up some of the ambiguities and settle some of the outstanding demands before entrenching Meech. Eventually, my views were echoed in the report of the all-party parliamentary committee headed by Jean Charest.

When Mulroney's pal Lucien Bouchard got wind of a new deal in the making, however, he resigned from the Tory cabinet and went out to form the Bloc Québécois. That prompted Mulroney to abandon the Charest report. Instead, he decided to "roll the dice" in June, 1990, and lock the premiers into a pressure cooker to force them to accept Meech as it stood.

All this was happening at the same time as the race for the Liberal leadership. Though Turner had announced his retirement in May, 1989, the convention wasn't held until the third week of June, 1990. As in 1984, I figured that the winner would be the candidate who had the support of the majority of the Liberal caucus, and I decided

I would only run if I had that support. It didn't take long to get it. Most of the MPs were quick to jump in the boat. So I was the strong frontrunner the moment I decided to enter the contest.

That didn't make this campaign any easier than the one in 1984. While I was strong among members of the federal Liberal Party, I met fierce opposition from the Liberal premiers of Quebec and Ontario. Perhaps because Robert Bourassa wanted to see his friend David Peterson as federal leader, perhaps because they were ardent defenders of the Meech Lake Accord, both tried to block me through their control of the provincial organizations. Though I soon picked up the lion's share of the delegates from every region, the opposition toughened with each passing week. My principal opponents, Paul Martin and Sheila Copps, were superb candidates.

At the same time, Canada was in a difficult political situation, what with the resignation of Lucien Bouchard, the rejection of the Charest report, and the collapse of the Meech Lake process. Though its fate was not in my hands, I could not help but be caught up in the emotion and controversy that Meech had aroused among Canadians. The accord died on June 23, the very day I won 60 per cent of the votes on the first ballot and was elected leader of the Liberal Party of Canada.

CHAPTER ELEVEN

THE ROCKY ROAD TO
SUSSEX DRIVE

T HE LIBERAL PARTY emerged from the leadership convention reasonably united, though we did suffer some fallout from the collapse of the Meech Lake Accord. Two of our MPs, Jean Lapierre and
Gilles Rocheleau, immediately quit the caucus, and the Quebec media
remained unbelievably hostile toward me for months afterwards.
Every morning they dumped on me in the newspapers, and every
night on TV they replayed in slow motion a scene of me hugging
Clyde Wells, the premier of Newfoundland, in the euphoria of my
convention victory. It cost me a lot of popularity in my home province. Nobody ever insulted me directly, but there was a coolness that
made me feel uncomfortable even among my golfing buddies.

That was just one of the problems I faced in my early days as leader
of the party. During the native uprising at Oka that summer, I suggested that it would be cheaper and more effective to let the trou-
blemakers go for the time being and pick them up later one by one,
since the police had their names, than to hole them up behind bar-
ricades at the risk of losing human lives and the cost of millions of
dollars a day. The media twisted that into a total surrender. Then, in
September, Bob Rae's NDP won the Ontario election. The federal
Liberals were caught in the popular backlash against David Peterson's

228

government, and we dropped from 50 per cent to 32 per cent in a couple of months. And, until Mulroney called a by-election for the New Brunswick riding of Beauséjour in December, I still had to win a seat in the House of Commons.

The initial concerns about my leadership made it harder to attract good people to work in my office, which wasn't functioning very well because I lacked a strong manager to run it properly. Around that time, too, I started using a teleprompter to deliver my speeches. I liked the device, but it was seen as a plot by my handlers to make me seem more "prime ministerial." The press was full of stories about the disappearance of the good old Jean Chrétien.

Reading those reports, I even began to doubt myself. Why had I done things that way? What had happened to my instincts? Was I cut out to be a leader? Perhaps I was just a good number two, after all, and could never be a good number one.

In February, 1991, I got sick. The doctors found two nodules on my lung and feared they were malignant. I didn't want to take any chances. Three days later I went under the knife. To my great relief and good fortune the nodules turned out to be no danger at all. I used to refer to them as Lapierre and Rocheleau.

During my recuperation in Florida I had time to review all that had happened since the beginning of the leadership race fifteen months before. One night, unable to sleep, I had a long discussion about it with Aline. "You're not the Chrétien that you were," she said. "There's something missing. You listen too much. You take too much advice. Why don't you just be yourself?"

It was fantastic advice. When I returned to the office I was ready to take charge. One of my first achievements was to recruit Jean Pelletier, the former mayor of Quebec City, as my chief of staff. I boxed him into accepting, in fact. "Some years ago," I said, "you told me that if I ever needed you, you'd be with me. Well, now I need your help. But I know that you will be like everyone else. I know I'm still not very popular. I know it wouldn't be fashionable for you to work with me. So I expect that you will say no." But he is a man of his word, with a strong sense of public duty. He came, and he soon brought order to my office.

229

We began doing better on the policy side, too. Besides the Meech Lake Accord and Canadian-American relations, there was Mulroney's economic record to combat. He had come to power in 1984 promising to reduce the debt, create jobs, and protect universal social programs. By the time he retired in 1993, he had tripled the debt produced by the 1981-82 recession, left one and a half million Canadians out of work, and slashed away at what he himself had called the "sacred trusts." His monetary policies got us into the latest recession before the Americans and killed a lot of enterprises that will never come back.

Some of his advisers were reported to have said that they would tolerate 25 per cent unemployment in order to wrestle inflation to the ground. When you have 25 per cent unemployment, I always replied, you won't have to worry about inflation or interest rates or the debt or anything else, because you'll have a revolution on your hands!

Meanwhile, many Tories seemed to be doing very well, thank you very much. Finding qualified people to fill the jobs that have to be filled is a normal part of government. That requires good judgment and proper balance. The issue isn't what party they belong to. The issue is their competence. Under the Tories, however, hundreds of people were appointed to public office with no other qualification than their friendship with the prime minister.

Simultaneously, the lobbying industry was encouraged to set up shop in Ottawa. I was shocked to discover its depth. One evening I met a good friend of mine, the president of a large company, at a dinner with a bunch of businessmen. The very next morning I got a call from a lobbyist who wanted to arrange a meeting between myself and this same guy with whom I'm on a first-name basis. Naturally, I was confused. So I asked my friend why he had bothered to hire the lobbyist. "Everybody has to," he said. "We've been told that's the only way we can do business with the government now. It's become part of our operation costs."

One day a Liberal MP was phoned by a lobbyist who wanted him to help one of his own constituents with an immigration problem!

No Canadian should have to hire anybody in order to get to see his or her MP. And what exactly were the lobbyists selling? Knowledge, sometimes. Too often, I suspect, influence. But lobbying has become such a big and integral part of the system that it's very difficult to tackle. Though no one is forced to go to a lobbyist, there's now a belief — which my government is determined to change — that you can't succeed without one.

The patronage, the scandals, and the lobbying were just manifestations, however, of the attitude the Tories brought to Ottawa. Government became a matter of money. All the talk of the town was about who had become rich on such and such a contract. The entire approach to economic and social policy was, if the rich got richer, there would be more crumbs for the poor. Even when not crooked, this constant praising of money contradicted the traditional values of Canadian society and the very notion of public service. It reflected, in fact, the "greed society" prevalent in the United States and the business community during the 1980s, when people made fortunes by getting huge loans from the banks, or pushing paper for easy bucks, without ever thinking of the social consequences. No wonder there was an unprecedented cynicism about politicians and our public institutions.

I never really felt comfortable as Leader of the Opposition. There can't be a worse job in the entire parliamentary system. You're only there to criticize. If you make a positive suggestion, nobody pays any attention. If you're constantly on the attack, then you're news. But it went against my nature to be negative, negative, negative all the time, and I didn't like being seen as a negative person. All my previous experience in public life, furthermore, had been on the government side of the House. My satisfaction had always been with getting things done, not with criticizing, and because I had been a minister for so long, I knew that the government ministers were doing their best, even when I disagreed with their policies. Many times I even knew how they were going to answer my questions.

I set myself four goals as leader of the Liberals in opposition: to unite the party, to get its finances into order, to recruit good candidates for the next election, and to develop new policies. An opposition party must be more than a vehicle for taking power. It must also propose new solutions and establish different priorities. That's why Mackenzie King organized a policy conference in Port Hope, Ontario, in 1933. That's why Lester Pearson organized one in Kingston, Ontario, in 1960. And that's why I asked my research director Chaviva Hosek and my principal secretary Eddie Goldenberg to organize the three-day non-partisan think-tank in Aylmer, Quebec, in November, 1991. I wanted to find constructive alternatives to the Tory agenda.

The Liberals' defeat in 1984 and 1988 had given us clear cause to reassess ourselves, and the world had changed enormously during the years we had been out of power. The collapse of the Soviet Union, the expansion of the European common market, the transformation of Eastern Europe, and the emergence of new economic powers in the Pacific had created new challenges and new opportunities, as had the liberalization of world trade and the technological revolution. So I wanted to explore, with experts from home and abroad, the economic and political implications for Canada and Liberalism on the eve of the twenty-first century.

Being a Liberal is more than carrying a card or accepting a policy. It's an attitude to life. It's caring about the creating of wealth, but it's also caring about the sharing of wealth. It's remaining loyal to the principles of social justice and national unity, but it's also responding flexibly to the changing circumstances of the times. Because of Canada's distances, its small population, and its diversity in language and interests, it is a complex structure always threatened by powerful centrifugal forces. As a result, our solutions to its problems can never be doctrinaire, and no doctrinaire party of the left or right beholden to specific groups can ever succeed at the national level. What may be valid in one part of the country or one period of time won't necessarily work in another. And if you're in the centre, the centre moves.

The Liberal Party has been particularly skillful at covering a lot of ground by staying in the centre. That is the natural instinct of Liberals, and Canadians have looked to the Liberal Party in times of national crisis because its moderation made it the best agent for resolving conflicts and finding pragmatic solutions. Thus, we believe in a healthy capitalism so long as it doesn't become a harmful disease. Thus, we believe that a government can be a force of good so long as it doesn't become arrogant and oppressive. The broad consensus that emerged out of the Aylmer conference struck that balance. Canada had to preserve and consolidate its social programs while adapting to radically different economic conditions. Our competitive advantage will be found by investing in human capital and maintaining universal medicare, safe cities, and access to quality education.

In the nearly two years following the Aylmer conference, Paul Martin and Chaviva Hosek consulted further and laboured to shape that consensus into a complete election program. It had to be fiscally responsible; it had to avoid exaggerated promises; and it had to create hope. If its priorities were the right ones and offered light at the end of the tunnel, then we felt it would overcome the cynicism across the land, and earn us the trust and respect of the Canadian people.

Despite the obvious risks, we unveiled our entire platform, with all its costs, on the eighth day of the election campaign in the form of a 112-page Red Book. We were both pleased and proud that it was received so well. It demonstrated how serious we were about the issues. It became a measure of our sincerity, purpose, ingenuity, and hard work. And, not only did it help us win, I believe it changed for the better the way elections will be fought in the future.

People always ask me if I expected to win the election. In truth, I didn't have many doubts. The strength of the Mulroney Tories, their close alliance with the Quebec nationalists, had become their weakness. It led, first of all, to the betrayal by Lucien Bouchard and the formation of the Bloc Québécois. And it led, secondly, to the popularity of the Reform Party among those Tories who thought Mulroney was in Quebec's pocket. So his vote was split in three. Simple arithmetic suggested that the Liberals only had to win around 38 per cent of the popular vote to form a government — which was not, in my judgment, a tall order. We had been riding above 40 per cent in the polls for more than a year, and the rest was divided among four parties.

Throughout 1992, Mulroney had been trying to build the Constitution into the one big issue of the upcoming election, just as he had made free trade the one big issue of the 1988 election. It was clever politically. If Turner had campaigned against Mulroney and the Tories' entire record, not just against the free-trade deal, I think he could have won. But because free trade had split the society in half, and because the antis had been divided between the Liberals and the NDP, Mulroney won. This time, however, his strategy failed, because his referendum on the Charlottetown constitutional agreement failed.

I supported the Charlottetown Accord as a compromise on the grounds that it answered most of my problems with the Meech Lake Accord. It wouldn't, I thought, have any substantial effect on the Charter of Rights. It reformed the Senate for the West and satisfied the demands of the native leaders. It devolved certain powers to the provinces, but in secondary areas. Best of all, even if it wasn't perfect, it had to pass a national referendum. Because I saw the country as an alliance of people, not as an alliance of premiers or institutions, I had always wanted the people themselves to be able to ratify their constitution. Indeed, I had insisted on a referendum as a condition of my support, and I was proud to have won that point.

Historians will debate for a long, long time why the October referendum failed. The intervention of Pierre Trudeau on the "No" side was certainly a crucial factor. It caused me, and every Liberal who admired him, some trouble, but I managed to keep my troops together. A second crucial factor was Brian Mulroney's desire to make the victory his personal project, as a way of restoring his reputation in the public mind and setting the stage to win a third majority government. He should have gone to Florida instead. The Charlottetown Accord became tainted by his lack of credibility, and Preston Manning was able to dismiss it as the Mulroney deal.

In February, 1993, Brian Mulroney gave up hope for his "triple crown" and announced his resignation, which was more of a disappointment than a surprise to me. The press, not waiting for the convention, immediately announced that Kim Campbell would be his successor, and everybody got excited, including some Nervous Nellies in my own party. Not me. She was bound to encounter problems during the leadership race. If you start high, you can only go down, and you have to be an old pro to survive the fall. She was no old pro. Though the media showed an abnormally high level of forgiveness for her mistakes, she almost lost the leadership to Jean Charest.

A Charest victory would have removed my vulnerability among those who didn't want to see yet another prime minister from Quebec. (The Tories tried that attack subliminally during the election, by showing me with a Quebec flag in their ads, but it never caught fire as an issue.) But, in pitting my age against his youth, I would have evoked the example of the Newfoundland fishermen who always turn to the most experienced sailor in times of trouble. Ultimately, however, it wasn't up to me to choose my opponent, and the Tories chose Kim Campbell.

Even during the summer, when everything was again forgiven because she was Canada's first female prime minister, I didn't panic. I only had to remember what had happened when the Liberals replaced Trudeau with Turner in 1984. (It didn't change a thing.) And I still had arithmetic on my side, thanks to rise of the Bloc Québécois and the Reform Party, and the collapse of the NDP. In August, in fact, at the height of Campbell's personal popularity, I gave Claude Charron my predictions for the election, not realizing that he would publish them in his newspaper column: twenty-five seats or more in Atlantic Canada, seventy-five seats in Ontario, between twenty-five and thirty seats in the West, and twenty seats in Quebec. (As it turned out, we won, respectively, thirty-one, ninety-eight, twenty-nine, and nineteen.)

When the election was finally called in September, I was ready, the party program was ready, and the Liberal team was ready. At a time when so many were cynical, I was grateful for the number of quality candidates and talented volunteers who offered to help. And it snowballed. When others saw people of such high calibre on our team, whether a former mayor of Toronto like Art Eggleton or a distinguished ex-bureaucrat like Marcel Massé, they, too, came on board. Eventually it gave me a big problem, the best kind of problem, because I ended up with too many good people. My "B" team in the caucus is probably as good as my "A" team in the cabinet. That keeps the "A" team on their toes, let me assure you, and it should make Canadians feel better to know that their affairs are being managed by such honest and competent people.

I am reluctant to add any more to the hurt Kim Campbell must have suffered from her party's devastation. Though the problems evident during her leadership race returned on the very first day of the election campaign, much of the result was not her fault. Ironically, if she had been stronger, I believe the Liberals would have done even better. The collapse of the Tory organization in the final week probably cost us more than a dozen seats in Alberta and British Columbia. It resulted in Reform's taking too many Tory votes to let the Liberals slip between them to victory, while the breakdown of Mulroney's alliance in Quebec prompted many more Western Tories to vote Reform to prevent Lucien Bouchard from becoming Leader of Her Majesty's Loyal Opposition.

Nothing hurt the Conservative Party more than the TV ads aimed at hurting me. I was expecting them. As a kid I had had to put up with jokes about my physical handicap. "I may have a twisted mouth," I used to joke, "but at least I don't have a twisted mind like you guys." All my political life, too, I have been put down with exaggerated insults about my English or my French. So when I woke up one morning in Saint John, New Brunswick, and heard about the terrible ads that had been on the night before, I knew they were about my mouth.

"Worse," I was told, "they're trying to make you look stupid."

"Don't worry," I said. "Those ads will be off by tonight."

Even the reporters felt emotional. Some had tears in their eyes when I thanked God for having given me some qualities as well as some afflictions. By the end of the day the ads were gone.

I also had to deal with a lot of speculation that I was going to lose personally in St-Maurice. Though my own polls gave me confidence, some published reports (whose methods I found questionable) showed me behind. Those negative reports may have harmed us in other parts of Quebec, where people told Liberal candidates, "Why should I vote for you when your own leader is going to be defeated?" In St-Maurice, however, they may have helped me. Hundreds of volunteers came out in response, and I finished with a majority of more than 6,000 votes. At my first press conference after the election I felt the same pleasure as Harry Truman when I held up the two major French newspapers whose headlines trumpeted my defeat.

The election clearly changed the character of the House of Commons. While the Conservatives and the NDP lost their official party status, the Reform Party emerged as the latest version of the populist Social Credit movement in which Preston Manning's father had been a player. Primarily rooted in the right-wing ideology of Western Canada, which is not the same as the right wing in Ontario or the Maritimes, Reform's success had more to do with the failure of the Tories than with its own intrinsic virtues. Unless it becomes the Conservative Party, I believe, it will ultimately meet the frustrating fate of all doctrinaire parties in Canada.

The success of the Bloc Québécois was also based on a populist protest. The Bloc benefited from the general discontent with the established parties and the particular problems of the Tories. As Lucien Bouchard himself admitted during the campaign, the Bloc's vote was not solidly separatist. We Liberals were even able to increase our support substantially during the course of the campaign. That's why I remain optimistic about the future of the country. In an era when the 1.2 billion people of China are gearing up to create an economic superpower, to take but one example, why should the 7 million people of Quebec toss away the advantages of Canada's membership in the Group of Seven industrialized countries and its presence on the Pacific?

It took a while to realize that I had been elected Prime Minister of Canada. It was nice when my wife woke me and said, "Do you want a coffee, Prime Minister?" It was nice when the President of the United States phoned me at the cottage and I was able to let my grandchildren listen in on the call. But then I flew to Ottawa and got right down to work. I had been a cabinet minister for so many years that nothing seemed particularly strange or difficult. The transition, long planned, took place without a problem. I reduced the cabinet to twenty-two and selected its members. I met the caucus and contacted the bureaucrats. And, on November 4, I was sworn in as Canada's twentieth Prime Minister.

There came a moment, however, when I felt the emotional impact of what had happened. On November 11, while attending a Remembrance Day ceremony on behalf of the Canadian people, I had to stand for a long time in the centre of a large, friendly crowd. With nothing pressing on my mind at the time, I began to study the dates on the cenotaph. And "1914-1918" made me think about my parents and grandparents, what they had been doing then, what dreams and ambitions they had had for their families. Suddenly I thought, if Wellie and Marie are watching now, they must be rather pleased.

I owe it to them, to myself, and to Canada not to fail. Everyone in my cabinet and on my staff knows that this is my last job and that I'm determined not to leave public life with a damaged reputation. If anyone disappoints me, I will act forcefully, because if I disappoint the Canadian people, they will throw me out — and they will be right to do so. Though I avoided making extravagant and unrealistic promises during the election campaign, there are some criteria by which the voters will measure my success. Has the number of unemployed been reduced? Has faith in the country been restored? Has Canada's independence been reasserted? Have we done as well as our competitors in meeting the global challenges of the 1990s? Have the people regained trust in the honesty and usefulness of their government?

Canadians don't expect miracles. They expect judgment, integrity, and hard work. If I can create that atmosphere of confidence, then we will feel good about ourselves again, and through millions and millions of positive decisions made every day by every one of us, we will be able to resolve most of the difficulties we now face.

Many challenges lie ahead. To overcome them, we have to overcome our despair about ourselves. Every one of us will have to become the best at everything we do, to be an example to our community and an example to the world. Canadians are good workers. We have education, we have experience, we have imagination, and we have the fantastic opportunity that our citizenship gives us. Millions of people would give their shirts for the chance to share our so-called miseries. I've been teased for talking all the time about the greatness of Canada. But if we don't have pride, we will never be able to succeed. And that is why I will continue to say, as long as God gives me life and a chance to serve my country: Canada is the best!

Cabinet Portfolios Held by Jean Chrétien

April 1967	Minister without Portfolio attached to Ministry of Finance
January–July 1968	Minister of National Revenue
July 1968– August 1974	Minister of Indian Affairs and Northern Development
August 1974– September 1976	President of the Treasury Board
September 1976– September 1977	Minister of Industry, Trade and Commerce
September 1977– June 1979	Minister of Finance
March 1980– September 1982	Minister of Justice and Attorney General of Canada, Minister of State for Social Development
September 1982– July 1984	Minister of Energy, Mines and Resources
July 1984– September 1984	Deputy Prime Minister and Secretary of State for External Affairs
November 1993–	Prime Minister of Canada

INDEX

244